Class, Kinship, and Power in an Ecuadorian Town

Class, Kinship, and Power in an Ecuadorian Town

The Negroes of San Lorenzo

NORMAN E. WHITTEN, JR.

1965
Stanford University Press
Stanford California

Stanford University Press
Stanford, California
© 1965 by the Board of Trustees of the
Leland Stanford Junior University
Printed in the United States of America
L.C. 65-18979

To Sibby

Acknowledgments

This study was made possible by Public Health Service Fellowship MH 14333 and by supplements M-54447 SSS and MH 06978-01 SSS R04 from the National Institute of Mental Health. Final preparation of the manuscript was aided by a Tulane University faculty research grant and by National Institutes of Health Grant 1-S01-FR5444.

The material upon which this book is based was first presented as a Ph.D. dissertation in Anthropology at the University of North Carolina, and rewritten for publication during my spare time while I conducted field research among Colombian Negroes. My first acknowledgment is to the anthropologists of the University of North Carolina, who created a stimulating, challenging, and rewarding academic environment, who taught me anthropology, and who allowed me to develop my own research interests. I am most grateful for the aid extended to me by Professors Charles J. Erasmus and John Gulick. To them I owe an intellectual debt far exceeding their involvement in the present study. John J. Honigmann, Guy B. Johnson, Joffre L. Coe, and Rupert B. Vance all contributed to the initial preparation of the manuscript.

I wish to thank Mr. Herbert Hunter, formerly of the Servicio Cooperativo Interamericano de Salud Pública for his aid, and the many officials of the Junta Autónoma del Ferrocarril Quito–San Lorenzo for permission to use their materials and facilities. Among the many residents of San Lorenzo who helped me, I am particularly indebted to Dr. Aurelio Fuentes Contreras, especially for his insights into highland-coastal relations and problems facing the highland in-migrant to San Lorenzo. The Reverend Lino Campesan made documents and maps available, and Teniente Político Manuel Montaño gave me access to all official statistics and assisted me in my household survey. Edelberto Rivera Reascos, Rosendo Quintero, and Luis Ante were my principal informants and trusted companions. In one way or another, dozens of other San Lorenzeños contributed directly to this study: I am grateful to every one of them.

Finally, I wish to thank my wife, Dorothea Scott Whitten, to whom the book is dedicated, not only for her constant help in reading and creatively criticizing every draft of the manuscript, but for the many intangibles that contributed directly to its completion.

Any errors of omission or commission are attributable only to me, and not to those who have so generously aided this endeavor.

N. E. W.

Contents

Eight pages of photographs follow p. 166

Introduction

The central concern of this book is to describe the changing social structure of a northwest Ecuadorian port town. Sociocultural change in San Lorenzo is characteristic of, but more rapid than, change taking place throughout the northern sector of Esmeraldas province. Change in the sector was largely stimulated by the construction of a railroad line, which reached San Lorenzo in 1957, linking the Ecuadorian highlands with the tropical rainforest coast. The central thesis of this study is that the Negroes of San Lorenzo have successfully adapted their social system to new and expanding economic, social, and political orders. The system shows no signs of disorganization; Negroes are still able to get things done in San Lorenzo. At the same time, an increasing emphasis on formal voluntary organizations that can influence national decisions has allowed newcomers, together with native townspeople, to accomplish things in the larger society.

I first visited San Lorenzo during an ethnographic reconnaissance trip to northwest Ecuador in July and August 1961, spending about one month in San Lorenzo and the surrounding hinterland and about three weeks in other parts of northern Ecuador. It was obvious at the time that San Lorenzo was a focal point of interest in Ecuador, and that within its own geographical niche it was regarded as somewhat special.

I returned to the town in January 1963 and remained through mid-August, traveling intermittently in the hinterland. In general, I lived the life of the people. Almost daily work with informants from various walks of life, consultation of all written material in the

town, and a survey of economics and family organization, which I
conducted in April, May, and June, all contributed to my understanding of life in the town.

San Lorenzo is a hot, rainy setting for life. It is reached from the
highlands by a train trip resembling a roller-coaster ride down the
western slopes of the Andes. Landslides make the trip particularly
treacherous between December and June. From the coast the only
means of transportation are the small, rugged banana and cargo boats
that ply between Guayaquil and Limones and occasionally put in at
San Lorenzo. Otherwise, the interior can be reached only by dugout
canoe or "launch." The only scheduled ferry service is a near-daily
Limones–San Lorenzo launch service, the launch being a dugout
canoe with balsa floats and built-up sides, powered by an outboard
motor.

In spite of such difficulties in traveling to and from this Ecuadorian frontier, growth and development are continuous. The expanding population and growing commerce are bringing a measure of
prosperity to San Lorenzo, but they are also taking their toll in
health (Fuentes Contreras n.d.). There is virtually no sanitation;
rats and flies seem to be everywhere; infant mortality is very high,
venereal disease rampant, and tetanus infections increasing. At the
same time, malaria and yaws have been nearly eradicated by government programs. The people are poor, but far from miserable.
People in San Lorenzo generally believe that something good is going to happen; on the whole they are outwardly oriented, open to
changes that promise a tangible benefit, and inquisitive about the
ways of others.

San Lorenzo may be viewed in both national and cultural-regional
contexts. In its national context, San Lorenzo is a new and potentially valuable port, inhabited by Negroes whose patterns of life are
quite different from those of other Ecuadorians. Migration of highlanders in the past ten years has given the town a more heterogeneous ethnic composition. Culturally, the Negroes of San Lorenzo
are part of what West (1957: 1–4) calls the "Pacific lowlands culture area." This area, inhabited primarily by Negroes with a common culture and scattered Indian groups from dispersed tribes—
Chocó, Waunamá (Noanamá), Cayapa—extends from Darién province of southeastern Panama south through western Colombia to

southern Esmeraldas, Ecuador. The Pacific lowlands strip is 50–100 miles wide and about 600 miles long. (See map in West 1957: 2.)

My description and analysis of San Lorenzo is set in the national, rather than culture-areal, context. I am concerned here with the changing structure of San Lorenzo as an Ecuadorian town, not with San Lorenzo as a representative of Pacific lowlands Negro culture. There are several reasons for my choice of emphasis.

First, Ecuadorians from the highlands and from other coastal regions are concerned with the town, with its development and potential, and with the possible political and economic impact of the new northwestern port. Second, the Negroes of San Lorenzo, for their part, are aware that they are important to the nation. Their conception of the role of San Lorenzo in national economics and politics does not always coincide with that of the highlanders, but this does not alter the fact that Ecuadorians from all parts of the country regard the town as a very important factor in the development of an economic base for the Ecuadorian nation.

Third, the acculturation of the Negroes in northern Esmeraldas has differed somewhat from that of their counterparts to the north during the last 150 years because of a series of economic booms exploited by English, German, French, and American interests. Fourth, focusing on the Negroes of San Lorenzo in the context of their culture area would have meant slighting the data on the effect of the incoming highlanders. And I did not feel that the Negroes' life could be adequately understood without a concomitant knowledge of at least some aspects of the newcomers' lifeways.

Last, and perhaps most important, the future of San Lorenzo is now bound to the future of the developing nation. For this reason it would be doing a great disservice to the town not to see its social system as a segment of an underdeveloped region in a poor country. As Ecuador develops, it will most likely develop as a plural society. San Lorenzo will be a component of that society, not a static, "quaint," Negroid region, but a functioning, contributing part of the nation. Within the national economic and political framework, then, San Lorenzo can be studied as a dynamic social system, which should have more significance for theory than studying it as a part of a culture area.

On the negative side, this focus leads me to slight some interesting aspects of the Pacific lowlands culture area. I have, for example, minimized (but not omitted) descriptions of material culture, daily life, ritual, and folklore. I have not discussed the possible African provenience of many characteristic features of Negro life: the family system, cooperative work associations, mothers' methods of trapping mates for their daughters by involving local politicians and mid-wives, funerary rituals, ghost beliefs, music, and dancing. I have, however, endeavored to include enough data to allow the reader concerned with trait provenience to satisfy at least some of his curiosity.

At the same time, I have had to include a good deal of material on San Lorenzo's development, including a description of the economic situation of the newcomers in addition to that of the native towns-people. This book is thus a study of an entire ethnically plural community, although my main interest is the place of the Negroes in the community, their economic, social, and political means of coping with change, and their capacity for controlling their own fate in a world of changing systems.

Chapters I and II present background information necessary for understanding the changes occurring in San Lorenzo's social system. Chapter I describes San Lorenzo's national and regional setting, its history and ethnohistory, and Chapter II the development of the railroad, port, and town. Chapters III through VI present the economic and social structure of San Lorenzo. The last three chapters synthesize material presented earlier and deal with structural change by focusing on kinship and social mobility in Chapter VII and on the political order in Chapter VIII. The Conclusion reviews the nature of San Lorenzo's changing social system. The town ecology, illustrated by two maps, is described in the Appendix.

In describing a changing social structure, I have had to deal with different areas of life and different types of data, which called for different field and analytical techniques. Chapters III and IV are concerned with the objective class situation. By class I mean the relative economic situation of a given person (or family), his position in relation to the other people in the community. For example, the upper class in San Lorenzo is by no means made up of people wealthy by national standards, but simply the most well-to-do in town. The class lines I draw are my own, and they are based on real income. San Lorenzo's class structure is pyramidal, divided by economic differences into upper, middle, and lower classes. To repeat, my sole criterion for class is income, as it relates to the general economy of northwest Ecuador. The divisions are my own; in general, the Negroes recognize the same divisions I do, but most of the newcomers from the highlands do not, for reasons to be discussed later.

Economic stratification is important for an analysis of daily life; it also has some importance for the Negroes themselves in their relations with each other, but not always in the place they assign to a given person. The class hierarchy defined here is indispensable for the presentation of data, but it is to be considered an essential framework, not a system in itself. Within this framework I discuss occupational patterns, including subsistence techniques and reciprocal work relationships and groupings.

Chapter V analyzes the ethnic and status system or the system of personal and group placement and social honor. Here I draw on concepts held by the people themselves for my analytical categories. In this chapter I also discuss formal and informal groupings in San Lorenzo, and find that the crucial feature of the system of social honor, *as it relates to the changing structure,* is a community orientation which has economic and ethnic ramifications and which defines potential and existing alliances.

Chapter VI, Family, Household, and Kinship, is crucial for subsequent chapters, in which the description of the social structure is merged with data on how it is changing. Basically, it is found that the crucial kinship grouping is the kindred, and that kindred ties have ramifications in all spheres of sociocultural activity.

Kinship data were derived by several methods. First, almost daily work with a very insightful informant, who became particularly interested in plotting genealogy and household composition, led to a rough scheme of about one-third of the San Lorenzo households with their interlocking consanguineal and affinal ties. In order to fill in genealogical data, my informant supplied me with other informants who could supplement our information. Work with my principal informant (a lower-class Negro) and the people he recommended covered personal data on all members of the households discussed, past and present sexual liaisons, personal attributes, education, social prestige. The informants' distortions and prevarications were as useful as their facts, since they gave me insights into the functioning of kindreds and the way in which kinship bonds can be manipulated as sources of prestige and power. The data gained from these informants were constantly checked against information supplied by other members of the community.

After I had a fair notion of the household composition and consanguineal and affinal links of about one-third the community, I worked daily with a member of the upper class, a highland mestizo who had been in San Lorenzo for a number of years and was especially interested in local economic, social, and political relationships, and in relations between the highlanders and the native Costeños. I was primarily interested in the extent of his knowledge, or even vague awareness, of aspects of the Negro system. I wanted to know how well the group he represented understood the articulation of the Negro system with the broader network of highland-coastal sociocultural relationships. And I needed to understand highlanders' conceptions of their own place in San Lorenzo. This informant also gave me invaluable data on the family and kinship of the other highlanders, including extensive information on the linkages and alliances between highlanders and coastal people.

Finally, I administered a systematic house-to-house survey, designed and developed in the field, to check data gained from work with informants, more general interviewing, and participation in community and hinterland life. In conducting this survey, I was accompanied by the *teniente político* (political lieutenant), a highly respected Negro who had lived in San Lorenzo for 17 years. The responses that his presence evoked, together with his intimate knowledge of all the old families (he had married a daughter of one of the most prominent Negroes in town), and of most of the recent marriages and births, provided me with a wealth of detail I should never have been able to gather on my own. I paid the teniente político three sucres (about 15 cents) for each household; everyone knew that I was paying him, and for the most part members of the community took great pride in a local Negro's being paid to help the North American anthropologist. All data from the survey were again checked with several other Negroes, who were persuaded to give me more detail on families suspected of having been reticent—

or inaccurate. Information on marriage was checked against official records in San Lorenzo and Limones and the archives of the Catholic missionaries. Finally, I returned to many households without the teniente político, to check seemingly contradictory or unusual information.

Chapter VII presents a model of kinship and socioeconomic mobility. In this chapter I begin to describe the dynamic features of the social system and to relate the data on history, development, economics, and social status to the material on kinship. My central thesis is that for natives of the coast, lower-class personal kindreds aid members in spatial mobility and subsistence economics, whereas middle-class stem kindreds contribute to socioeconomic mobility from the lower to the middle class. The middle-class stem kindreds are classified as small rising, corporate established, and large disintegrating kindreds, representing the second, third, and fourth generations of socioeconomic mobility. It is the third-generation stem kindred that unites cash and subsistence economics and buffers highland-coastal socioeconomic relations. Data for this chapter were gathered in extensive interviews with prominent and once-prominent members of large kindreds and in general interviews concerning prominent people with many townsmen and people from the rural hinterland.

Chapter VIII sets forth the formal political order as it relates to political behavior at the community level. Political success is seen as a necessary condition of socioeconomic mobility for second-generation kindreds, and of socioeconomic domination by any third-generation stem kindred. Party affiliation follows class, status, and kinship lines, though interparty cooperation is possible when prominent members of different parties emphasize their kinship linkage. Lines of socioeconomic cleavage are most marked when behavior clearly directed toward achieving a goal by political means fails, and most obscure when it succeeds.

The crucial data for the chapter on politics, and for other sections in the book that deal with politics, are derived strictly from first-hand observation and experience. For the period between 1961 and 1963, when I was not in Ecuador, I used data supplied by informants only to the extent that they could be corroborated by newspaper reports, official reports or other relatively reliable printed materials. A series of local and national crises in 1961 and 1963, which culminated in a national military take-over in mid-July 1963, shed light on many aspects of political life. In the Conclusion it is found that the Negro kinship system has ramified into new contexts but shows no signs of breakdown. Traditional labor groups continue functioning, with some modifications, in a new context of cash labor in the lumber industry. A new feature of the social structure is the growth of formal associations dedicated to economic, social, and political ends.

The structure of San Lorenzo seems to have moved in the direction of increased rationalization, while at the same time traditional ways of getting things done have remained viable. Rationalization of the structure seems to link this northwest Ecuadorian community to the larger Ecuadorian society, while intra-community affairs continue to be handled in traditional ways. Because the traditional means of social control and manipulation are successful at the community level, and the formal organizations are relatively effective in dealing with outside agencies fostering development, neither Communism nor the labor union is as popular in San Lorenzo as in other coastal towns.

San Lorenzo is not a pseudonym; it exists today in the geographical and, to the best of my knowledge, sociocultural context set forth below. In writing about people and events in the town I have walked a thin line between disguising the names of people involved in potentially damaging situations, and reporting events accurately in order to analyze them properly. I have changed everyone's name, but almost every name used in this book is common in San Lorenzo. I greatly appreciate the more obscure and emotionally charged data given me, and trust that I have betrayed no one's confidence. In the long run I hope that such information will contribute solely to the advancement of our knowledge of communities undergoing change, and will not work to the detriment of my friends in northwest Ecuador.

The Setting

Ecuador, second smallest of the South American Republics, has shrunk in a little more than one hundred years from an area of about 400,000 square miles to its present 100,000 square miles.[1] Geographically classified as an "Andean country," Ecuador is bordered by Colombia on the north, by the Pacific on the west, and by Peru on the east and south. In their writings, travelers to Ecuador stress its vivid cultural contrasts, which reflect the country's division into four distinct geographical areas: the Sierra (Andean highlands), the Oriente (eastern jungle), the Litoral (western coastal plain), and the Archipiélago de Colón (Galápagos Islands).[2]

The Sierra is formed by two north-south mountain ranges, the Cordillera Oriental and the Cordillera Occidental. In its habitable areas, Quechua-speaking Indians eke out a meager existence (Sáenz 1933; Jaramillo Alvarado 1954) and the country's elite live in luxury (Saunders 1961). In 1958, an estimated three-fifths of the population of Ecuador lived in the Sierra (Herring 1961: 525). Quito, the national capital, is situated in a valley in the western range at an altitude of 9,350 feet; around it snow-capped volcanic mountains rise as high as 20,577 feet. Other large towns in the Sierra, each the capital of a province, are Ibarra and Tulcán to the north of Quito, and Latacunga, Ambato, Riobamba, Cuenca, and Loja to the south.

1. For historical information relating to the decrease in Ecuador's territory, see Herring (1961: 181, 261–68, 525).
2. Fairly detailed travelers' accounts stressing the geographical and cultural contrasts are given in Simpson (1886); Kolberg (1897); Niles (1923); Franklin (1943); Von Hagen (1940, 1949); Eichler (1955).

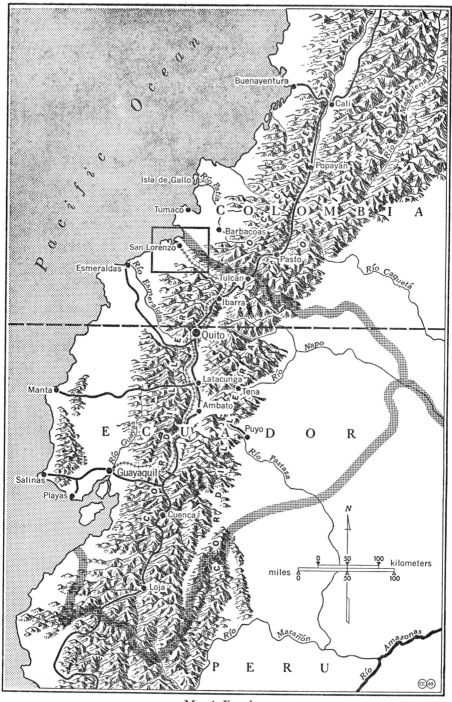

Map 1. Ecuador

The tropical and subtropical forests of the Oriente comprise approximately half the territory of Ecuador, and contain a scant 5 per cent of its population (Herring 1961: 525). The most famous inhabitants are the head-shrinking Jívaro Indians (Stirling 1938; Karsten 1935, 1954; Harner 1962) and the so-called Auca ("unbaptized") Indians (Elliot 1961). The Oriente, like the Galápagos Islands, which contain 2 per cent of the national population, is today undeveloped and only partially explored.

The Litoral, or coastal plain, covers little more than one-quarter of Ecuador's surface but contains about one-third of its population. Its population growth rate between 1950 and 1960 was 50.4 per cent, compared with 34.9 per cent in the Sierra (*El Comercio*, Feb. 15, 1963). An alluvial plain cut by rivers and a few chains of hills, the Litoral varies in width from twelve to one hundred miles. Its population is composed of Negroes, Indians, mestizos, Asiatics, whites, and all possible combinations of these. Guayaquil, with a growing population now exceeding 600,000, is the commercial and industrial center of the Litoral and the largest city in Ecuador. Manta, on the central desert coast, and Esmeraldas, in the northern rainforest, are the other leading towns of the Litoral.

The coast is crucial to Ecuadorian development. Nationalism in underdeveloped countries seems to require an expanding economic system (cf. Kunkel 1961: 51–53), and the most accessible economic resources in Ecuador lie along the coast. For Ecuador to develop as a nation, the coastal potential must be tapped and adequate communications between coast and highlands must be established. Responsible Ecuadorians are well aware of this, and they are striving to develop their coastal lands and to bridge the sociocultural gap between Serranos and Costeños.

The development of the coast is inextricably linked to national politics, which are dominated by the regional antagonism between a northern, conservative bloc, centered in Quito, and a southern, liberal bloc, based in Guayaquil. This political schism, reflecting large social, economic, and cultural differences, is as old as the nation (Dozer 1962: 321; Herring 1961: 526–28). Each side struggles constantly as a locus of the national political schism, and dedicates itself to making invidious comparisons in all areas of life.

The Province of Esmeraldas

The province of Esmeraldas is a tropical rainforest in which the northern slopes of the Ecuadorian Cordillera Occidental grades into an alluvial delta marked by two large river basins, the Esmeraldas basin in the south and the Santiago basin in the north. Over 120 inches of rain falls every year in this region (West 1957: 3); the temperature averages around 80° F (Acosta-Solis 1959b: 41); and the humidity is usually 90 per cent or higher (West 1957: 3). Esmeraldas has a vague two-season variation in climate. "Winter" refers to the rainy season, which lasts from November to June and reaches its height between January and May. It features incessant rainfall, interrupted by bright days and nights with occasional crystal-clear skies. During the dry "summer" season, June through October, some rain falls every day and it is almost always cloudy.

Esmeraldas, the capital of the province, is situated at the mouth of the Esmeraldas River, in the southwestern part of the province. Rubio Orbe *et al.* (1961: 258–59) describe the history of Esmeraldas as a series of alternating booms and depressions. A rubber and balsa boom during World War II was followed by a depression lasting from 1945 to 1947. A banana boom began in 1948 but was ended in the late 1950's by two simultaneous disasters, a banana blight and an earthquake that razed the entire town.

In the early 1960's, Esmeraldas appeared to be booming once again. In part, this prosperity was due to the opening of the Quito–Esmeraldas road. The largest banana plantations in the province are near Esmeraldas, and the town is now the northern center for exports of forest products. Around Esmeraldas, and just south of Limones, there are a number of profitable cattle ranches, which were apparently established with the wartime profits from balsa and rubber (Rubio Orbe *et al.* 1961: 258).

The Santiago basin in the north of the province is drained by the Santiago and Cayapas Rivers. Smaller important rivers are the Ónzole, which has cut a channel toward the Esmeraldas basin; the Sapallo Grande, which flows into the Cayapas; and the Bogotá and Cachabí Rivers, which flow into the Santiago. Lumbering operations are carried out on all these rivers, but chiefly on the Santiago. Principal towns in the Santiago basin have been Borbón, at the confluence of the Santiago and Cayapas Rivers, and Limones, at the mouth of the Santiago. Changes taking place since the completion of the Quito–San Lorenzo railroad have favored the growth of other towns. Limones remains a major town, but Borbón, described in 1942 as "the busiest little town in all northern Esmeraldas" (Ferdon 1950: 16), is now decaying and has given way to many other towns in size and importance. Its population rose from 600 in 1939 to an estimated 1,200 in 1942 (Ferdon 1950: 17), then shrank to 445 by 1963, and is still decreasing.[3] Today the leading towns of Esmeraldas province are San Lorenzo, Limones, and Esmeraldas. All three ports serve as export centers for tropical products—fruit, rice, lumber, balsa, fish, shellfish, and tagua—and, increasingly, for cattle raised on the newly cleared lands. The towns also serve as trading centers for the interior.

Racially, the population of the province is predominantly Negro, mulatto, and *zambo* (Negro-Indian racial mixture). Native Chibchan-speaking Indians (Colorado Indians in the south, Cayapa in the north and to a limited extent the south) supposedly retreated along the rivers as Negroes moved inland (Wolf 1879: 54; Barrett 1925: 37). The principal settlement of the Colorados is now at Santo Domingo de los Colorados, east of Esmeraldas, where their declining numbers are viewed by more and more tourists each year.

The Cayapa occupy the central and upper reaches of the Cayapas River and the various rivers flowing into it, especially the Sapallo Grande and the Ónzole and their tributaries. In 1963, many Cayapa were abandoning their subsistence farming, fishing, and hunting activities, as well as their handicrafts, and were moving from the smaller rivers to the Cayapas River itself, where they were clearing land for the cattle they hoped to buy or receive gratis from agencies working with the Alliance for Progress. Cayapa can be encountered almost any day in Borbón and Limones, and occasionally in San Lorenzo and Esmeraldas, where they come to sell bananas, plantains, wood, fire fans, and the finest dugout canoes on the Ecuadorian coast, which are in some demand from San Lorenzo to Guayaquil.

Negroes live along all the rivers and streams and along the coast of the province, as well as on the islands in the north. A smaller number live in the jungle interior on small farms, usually within

3. Unofficial statistics of the Servicio Cooperativo Interamericano de Salud Pública, supplied by the SCISP office in San Lorenzo.

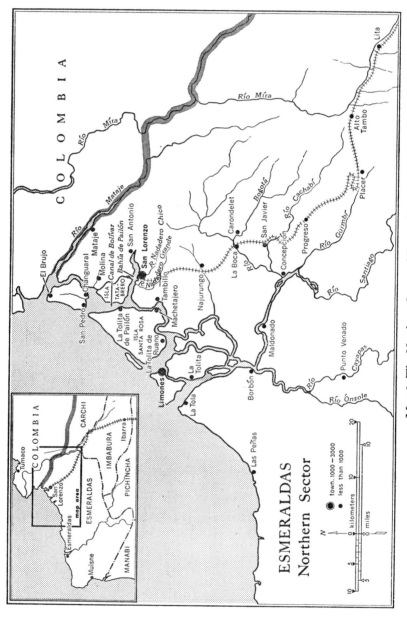

Map 2. The Northern Sector of Esmeraldas

an hour's walk from a stream, river, or railroad. Negroes, unlike Indians, work on shrimp, fishing, cargo, and banana boats, or in other jobs that are part of the cash economy; they make up most of the provincial labor force.

The Northern Sector of Esmeraldas

The northern sector of Esmeraldas is not a formal political division, but a geographic sector, now characterized by change in many areas of life. The changes have been stimulated by the Quito–San Lorenzo railroad, which cuts through the area. These changes are not restricted to San Lorenzo. On the basis of extensive travel and observation in 1961 and 1963, it can be stated that similar though less extensive changes are taking place in the rest of the sector.

The accompanying map of Esmeraldas province shows that the northern sector forms a triangle, with the little jungle town of Mataje on the northern border, the tiny coastal village of Las Peñas on the southern border, and the train stop of Lita at the eastern point. The entire northern sector is tropical rainforest, which dips sharply from 3,000–5,000 feet at Lita to sea level at San Javier. Temperature and humidity are high and streams appear everywhere, sometimes swollen with rain, at other times almost dry. Although the swelling and drying of streams corresponds generally to the wet-"dry" seasons, this correspondence is not absolute.

Ferdon (1950: 13) described the sector as it appeared to him in 1942:

Scattered here and there along the waterways are small agricultural settlements, while such villages as Concepción, Borbón, and probably Carondelet are primarily trading centers, buying tagua, rubber, and gold, and selling manufactured dry goods and some food. Conspicuous in the basin is the absence of haciendas and the presence of many small, individual land holdings. Subsistence agriculture based upon sweet manioc, plantains, bananas, rice, and sugarcane is typical of the region. On the upper waters of many of the streams, placer gold is panned out of the gravel as a source of cash. However, the dominant income source is the raising of tagua and rubber.

Today, rubber is no longer grown and placer gold no longer panned to any appreciable extent. The cultivation of tagua (palmnut ivory, now used chiefly for dice, carved jewelry, and toys) has only very recently been revived, on a small scale, along the Bogotá and Santiago Rivers. Lumber is now the main export of the interior; along the coast, there is profitable trade in such items as shellfish, fish, and mangrove bark. Subsistence agriculture is still based on the mainstay crops of 1942, and, as yet, there are no real plantations. The biggest change, except for the growth of the lumber trade, is the introduction of cattle raising, which is just getting under way and rapidly gaining popularity. Although cattle have been kept in the area for over a hundred years, moderate-scale ranching (25 or more head) is new.

The northern sector is not a completely homogeneous zone. From Lita to Progreso there are jungle-covered mountains, whose sparse population consists primarily of in-migrants from the Sierra. From San Javier southwest or northwest along the rivers in the lowland rainforests, Negroes live by farming and trading, cutting logs and killing a little game; those to the southwest are better off economically and culturally less isolated. The Negroes who live along the railroad do much the same thing, except for those who are beginning to take up cattle raising.

A second ecological zone is formed by the islands that extend from San Lorenzo to the Colombian border. One could argue that racially, culturally, and socioeconomically the inhabitants of these islands are not really a part of the northern sector. The island people show a heavier Indian admixture, and they rely more on coconuts and sea fishing than the mainlanders. The islanders also maintain subsistence farms, cut mangrove bark for export, engage in logging, and gather shellfish; all in all, they are the wealthiest non-trading people on the northern coast. Island villages have a more marked tendency to specialize than any other towns in northwest Ecuador: San Pedro, for example, is known for its coconuts, sugarcane, and bananas, Changuaral for its mangos and cattle, and El Brujo for its deep-sea fishing.

The mangrove swamps, which thrive in the protected bays of the Pacific coastal plain, form a third ecological zone between the rainforest and islands. The brackish swamps are cut by deep sea channels and smaller tidal rivers (*esteros*). They are interlaced with smaller streams, the navigation of which, even by canoe, is dependent upon the tidal flow. These mangrove swamps, like their Colombian counterparts, described by West (1957: 62) as among "the most luxurious in the world," restrict habitation to points of high ground. Places where the ground rises sharply and the sea channels are broad and deep make excellent habitation sites; San Lorenzo is one such place. The mangrove bays and estuaries protect the town from the force of sea winds but at the same time allow a refreshing breeze to penetrate, which makes living more comfortable than it is farther inland. Some of the largest towns in northwest Ecuador are found in the mangrove estuaries and bays.

The most important sources of income in the swamps are the cultivation of coconuts, stripping mangrove bark, and fishing for shellfish (crabs, mussels, and shrimp) and such popular and plentiful channel fish as the *corvina* and the *pargo*. The deep, protected harbors and estuaries connecting one town to another encourage shipping and commerce and make it possible to travel in light craft without fear of punishing storms from the sea.

San Lorenzo, jutting into the mangrove delta on an elevated point of land, embodies elements from many regions of the northern sector, of the coast in general, and of the country as a whole. Its population reflects the rural orientation of inland and island areas of Ecuador and Colombia, and of the small but growing sea-channel villages. It includes migrants from the larger coastal towns of Esmeraldas and Limones, Ecuador, and Tumaco, Colombia. Highlanders from Loja, Cuenca, Ambato, Riobamba, Ibarra, and points between, as well as from the capital city of Quito and the coastal metropolis of Guayaquil, also reside in, or visit, San Lorenzo. A few highlanders living there have spent time in the Oriente. Cayapa, Otavalo, and non-tribal Indians from northern Ecuador visit or pass through San Lorenzo, as do occasional Indians from the Putumayo region of Colombia. Heterogeneous socioeconomic, political, and cultural currents sweeping the country, coast, and sector often crystallize in San Lorenzo, allowing the observer to study the dynamics of change while analyzing community structure.

According to unofficial estimates, the population of the northern half of Esmeraldas province was 29,590 in 1963.[4] The major towns in the northern sector were as follows:

4. Unofficial statistic of the Servicio Cooperativo Interamericano de Salud Pública, supplied by the SCISP office in San Lorenzo. The SCISP figure covers a larger area than the "northern sector" under consideration here; it includes the population of the Cayapas and Ónzole Rivers, plus their tributaries and nearby streams.

Limones . . .	2,975	Borbón	445
San Lorenzo .	2,221	Concepción . .	419
Maldonado . .	689	Carondelet . .	328
La Tola . . .	641	San Javier . .	295
La Boca . . .	453		

Borbón has been steadily shrinking since the beginning of lumbering expansion about ten years ago, as has La Tola; Maldonado has replaced Borbón as the last deep-water town a small seagoing ship can reach to collect cargo. Concepción, a river trading town, has grown slowly since 1942; and Carondelet, the capital of the parish (in the civil, not ecclesiastical, sense) of Carondelet, is shrinking, its population shifting to the new railroad towns of San Javier and La Boca. Population movements in San Lorenzo will be discussed in detail in Chapter III.

To make the dynamics of change within the sector clear and to set the scene for an intensive consideration of San Lorenzo, certain factors involved in the development of the Ibarra–San Lorenzo section of the Quito–San Lorenzo railway must be set forth at this point.

Crucial for understanding the development of the railroad is knowledge of the political schism between Quito and Guayaquil and some of the speculations concerning the possible strengthening of Quito and the whole northern area as a politico-economic power. In 1942, Ferdon (1950: 18) noted:

The people of the northern highlands want the railroad completed so that they may have a cheap outlet to the sea. The people of Guayaquil fear that the development of a northern port and railroad terminus would lessen the importance of their city. Since Ecuador's exports are largely tropical products grown on the coast, the fullest development of San Lorenzo will depend, in large part, upon the eventual agricultural development of the Esmeraldas hinterland.

The highlanders feel that the Guayaquil industrial and commercial bloc has become too powerful. They have been feeling this way for some time, and have been looking to alliance with Esmeraldas province for support. The development of the road from Santo Domingo to Esmeraldas, and, more important, the Quito–San Lorenzo railroad, were attempts to politically and economically solidify the northern provinces. The eventual hope of Quiteño politicians is to colonize and industrialize the northern sector so that it can in fact, as well as propaganda, compete with Guayaquil and the southern political bloc. Before sufficient funds can be allocated for full-scale development of the northern sector, however, the Esmeraldas area must be developed economically and its population must increase and become urbanized. But to develop Esmeraldas, Quito must gain legislative support, and to gain this support she must have a majority in the legislature, which in turn depends on a stronger northern sector.

Development has thus far slowly taken place on small, sporadic appropriations conceded by the Guayaquil bloc. At the same time, the southern bloc has missed few opportunities to ridicule the slow development of the north and to point to the allegedly rapid progress of such enterprises as the new Guayaquil port and the projected port at Manta (*El Comercio*, April 12, 1963).

The northern bloc, by contrast, extols the virtues of Esmeraldas province and especially of the northern sector. A series of articles that appeared in Quito's daily newspaper, *El Comercio*, in 1961 was entitled "Esmeraldas—Piedra Preciosa Sin Labrar." Esmeraldas, the "precious, uncut stone," was presented as a rich, underdeveloped region that would someday shine as the jewel of the country. Like earlier and later articles and reports, this series emphasized the potential of San Lorenzo. One effect of this controversy has been to stimulate interest, both along the coast and throughout the highlands, in northern Esmeraldas.

More important than the immediate problem of victory in the battle for regional prestige is the question of what the northern sector can do to help the severely impoverished provinces of Carchi and, to a lesser degree, Imbabura and Pichincha. The shipment of goods from Guayaquil to Quito and on to the north leaves little trade for the particularly impoverished province of Carchi, which is, perhaps, the region of Ecuador most desperately in need of a more certain inflow of goods. San Lorenzo, the northern railroad terminus, is situated on a deep-water estuary, in one of the most accessible agricultural and foresting regions of the country (cf. Acosta-Solis 1959a, b; Conforti 1962; Houssin 1954). Nowhere else in Ecuador can large seagoing ships come directly to the wharf (though only at high tide) to meet the railroad, which takes goods into the interior. Northern Esmeraldas is a potential region for colonization from the arid mountains of Carchi and Imbabura. Colonization is certainly a major hope of engineers and planners, and, apparently, of an increasing number of lower-class highlanders.

The dream of a new land, rich and free, warm and friendly, attracted a great many people some eight years ago, when the railroad first opened a route from Ibarra (the capital of Imbabura) to San Lorenzo; it still attracts people interested in settling down in a wealthy land, or in accumulating a financial stake and returning to their beloved highland homes. The development of the section will be considered in Chapter II. Here I only wish to point out the most striking social phenomenon of the early attempts at colonization: two cultures, previously in sporadic contact, were conjoined, and this occurred within the sociocultural milieu of the Negro. It was his culture, his social system, his way of manipulating the world, into which the highlanders moved. Perhaps what initially led to the acceptance of the highlander by the Negroes was his introduction of things of interest and benefit to the coastal system: foods from the Sierra; an opportunity to work for the agencies involved with change; a stimulus for more ships to enter the harbor bringing goods and providing an outlet for exports; a rising population to stimulate local business; and certain material improvements. Whatever the reasons, the highlander, though ill at ease in his new sociocultural milieu, was treated with deference, and, from all reports, has often been accorded more prestige than he could have expected from his peers in the Sierra.

Northwest Ecuador is a frontier, but it is not a frontier where the original inhabitants (except possibly the Indians) are in decline. It is, rather, a region where the local people can flourish alongside the in-migrant frontiersmen.

Prehistory, Protohistory, and History

The prehistory of Esmeraldas province and the surrounding area remains to be set forth by archaeological work. The possibility of early intermittent contact with Mexican and Mayan cultures (Borhegyi 1959; Coe 1960: 367–93), and even transoceanic contacts

(Estrada and Meggers 1961), is stressed in recent articles on the provenience of figurines characteristic of the area.[5] Future archaeological work will be rewarding: deposits of utilitarian and ritual forms of pottery are so numerous and so rich that it is difficult to travel through the area without traipsing over an ancient residence or ceremonial site of prehistoric Indians.

For protohistoric times we have scarcely more information:

The place assigned to Ecuador in traditional culture-area divisions of the Andean chain is a marginal one. Within the territory of this country we find the southernmost extension of Chibchan-speaking groups as well as peoples for whom affiliation with the north coast of Peru has been suggested. In addition, the tribes of Ecuador were the last to be subdued by the Inca, and as such were never thoroughly integrated within the feudal structure of the Empire. (Murra 1946: 785.)

There seem to have been two different "tribes" in the northern sector of Esmeraldas, both of which existed into historic times. They were the Malaba Indians of the Mataje River valley, who were encountered in the eighteenth century (Murra 1946: 807), and the Esmeralda Indians, whose language, believed to have been Chibchan, was spoken in the nineteenth century (Murra 1946: 802; Jijón y Caamaño 1941), and who figured in travelers' reports from the mid-sixteenth century to the early nineteenth (Garcilaso de la Vega 1723; Stevenson 1826; Cieza de León 1932). The Cayapa Indians speak Chibchan; they are believed to have entered the area from the Andes to the northeast. They may have been forced into the western forests by encroaching Quechua-speaking Indians (Barrett 1925: 31; Murra 1948: 277–78), and kept from the coast by the so-called "Indios Bravos," fierce coastal Indians, sometimes reputed to have been cannibals (Barrett 1925: 32–39). The general movement of Indians into the area in protohistoric times seems to have been from the north and northeast. There was a later swing back from Peru, but this never had the cultural and political impact on the Esmeraldas coast that it had in, and adjacent to, other Andean regions;

5. The figurines are described in Acosta-Solis (1944), Ferdon (n.d.), and Collier (1946: 781). The results of several excavations have not yet been taken into account by the literature on provenience (see Uhle 1927; Costales Samaniego 1957; César Cubillos 1955).

it was truncated by the advent of Francisco Pizarro and the beginning of the Spanish Conquest.

There is some evidence that on his second voyage (1526–27)
Pizarro touched on the area that is the subject of this study. Having
left Pizarro to his booty on the San Juan River, his pilot, Bartolomé
Ruiz, sallied forth to reconnoiter the country to the south.

Coasting along the great continent, with his canvas still spread to favorable
winds, the first place at which Ruiz cast anchor was off the little island of
Gallo, about two degrees north. The inhabitants, who were not numerous,
were prepared to give him a hostile reception,—for tidings of the invaders
had preceded them along the country, and even reached this insulated spot.
As the object of Ruiz was to explore, not to conquer, he did not care to
entangle himself in hostilities with the natives: so, changing his purpose of
landing, he weighed anchor, and ran down the coast as far as what is now
called the Bay of St. Matthew. (Prescott 1874: I, 242.)

Bartholomew (1930: 133) locates the Bay of St. Matthew south of
Barbacoas, Colombia, and north of the Santiago River, Ecuador,
which places it in either what is today called the Bahía de Tumaco,
in Colombia, or the Bahía de Ancón de Sardinas, in Ecuador. Pedro
Vicente Maldonado (Rumazo 1948: I, map facing p. 354) locates
the bay further south, between the Esmeraldas and Verde Rivers.
In any case, the bay lies within the area under discussion, and can
serve as a geographical and historical locus.

Pizarro's arrival on the coast, his encampment on Gallo Island,
and his subsequent exploration of the Bay of St. Matthew (Prescott
1874: I, 249) may have introduced the first Negro to the area. According to Paredes Borja (1963b: 47), at least one Negro was with
Pizarro on Gallo Island.

Negroes in Esmeraldas Province

Esmeraldas province today is populated predominantly by Negroes whose ancestors came from Africa within the last four hundred
years. Paredes Borja (1963b: 47), along with other Ecuadorian
historians, asserts that the Negro population originated with slaves
who were imported by Negro slave traders, shipwrecked on the
Esmeraldas coast, and led by a Negro named Illescas.

Victor Von Hagen (1940: 282) holds that the Negroes of Esmeraldas "are descendants of slaves from a Negro slave ship which

was wrecked on the coast of Esmeraldas in 1650. Here the slaves had put their Spanish captors to the knife and regained their freedom." (See also Von Hagen 1955: 32–33.) Emilio Estrada and Betty J. Meggers (1961: 935–36) apparently have no qualms about repeating this version of the beginning of Negroes in Esmeraldas:

A few years after European discovery, in the early sixteenth century, 17 Negroes survived a shipwreck off the coast of Esmeraldas. Intermarrying with Indian women, they were able to gain political control of the whole province in a short time. Their domination continued for several decades, during which time the Spaniards were unable to conquer the area.

Such references to the wrecked slaving ship seem to begin with a work by the traveler Miguel Cabello de Balboa.[6] According to Jijón y Caamaño (1943: II, 71–73), who refers to the original archival source, 17 Negro men and six Negro women, the property of Alfonso Illescas, a ladino, landed near Esmeraldas.[7] Fighting among the Negroes reduced their number to seven men and three women, all of whom supposedly married Indians rather than one another, and, led by Illescas, came to dominate political life in what is now Esmeraldas province.

The Negroes today hold no socially standardized legend of entry to the province. Indeed, it is uncommon to encounter a Negro who will describe entry further back than his father's or grandfather's generation, but now and again an imaginative informant gives a more elaborate account. Usually, such a conversation arises when a Negro denies African heritage. He did not come from Africa, his ancestors came from Colombia, in the north, or as the Negroes say "abajo" (down) the coast. One such story involves the founding of the town of San Lorenzo:

Long, long ago a man came paddling into the Bahía de Pailón, which was always so named. He came from the direction of the Canal de Bolívar. He was a fisherman come from the north in search of new territory. The fishing was so good and the area so agreeable that he went back down the

6. Jijón y Caamaño (1943: II, 71) gives the original source for Cabello de Balboa's journey as a manuscript in the Archivo de Indias de Sevilla (n.d.: 70-4-7) entitled, "Verdadera relación de la Provincia y Tierra de las Esmeraldas." Cabello de Balboa was in the province of Esmeraldas in 1577 (Merizalde de Carmen 1921: 123).
7. A ladino in this sense is a Negro born in Africa but acculturated in hispanic language and culture. Cf. Mellafe (1964: 69.)

coast [north to Colombia] and found a woman. He returned with her to the Bahía de Pailón. Later, more and more people settled in San Lorenzo, while others settled or established farms in the hinterland streams and rivers.

Available information on the entry of Negroes to northwest Ecuador does indicate a north-to-south movement. Robert C. West (1952: 9–51, 83) clearly establishes the fact that the Negroes of New Granada entered through Cartagena, on Colombia's Caribbean coast, and moved south and west to areas just north of the Ecuadorian border. For example, Negro slaves were brought into the upper Cauca River area as early as 1544, to the northern Chocó, near Ríosucio, by 1583, and to the northern edge of the Popayán plateau by 1640 (West 1952: 10–13, 37; Hernández de Alba 1946: 927; 1948a: 299–300; 1948b: 331). There is ample evidence that Negroes lived in the highlands of Ecuador as early as the 1550's (Kubler 1946: 367–70; Murra 1946: 817), but no indication of how they got there.

In the early nineteenth century more Negroes arrived in the Sierra, in the armies of the liberators. "The Negro distinguished himself as a leader and soldier in practically all the campaigns for independence in the New World. He brought his talent and aptitude for warfare to the campaigns of both Simón Bolívar and San Martín, in which there were well-organized and well-disciplined troops of Negro soldiers." (Herring 1961: 113.) Apparently some of these soldiers remained in Ecuador. According to Dozer (1962: 320), Vicente Rocafuerte, a liberal reformer and President of Ecuador from 1834 to 1839, "opposed and sought to reduce the power of the Negro troops" whom Juan José Flores (military leader under Simón Bolívar and later responsible for Ecuador's separation from Gran Colombia) imported from Venezuela.

West (1957: 106) claims that the Negro population of Esmeraldas originated partly with migrations during the last one hundred years of the Negroes known to have been living in the Sierra. Although I have frequently heard educated Ecuadorians speak of Negro migrations from the Sierra to the coast, this is still undocumented speculation.

The Negroes who were imported to work the mines of the Barbacoas area of Colombia in the mid-seventeenth century are the first

whose presence near northern Esmeraldas is really well-documented
(West 1952: 18; Merizalde del Carmen 1921: 143, 149). It seems
much more reasonable to suppose that Negroes reached Esmeraldas
by filtering southward from Colombia than to explain their presence there by one shipwreck off the coast, or by undocumented migrations from the Sierra during the past one hundred years.

English and German Influences

The recorded history of San Lorenzo began with the founding of
two land companies, one English and the other German, to exploit
the resources of the region. Information about the original English
company, reported here because San Lorenzeños regard it as a fact,
is vague and likely to be inaccurate. However, my description of the
German company's activities is drawn, unless otherwise noted, from
conversations with old men who had worked for the company themselves or whose fathers had worked for it.

In her fight for independence from New Granada, Ecuador incurred a debt to the British Crown, which it repaid by granting exploitation rights in the province of Esmeraldas to an English company, named La Compañía Inglesa Limitada del Ecuador (Wolf
1879). Informants claim that the English wrote "Ecuadorian Land
Company" and "English Land Company" on their belongings. The
English began studying the area as early as 1837, but the company
actually began operations around 1860 (Suárez Veintimilla 1942:
273).[8] Although old informants in San Lorenzo state that the English company remained until 1902, when it granted a subcontract
to a German company, Linke (1955: 157) dates the turnover from
English to German operation at about 1870.

The English company purchased tagua, fine wood, balsa, gold,
mangrove bark, pelts, and medicinal herbs. The company's home
office was in Mataje, which, according to Wolf's map (1879), was
named Compaña. Local men were hired to work as clerks and pur-

---

8. It was with a letter from the British Admiralty, dated 1837, that exploration of the
northern sector of Esmeraldas began; the English pursued their investigations so long as
their company was active (Acosta-Solis 1944: 575). In part, such studies were intended to
determine the best entrance to the port of San Lorenzo and to facilitate the export of forest
products (Suárez Veintimilla 1942: 273–75). The English exploration of the area is described in more detail in *El Comercio*, Aug. 5, 1962, and in documents in the Archives of
the San Lorenzo naval base.

chasers in hinterland towns, the most important of which were Borbón, Concepción, and San Lorenzo. Some buildings were constructed
in San Lorenzo, supposedly on and near the site of the present Hotel
Imperial. The English are also reputed to have made pastures for
their horses and mules, and for the Brown Swiss cows they are said
to have introduced into the region. According to San Lorenzeños,
the Englishmen and their families all lived in one large house. Although the men reputedly refused offers of Negro concubines, they
are said to have treated the local Negroes with respect.

I know of only two San Lorenzeños who claim descent from Englishmen; one uses an English first name as his surname, the other
an English surname as his surname. I have collected over three
hundred English names, mostly first names, of Negroes in the area.
Milton, Joffre, Jenny, Gilbert, Douglas, and Daisy crop up frequently; the pronunciation is Spanish, but the spelling (for the literate) is as given here. Such words as Lover, Limber, Liver, Klever,
and Timber are also used as first names. One street in San Lorenzo
is named "Mister Corner."

Sometime after the mid-nineteenth century, trouble between the
townspeople and the head of the English company is said to have
broken out in San Lorenzo. For one reason or another, a fence, or
perhaps many fences, had been erected in the town. One May 24,
Negroes are reported to have razed the fences. The head of the company, whose office was in San Lorenzo (or Mataje—stories vary),
sent word to Britain that the razing of fences and other, unspecified
acts of minor violence constituted torts against the British Crown. A
warship, sent to investigate, supposedly sailed into the Bahía de
Pailón and trained its guns on San Lorenzo. An inquest was held,
at which it was decided that the hostile acts were personal and directed toward the company head, not the Crown. All expenses of
the trip were accordingly charged to the English company. For all
practical purposes, this marked the end of English interests in the
area. In the absence of supporting evidence, this story must be regarded as an important part of the Negroes' folk history, rather than
fact.

The name of San Lorenzo during, or just preceding, British exploitation was reputedly Pueblo de Pailón, which later became San
Lorenzo de Pailón, and finally San Lorenzo. At this time, all of

Esmeraldas province was one *cantón* (canton) and San Lorenzo was the head of one of the seven civil parishes in the canton (Wolf 1879: 47).

The German company, called Casa Tagua, continued operations until 1930. The tenure of this company extends into the period when the railroad from Ibarra to San Lorenzo was under construction (Linke 1960: 117; Acosta-Solis 1959b). As the name indicates, the company's main interest was in the tagua trade; it also dealt in gold, wood, and other forest products. It had its head office in Mataje, with branches in San Lorenzo, Concepción, Borbón, Limones, Muisne, and Esmeraldas.

German engineers completed two studies of the northern sector in 1918 and 1919 (Acosta-Solis 1944: 576), and later several conservation studies were made, sponsored in part by the government agency responsible for the Ibarra–San Lorenzo railroad (Suárez Veintimilla 1942: 273; *El Comercio,* Aug. 5, 1962). In 1926 a study was made by an American engineer, and four more studies were completed by Ecuadorians prior to 1940 (Acosta-Solis 1944: 576–77). Since 1940, French, American, and Italian engineers have made surveys of the area.

Throughout the modern history of northern Esmeraldas, pressures coming from outside the area itself have given it an atmosphere of impending change. First came the Negroes, a potential labor force, with their successful encroachment on Indian lands. Next came the foreign exploiters, who provided a market, albeit a small one, for forest products. Foreign entrepreneurs provided sporadic boom periods for the expanding Negro labor force, while the rich environment sustained subsistence labor between such booms. Finally came the Quito–San Lorenzo railroad (to be examined in the following chapter), which linked the northwest to the rest of the country. It began a new boom period, but, more important, it established the potential for sustained development.

II

Change in San Lorenzo: 1942–1963

According to Ferdon (1950: 18), who visited San Lorenzo in 1942, the town at that time had no electricity, no hotel or public restaurant, and apparently no school. The canoe was the only means of transportation in common use. He estimated that there were about one hundred houses in the town; if the average household in San Lorenzo had between five and seven people, as it does now, then there were between five and seven hundred people living there in 1942. Ferdon recognized the great potential of the town:

San Lorenzo impresses one as a small town waiting for someone else to do something. Some day, if the railroad reaches the coast, the town may become one of the principal ports of Ecuador. It is reached from the ocean by a short steamer run up the Canal de Bolívar estuary, in marked contrast to the long, time-consuming trip up the Guayas River to Guayaquil. The railroad, which has been in the process of construction for at least thirty years and is still less than 50 per cent complete, has been used as a political pawn.

Political pawn or not, the railroad did reach San Lorenzo, and ushered in an era of local growth and change. The modern history of San Lorenzo may be divided into four overlapping stages: railroad construction (1952–1957), railroad completion (1957–1959), port construction (1959–1961), and port completion (1961–1965). This study was undertaken during the end of the third stage, and completed during the fourth. At the end of the study, in 1963, San Lorenzo was still in the process of port completion. My description of changes in the town, unless otherwise noted, is based on extensive interviews with railroad officials and townspeople.

Railroad Construction

President García Moreno authorized the construction of a Quito–San Lorenzo railroad in a legislative decree issued in 1861 (Suárez Veintimilla 1942: 262–64), but it was not until 1915 that work actually began (Acosta-Solis 1944: 571). By 1928 the railroad had reached a spot some thirty miles north of Ibarra (Suárez Veintimilla 1942: 275). For years the proposed Quito–San Lorenzo railway moved very slowly westward from Ibarra toward San Lorenzo. Construction began from San Lorenzo eastward in 1952, as the westbound section reached Lita. "The additional ninety-four miles required to descend the slopes of the Andes in a northwestern direction to the coast were built by the CIAVE [Comptoir International d'Achats et Ventes à l'Étranger] simultaneously from both ends, under the most trying geographic and climatic conditions, and completed in 1957." (Linke 1960: 117.)

The story of the extension of the railroad from Ibarra to San Lorenzo begins around 1940, with the reorganization of the Junta Autónoma del Ferrocarril Quito–San Lorenzo (the Quito–San Lorenzo Autonomous Railroad Organization).[1] A Junta Autónoma is an organization created by executive decree, with the approval of the legislature, on petition of a town, region, or agency to the government of Ecuador. In the late 1930's, prominent citizens and political leaders of Ibarra and other parts of Imbabura province petitioned the government to reorganize the existing Junta Autónoma to enable it to construct and maintain the railroad from Ibarra to San Lorenzo; to develop the port town of San Lorenzo; to complete and maintain the port; and to colonize and develop the area bordering on the railroad, i.e., the northern sector of Esmeraldas province. The Junta Autónoma, which is still in existence, was similar in makeup to other such bodies; the government designated representatives from the Republic of Ecuador, the national Ministry of Public Works, the national economic council, the provincial council of Imbabura, and the *Consejo Municipal* (municipal council) of Ibarra to serve as directors. (Recently, a member of the Junta de Planificación was added.) A fixed percentage of the federal revenue, which has never been changed, was allotted to the Junta Autónoma.

1. For the predecessors of the Junta Autónoma and further details on its reorganization, see Suárez Veintimilla (1942: 164–70, 177–78).

The completion of the railroad was made possible by a contract between the Junta Autónoma and two French companies, CIAVE and Entreprises Métropolitaines et Coloniales. CIAVE subcontracted the actual construction to a company known as CFE.[2] CIAVE provided the funds to complete the railroad, supplied two diesel engines especially designed for the steep, twisting, narrow gauge track, and sponsored studies of the potential of the northern sector. It also enlisted the aid of another French company, the Sociedad Grenoblesa (SOGREA), to study the port and estuary and to recommend practical measures for developing the port. SOGREA's recommendations are still the basis for discussions of the needs of the northern sector (*El Comercio*, Aug. 5, 1962).

In 1952 the Junta Autónoma transferred its permanent field offices from Ibarra to San Lorenzo. A head engineer, several assistant engineers, secretaries, and other office workers moved to San Lorenzo. The executive offices remained in Quito, where the president of the Junta Autónoma and his aides, representing the board of directors, began a campaign to publicize the developing town of San Lorenzo. CIAVE and Junta Autónoma officials in San Lorenzo built their own office buildings, established their own medical center, and financed the construction of a small airstrip. To the reported dismay of the local inhabitants, they began to spend money allotted for the development of San Lorenzo on the construction of a so-called New Town, an outlying area which they designated as a new residential section.

The Junta Autónoma was responsible for the maintenance of the land for 20 kilometers on either side of the railroad—an area covering the entire town of San Lorenzo (Acosta-Solis 1959b: 27). Income from the sale and exploitation of this land was to supplement the tax funds allotted to the Junta Autónoma. Ownership of the town of San Lorenzo by the Junta did not appear strange to planners in Quito, for on paper no one owned any land there. The local inhabitants have no formal system of inheritance or landownership. A man owns the land that he works, and anyone has the right to occupy land that is lying fallow. It was not long before the Junta Autónoma's legal ownership of San Lorenzo came into conflict with

2. Railroad officials in San Lorenzo believed that CFE stood for Compañía Francaisa Entreprises, but they were not certain.

the Negroes' traditional right to work and live on the land of their choosing.

Two distinct classes, both composed largely of highlanders, took up residence in San Lorenzo during the construction of the railroad: one was a new elite of Ecuadorian and French engineers, planners, and other officials; the other was made up of Indian and mestizo construction workers. The new elite belonged to Ecuador's rising middle class, their advance contingent on achievement demonstrable to other highlanders. Though they felt that nothing less than a New Town could serve as their showpiece, they did bring electricity to San Lorenzo, establish a network of street lights, and build a pumping station on the Nadadero Chico River, which brought water to a few outlets in town.

The mestizo and Indian workers formed a sizable labor force numbering from one to three hundred at any given time. They lived in specially constructed camps, usually staying only long enough to complete the job for which they had been hired. In general, the mestizos and the Negroes regarded each other more or less as equals, and both looked upon the Indian, set apart by his non-western dress, as inferior. Mestizo-Negro relations in the early 1950's were characterized by frequent fights, typically over women. There were also many clashes between local Negroes and the rural police, who were brought into San Lorenzo in increased numbers. Allegations of police brutality toward the Negroes were common. Later these conflicts subsided as some upper- and middle-class newcomers (whites and mestizos) established good relations with Negroes and mulattoes, while other middle- and lower-class mestizos and Negroes learned to avoid one another.

Progress on the railroad brought a building boom to San Lorenzo. The French built a large building in the center of town (now the Hotel Imperial), supposedly on the site of the old land company building. The Junta Autónoma erected the Ciudadela (Citadel), complete with tennis court, to house engineers and other officials; the Junta also built camps, offices, and mechanics' sheds. (See Map 3, p. 210.) When port construction was nearing completion, a group of Junta Autónoma and CIAVE employees built a movie theater, in which they occasionally showed movies rented from a theater in Ibarra. Other new buildings reflected the townspeople's new commercial hopes. The Hotel Pailón and the Salón Ibarra were built by local mulattoes, who were informally guaranteed Junta Autónoma patronage. Several saloons and shops, and two small restaurants, also sprang up.

During the period of railroad construction, San Lorenzo was primarily a workers' town, in which most of the inhabitants benefited from the changes taking place. People involved in semisubsistence labor had expanded outlets for their goods and new work opportunities; wage earners and skilled or semiskilled laborers had a relatively steady income. Commercial activities expanded, and shop, restaurant, and saloon owners had a guaranteed clientele. The elite corps of engineers and planners saw in the development of the coast an opportunity to win national attention and prominent positions elsewhere in Ecuador.

Railroad Completion

Although President Velasco Ibarra paid an official visit to San Lorenzo in 1955 to forecast the completion of the railroad, it was his successor, Camilo Ponce Enríquez, who was credited with the accomplishment when work was actually finished in 1957 (Herring 1961: 535). Completion of the railroad generated much excitement in the Sierra, whose inhabitants had easy access to the northern coast for the first time. The San Lorenzeños, for their part, welcomed the highlanders with special fiestas. In this atmosphere of general enthusiasm Junta Autónoma officials in San Lorenzo, supported by propaganda from their home office in Quito (Acosta-Solis 1959b: 25–26), redoubled their efforts to build the New Town. The New Town came to consist of a number of sidewalks and unpaved roads in one of the more mosquito-infested areas adjoining San Lorenzo. The highlanders designated as "industrial and commercial zones" the areas in which most of the Negroes lived (in effect, the actual town of San Lorenzo), albeit without papers of ownership, and as "residential zones" (the New Town) areas much further away from the port. The Negroes could not afford to live so far from the sea, on which much of their livelihood depended, and they continued to reside in the "industrial and commercial zones."

During this stage many mestizo workmen, some Negroes, and most of the Indians returned to their highland or coastal homes, in some cases abandoning concubines and children. Some mestizos and Negroes had been hired by the railroad as carpenters, mechanics, and foremen; they either found other work in San Lorenzo or stayed on as railroad-maintenance workers (*carrilanos*). Others who had succeeded in establishing themselves as small shop- or saloonkeepers also remained.

Ambitious newcomers continued to arrive. In 1958, a German purchased a sawmill that had changed ownership repeatedly for more than ten years; five Italian immigrants built another sawmill after trying unsuccessfully to farm; and a highland Ecuadorian bought land for a third sawmill, which began operation the next year. The first permanent priest, an Italian missionary of the Comboniano order, arrived in 1958. The Combonianos (called the Vernon Brothers in the United States and England) are committed to proselytizing Negroes, and they have recently extended their activity to the New World. Before the Italian missionary arrived, the northern sector of Esmeraldas had received only sporadic attention from the Franciscan priests of Ecuador, who made yearly rounds, baptizing, confirming, and occasionally marrying people (mostly Cayapa Indians), but never settling. Protestant Evangelists from the United States also began intensive efforts in this period, but to this day they have had little success.

Although many mestizos and Negroes left San Lorenzo with the completion of the railroad, a steady in-migration began that is still going on. An unofficial census taken in June 1958 indicated that San Lorenzo's population had risen from 500–700 inhabitants in 1942 to 1,485 (Acosta-Solis 1959b: 24). Although the 1958 figure includes many essentially transient workmen, it is obvious that the population had grown rapidly.

Early in this period, members of the municipal council, at the request of the townspeople, began to reassert their authority in San Lorenzo. Since 1953 the Junta Autónoma had been virtually running the town, without any serious intervention by the municipal council. The Junta Autónoma had brought electricity to San Lorenzo but had prohibited the construction of private dwellings except in the so-called residential areas, where no one wanted to live and where, in fact, no houses were built. Some houses were built in defiance of the Junta's ban, but this always led to trouble. Reportedly, the Junta Autónoma was running San Lorenzo with the unofficial support of the local rural police, the teniente político for the town, and a few prominent townsmen.

For a brief time both the Junta Autónoma and the municipal council claimed the right to control the activities of San Lorenzo and to regulate commerce. At the same time, both denied any obligation to the townspeople, each holding the other responsible. The denial of obligation by the Junta Autónoma led the teniente político and prominent townsmen to withdraw their support, and in 1959 they were regularly siding with municipal officials in their desire for more control. The situation was further aggravated when the national legislature stepped in and passed a law—the only one of its kind in Ecuador—giving the Junta Autónoma full authority in all matters relating to the development of the town. This law explicitly confirmed the powers previously implied by the Junta's authority over all land for 20 kilometers on either side of the railroad.

Passage of the law did not put an end to the power struggle. The Junta Autónoma, acting on its new authority, tried to force the townspeople (newcomers and natives) out of their homes and into the residential section designated in its plans. A crisis developed when they refused to leave their homes, and were supported by prominent members of the municipal council and influential figures from the northern coast. The Junta Autónoma, finding itself opposed to town and municipio, reversed its policies and began to court prominent members of the municipal council. Shortly thereafter, Junta Autónoma and municipal officials agreed to share responsibility for the welfare of the town.

The crisis receded as people began to build homes where they wanted to build them—in the officially designated commercial and industrial zones. In-migrants from the highlands and the coast continued to arrive. The French building was converted into the Hotel Imperial by an absentee landlord, a highlander from Ibarra. Another small hotel, the Hotel Carchi, was built by another highlander to take care of the almost immediate influx of officials and tourists from the highlands, who came to see if San Lorenzo might be worth investing in. Many of the local inhabitants, too, were busy expanding commercial operations and making important political and social contacts. Two poolrooms, a number of saloons, and several new shops and additions to old ones were built during this time, as San Lorenzo became a focal point of national interest. Informants report a widespread sense of impending change in the town. All these developments, however, had not affected the mass of Negroes appreciably by the time San Lorenzo entered the stage of port construction.

Port Construction

This stage began in 1959 and ended in 1961. During the construction and development of the port, Junta Autónoma officials apparently gained in prestige. Some of them brought their families to live in San Lorenzo and set about trying to create a favorable environment for children. The second Comboniano priest arrived. A small naval base was established in June 1961, and the officers and enlisted men actively tried to fit into the life of the town. The town expanded internally, highlanders settling in the center of town or along the railroad tracks and Negroes spreading along the airstrip, toward the naval base, and along the railroad. Barrios became more densely populated. During the construction of the port, skilled laborers had work and menial jobs were not hard to find. Propaganda from the head office at Quito kept tourism alive and encouraged the townspeople's hopes of an improved future. In northern Esmeraldas people began to speak of San Lorenzo as the new capital of the canton. There was even talk of dividing the canton into two municipios, one centered in San Lorenzo, the other in Limones. Such a move would have been extraordinary, for in the Ecuadorian administrative system, municipios are coterminous with cantons.

In 1960, an unofficial census taken by the Servicio Cooperativo Interamericano de Salud Pública indicated that the population of San Lorenzo stood at 1,787.[3] This is probably too high a figure, since SCISP tries to establish the maximum possible population, and so may count a person once as a member of one household, and again as a member of another, and also includes people who are clearly transients.

The period of port construction was notable for the absence of crises. In 1961, during my first visit, most people seemed happy to forget the troubles of the recent past. Saloons (i.e., large dance halls)

3. Unofficial statistic, supplied by the SCISP office in San Lorenzo.

poolrooms, and new *cantinas* (small, one-room drinking establishments) were open every night, and the weekend tourist trade was thriving. Although old grievances were sometimes discussed, they seldom were exploited to provoke new conflicts. Land for a hospital in the New Town was purchased by Evangelical Protestants; wealthy businessmen from Limones purchased other land for speculative purposes. The Junta Autónoma gave the municipio land for a new school, which was erected on the east side of the New Town. All this land, as well as the school, remains unused and almost unvisited, except by women who wash clothes in the nearby Nadadero Chico River and by the few Negroes who pass by on the way to their small farms.

On July 31, 1961, CIAVE gave the town a 30-day departure notice, which signaled the end of the period of port construction.[4] The company left before the end of August, leaving the port incomplete and unopened. CIAVE's official withdrawal left the Junta Autónoma as the sole responsible agency for all that had been undertaken: colonization, maintenance of the railroad, port and town completion, and, finally, payment of the debt to CIAVE and associated companies, which came to $2,500,000 (Conforti 1962: 4). Railroad officials claimed that any of these ventures would have exhausted the total Junta Autónoma budget.

In mid-August 1961, the Junta estimated its losses at 10,000 sucres per day, and soon afterward ended most activities except maintenance. The head engineer, a doctor and his assistant, a radio operator, a topographer and his assistant, an accountant, the chief of equipment, and some thirty workers were retained in San Lorenzo. All of the other engineers and secretaries, and most of the workers (between 100 and 140), were discharged.

At the end of 1961, there was a great deal of talk in Quito, Esmeraldas, and San Lorenzo of abolishing the Junta Autónoma and changing the capital of the canton Eloy Alfaro from Limones to San Lorenzo. In effect, such a move would have made municipal and political officials, rather than an agency of the national government, responsible for governing and developing the northern sector.

---

4. Officials in Quito knew the departure date well in advance but did not inform anyone in San Lorenzo; no one in the town knew of CIAVE's plans until the day notice was given.

Port Completion

In 1962 and 1963 propaganda for and against San Lorenzo kept the town before the eyes of the nation. The railroad was maintained, and the new line from the coast to the highlands was kept open at a loss of 400,000 sucres per month (Conforti 1962: 4). Along the line the *autocarriles* (old Ford buses on railway wheels) ran daily from Quito to Ibarra and from Ibarra to San Lorenzo, carrying passengers, mail, and freight. The two large diesels continued pulling cargo trains. The Junta Autónoma remained active, and San Lorenzo did not become the center of a municipio or canton, although two new parishes were established within the canton Eloy Alfaro. Superficially, at least, San Lorenzo continued to change; but, as I shall show, the motivating force for change shifted somewhat from outside organizations to local agencies.

Before discussing the changes that occurred between 1961 and 1963, we should have some idea of the population growth for the period. SCISP took a census in July 1962, and counted 2,221 persons.[5] The first national house-to-house census was taken in November of the same year, and registered 2,426 people.[6] The SCISP figure is probably too high for the reasons given earlier, and the national figure is unreliable because it is dependent on the guesses of untrained census takers. My own census, based on house-to-house counts of the coastal Negroes, zambos, and mulattoes, and estimates of the highlanders, placed the population as of August 1963 at 2,418. Depending on movements of visitors and workmen, this figure may vary by as much as 300 in either direction. These data can be summed up as follows:

Date	Census	Population	Probable Error
1942	Ferdon	500–700	rough estimates
June 1958	Acosta-Solis	1,485	?
1960	SCISP	1,787	excess
July 1962	SCISP	2,221	excess
Nov. 1962	National	2,426	?
Aug. 1963	Whitten	2,418	± 300

5. Unpublished statistic, supplied by the SCISP office in San Lorenzo.
6. Unpublished statistic, supplied by the Tenencia Política office in San Lorenzo.

San Lorenzo's steady growth is reflected in the constant building going on in several barrios in the town, notably the one known as Las Tres Marías and along the railroad and airstrip. Maps of San Lorenzo, on which conscientious engineers tried to note every building in town, confirm the impression of steady growth. My data on the number of houses in 1961 and 1963, together with the maps, indicate an increase of 30–40 per cent in the number of houses between 1961 and 1963.

The growth of San Lorenzo cannot be accounted for by in-migration alone, although this is the explanation usually given by Ecuadorians. True, many Negroes are moving in, but many also seem to be moving out, following the patterns of spatial mobility discussed in Chapter VII. The growth of San Lorenzo can best be seen as the result of natural increase plus in-migration. Negroes born or raised in San Lorenzo are apparently less likely to move away than residents of other coastal areas. San Lorenzo's population is "younging" (Petersen 1961: 81). Many young people are staying, not moving away in search of work, and the majority of in-migrants are also young. For this reason, the population growth of San Lorenzo represents an increase in the labor force, and therefore an increased capacity to bring about material change.

Between 1961 and 1963, San Lorenzo seemed to have settled down to steady sociocultural change. Economic development still seemed imminent. During this period the Catholic charity CARITAS was established, and the CARE agency that had been established in 1959 increased its activity. The Catholic Church expanded its membership and brought in three nuns to manage a medical dispensary; the nuns taught first aid and sewing as the first steps toward a complete curriculum. SCISP moved its regional office from Borbón to San Lorenzo.

There was much excitement over the possibility of making San Lorenzo a free port for merchandise imported by Brazil; although this step was officially taken, it cannot benefit the town until a way is worked out to transport goods to the Napo River in the Oriente. At this writing there is a jungle hiatus between the end of the road from Ambato to Puyo and the Napo River. Nevertheless, a barrio was named Puerto de Manaos in honor of the town on the Amazon

River that would receive goods sent from San Lorenzo over the Andes and down the Napo and Amazon. (See Map 4, p. 213.)

New buildings were erected between 1961 and 1963, and the number of galvanized tin roofs increased. Among the mass of Negroes, no one owned transistor radios and not many owned shoes in 1961; by 1963 there was a striking increase in both items. Cantinas had increased from three or four in 1961 to over thirty in 1963, while the number of saloons had shrunk to only one that was regularly open.

The propaganda campaign for the development of San Lorenzo brought a *comisario nacional de policía* and two customs agents to the town. The comisario is a representative of the supreme court of justice; he decides criminal cases, usually for an entire canton. Most of his income comes from graft. Ordinarily, even the administrative center of an urban parish has only a teniente político, a representative of the executive branch of government, whose livelihood also depends on graft. The effects of bringing a comisario to such a small town will be seen in later chapters.

To say San Lorenzo settled down between 1961 and 1963 is not to say that all was serene. But the storms arising in this period generally originated at home, although some of them may have had outside inspiration. The most striking developments of these three years were the establishment of an apolitical agency oriented toward development of San Lorenzo; the revival of a political organization committed to similar ends; a strike of Junta Autónoma employees; a political crisis stemming from conflict between the navy captain and the teniente político; and the spread of Communism in the town.

The Junta Patriótica de San Lorenzo is a civic association, founded at a public meeting in mid-January 1962, for the purpose of protecting local interests and completing the development of the port and the town. There are other such organizations; San Lorenzo's is patterned after the one in Ibarra. The Junta Patriótica consists of both Negroes and highland mestizos who are active in commerce or hold some official position. The Junta Patriótica announced its formation on January 25, 1962, in telegrams to the President of Ecuador, a number of ministries, and other Juntas Patrióticas, as well as municipal councils in the northern highlands, the mayors of Ibarra, Tulcán, Quito, and Esmeraldas, the president of the Junta Autónoma, leading newspapers and radio stations, and other important agencies and officials.

The telegrams were followed up by letters to every person and agency in Ecuador that might conceivably be interested, listing San Lorenzo's specific needs: completion of the port and installation of buoys, better electricity, improved railroad maintenance, unpolluted drinking water, sanitation facilities. The Junta Patriótica also wrote to the Pan American Union, the World Health Organization, the Alliance for Progress, and the American Ambassador to Ecuador. On July 14, 1962, a long letter was posted to President John F. Kennedy, asking for buoys for the Canal de Bolívar.

The Junta Patriótica has had some effect in influencing outside agencies. But more important, its formation marks a shift from change prompted by outside pressure to change sponsored from within, even though outside help is still indispensable.

The Junta Parroquial is supposed to be a political party council that advises party members who hold office. Traditionally, coastal Juntas Parroquiales have been formed by the Liberal party. In San Lorenzo, members of the Liberal party, together with prominent Socialists, revived a long-defunct Junta Parroquial on a bipartisan basis in late January 1962, with the purpose of influencing decisions affecting the municipio, which is itself a social, not political, organization. The Junta Parroquial, then, is a bipartisan pressure group active in local politics (including the system of social administration), whereas the Junta Patriótica is an avowedly nonpolitical group that seeks to influence national and international agencies. Both have made the development of San Lorenzo their explicit goal, reflecting growing pressure for change from within the community. In 1963 the Junta Parroquial engineered the election of a San Lorenzo Negro as vice-president of the municipal council; through public meetings, it brought many issues facing the municipio to the attention of the townspeople.

The ties between the highlanders and the native San Lorenzeños were strengthened by the strike of the Junta Autónoma employees, which came on the heels of the successful strike of the carrilanos. After going without pay for over three months and without medicine for seven months, in March 1962 the Junta Autónoma employees struck against their Quito employers. The strike, which was illegal,

had repercussions throughout the highlands and received some notice in newspapers and government offices in Quito. Even though
the strike was illegal, it was informally supported by the head engineer of the Junta Autónoma, the Junta Patriótica, the Junta Parroquial, the president and vice-president of the municipal council, and
the comisario. Most of the strikers were highlanders; the people of
San Lorenzo were very pleased to see them defy their bosses, who
were also highlanders, for the first time. The strike was moderately
successful in achieving its goals, but its more important immediate
effect was to unite the strikers with other segments of the community.

San Lorenzeños were further united by a political dispute that
erupted in August 1962. Essentially, the dispute arose from a quar-
rel between the unpopular teniente político then in office and the Socialists, who had helped him secure his position. For some reason, the
lieutenant of the newly established naval station, who was second-in-
command, entered the public dispute on the side of the teniente político, and called in the sailors to guard him. Although the trouble
rapidly subsided, the sailors continued to patrol the streets of town.
The next day, while all the prominent townspeople were attending
a meeting, the captain of the naval base sent sailors to arrest all the
leaders of the Socialist and Communist parties, on the ground that
they were plotting an insurrection against the national government.

The three leading Socialists and two Communists were sent to
Quito as political prisoners. After a day and a half of political machi-
nations in Quito and San Lorenzo, the prisoners were released and
returned to San Lorenzo, where they were greeted with a fervor
that they had never before known. The significant point about this
episode is that for the first time in anyone's memory the military directly intervened in what townspeople considered a routine local dispute. This incident led to a community unity based on collective antagonism toward the naval base.

The spread of Communism in San Lorenzo seems to reflect a
search by some coastal Negroes and highland mestizos for an alterna-
tive to the traditional ways of doing things. The church and the military are disturbed and agitated by the spread of Communism, the
Junta Autónoma labor union interested, and the majority of the
populace curious and tolerant. More will be said about this later.

The United States Agency for International Development (AID)

and the Alliance for Progress are assisting San Lorenzo with excavations for a drinking-water supply. The United States government
bought buoys for the entrance to the port. American lumber interests are expanding their activity, and several cargoes of lumber and
raw timber have already been shipped to the United States. The
United Nations Food and Agricultural Organization (FAO) and
the Ecuadorian Junta de Planificación have recently made studies of
the area. Officials of virtually every government office visit San
Lorenzo regularly, and additional customs personnel and a representative of the Ministry of Development now have offices in the
town. All in all, the impetus to change increases, and San Lorenzo
is increasingly responsive.

To understand the dynamics of change in San Lorenzo, we must
first understand the structure of the community that is changing.
The following chapters set forth that structure, and then our attention is turned once more to change itself.

III

The Economic Order:
The Upper and Middle Classes

For my discussion of social structure, I have adopted Max Weber's (1958: 180–95) distinction between "class" (the life chances of people as a result of their objective economic situation), "status" (the shared style of life, determined by the amount of social honor people have within the subjective social order), and "party" (actual groups whose action "is oriented toward the acquisition of social 'power,' that is to say, toward influencing a communal action") (Weber 1958: 194). American sociologists (e.g. Parsons 1954: 69–88; Kahl 1957: 8–12; Warner, Meeker, and Eells 1960, to name only a few) have combined Weber's variables in order to scientifically measure American social strata. We do not have the wealth of data for Ecuador necessary to arrive at such sophisticated indices of position within the socioeconomic order. Our problem is to describe various parts of a system in order to see how they function in a changing community.

Like Chandra Jayawardena (1963: 29), I find Weber's distinctions particularly useful in analyzing the social dynamics of an ethnically plural society. They provide basic tools with which to describe and order the changing community structure by contrasting the objective economic order with the subjective social order. We can then ask how people use the power their economic and social positions give them in forming groups to influence community action.

Weber (1958: 181) defines class as follows:

We may speak of a "class" when (1) a number of people have in common a specific causal component of their life chances, in so far as (2) this component is represented exclusively by economic interests in the possession of goods and opportunities for income, and (3) is represented under the conditions of the commodity or labor markets. [These points refer to "class situations," which we may express more briefly as the typical chance for a supply of goods, external living conditions, and personal life experiences, in so far as this chance is determined by the amount and kind of power, or lack of such, to dispose of goods and skills for the sake of income in a given economic order. The term "class" refers to any group of people that is found in the same class situation.] (Bracketed material supplied by Gerth and Mills.)

Inhabitants of northwest Ecuador support themselves by occupations ranging from positions in a national bureaucracy to subsistence farming and fishing. It is fair to say that cash and subsistence economies are joined together in San Lorenzo, and that the former has penetrated the latter to some extent. Nevertheless, subsistence living and some of its sociological correlates still play an important part in the total economic order.

The Class Hierarchy of San Lorenzo: An Overview

The class hierarchy of San Lorenzo, like that of other developing towns in northwest Ecuador, can be described as a pyramid, composed of three major classes—upper, middle, and lower. Any subdivisions within the classes must be based on ethnic and other status criteria, rather than economic positions. Figure 1 represents the class structure and the major ethnic division, between Negroes and mestizos. I use "Negro" and "mestizo" in the following way. The mestizo ethnic type tends to identify with highland Ecuadorian culture. The Negro ethnic type tends to identify with coastal Colombian and Ecuadorian culture. Though the two types are not always in sharp contrast in all areas of life, the characterization of two ethnic orientations in racial terms is useful in the analysis of class in northwest Ecuador. Ethnic types will be differentiated further in Chapter V.[1]

The upper class is a white and mestizo socially self-conscious group, made up of Junta Autónoma employees, the clergy, naval officers, and men in the lumber business. The Italian priests and the three nuns are included in this class because their standard of living

1. This book considers the mestizos' lifeways only as they affect those of the Negroes. For a description of the characteristic society and culture of "mestizo America," see Gillin (1949).

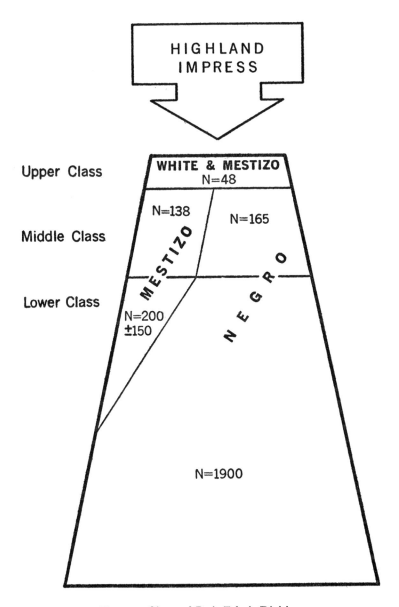

Figure 1. Class and Basic Ethnic Divisions

is equal to that of other members of the upper class. In 1963 this class totaled 48 persons (16 breadwinners and their families). It consists of Ecuadorians, other Latin Americans, and Europeans, all originally from outside the coastal system. Upper-class men earn at least 3,500 sucres per month, which is the equivalent of about $2,000 per annum.[2]

The middle class is ethnically divided between 138 mestizo highlanders (including 37 family heads and 23 transient sailors) making up 6 per cent of the town's population, and 165 Negroes (33 household heads) or 7 per cent of San Lorenzo's total population. The mestizo highlanders are minor officials and small entrepreneurs; the Negroes operate small-scale cash farms, run large stores, and are involved in the trade of such products as lumber, mangrove bark, shellfish, and pelts. The illegal sources of income furnished by local politics are also important to the Negro middle class. To anticipate later discussion, it should be noted that any given Negro kinship unit must have several sources of income to maintain its position in the middle class. The Negro middle class is defined by an income of at least 1,000 sucres a month, or $600 per year *per household*. The mestizo middle class characteristically earns $600 or more per year, *per employed man*. The members of the mestizo middle class come and go, but their Negro counterparts remain in town, though not always in the middle class. The movement of Negroes into the middle class, and their means of maintaining their position, are the subject of Chapter VII.

Some 1,900 Negroes make up San Lorenzo's lower class. The potential labor force is made up of 350–400 men and about the same number of women. At any given time, between 50 and 350 lower-class mestizos may also be in San Lorenzo, though they are for the most part transients looking for menial jobs. The Negro lower class lives on a day-to-day subsistence basis. The men fish, farm a little, load and unload ships, market forest products, and work in the lumber industry. The women wash clothes, sew, cook, gather shellfish, and take care of their own and occasionally upper-class households. Except for their greater opportunities for day labor, lower-class San Lorenzo Negroes lead a life not too different from that of their rural cousins.

2. A sucre is worth about five cents.

Upper-Class Occupations

Table I shows the occupations, income, and origin of members of the upper class in 1961 and 1963. To this could have been added Junta Autónoma secretaries, who in 1961 received a salary equivalent to the radio operator's.

Junta Autónoma Employees

Upper-level Junta Autónoma employees in San Lorenzo are "frozen" in their positions, because competition for better jobs takes place in the central office in Quito. To be sent to San Lorenzo is to be cut off from other employment opportunities. The only hope for advancement within the Junta Autónoma lies in accomplishing something of national political or economic consequence. Advance in the national class hierarchy outside the Junta Autónoma requires contact with officials of other agencies. The Junta Autónoma head office

TABLE I

Upper-Class Occupations

Occupation	Monthly income (Sucres)	Origin
Junta Autónoma:		
Doctor (including private practice) . . .	5,000	Quito
Head engineer	4,000	Quito
Special engineer	3,500	Highlands
Supply head[a]	2,500	Ibarra
Radio operator[a]	2,400	Quito
Government:		
Representative of Ministry of Development	3,500	Quito
Naval captain	5,000	Guayaquil
Naval lieutenant	4,000	Guayaquil
Commerce:		
Timber dealer	Over 5,000	Cuba
Lumber mill owner/manager	Over 3,500	Highlands, Italy, Germany
Clergy:		
Priest	?	Italy
Nun	?	Italy

[a] These men have other sources of income which supplement their Junta Autónoma pay.

discourages this by greatly restricting opportunities to visit Quito or other cities in Ecuador. Therefore, contact with important visitors to San Lorenzo, many of whom are superior to the local upper class in the national class structure, constitutes the major opportunity for advancement. Such contacts are dependent on the tourist trade, which is in turn dependent on development of the town and port. Thus the advancement of the top Junta Autónoma employees is directly dependent on the development of San Lorenzo and the successful presentation of this development to the nation.

Government Employees

One representative of the Ministry of Development in San Lorenzo was appointed in June 1963. At the time this new position was regarded by the occupant and his superiors as a stepping-stone to more important jobs in the Ministry. Whether or not it, too, becomes a dead-end position depends on the development of the timber business in San Lorenzo and the hinterland.

Military Personnel

San Lorenzo is a penalty post for captains and lieutenants in the Ecuadorian navy; it is a military Siberia second only to duty on the Napo River in the Oriente. Although there has been a naval establishment at San Lorenzo since 1961, there is still no permanent naval ship there. Reassignment out of San Lorenzo is contingent upon the performance of an impressive act, notably the quelling of a Communist insurrection or the interception of Cuban arms.

Although there is no obvious advantage for the naval officers in maintaining good relations with the rest of the town, very poor relations may result in further demotion. Because he had antagonized the community, the captain of the base was demoted to the Napo River post in the spring of 1963.

Sawmill Owners and Managers

There are three sawmills in San Lorenzo, in the barrios La Samuela, Puerto de Manaos, and Las Tres Marías. The first is owned and operated by a German Jew, the second by three Italian immigrants; the third is owned by an absentee Quiteño and managed by another highlander. (There is also a new mill in the Bahía de Pailón, owned

by a resident of Guayaquil.) Until recently the mills purchased timber from Negroes who cut and moved it, working together in a traditional form of reciprocal labor organization.[3] Recently, the Italian
mill owners, and to a more limited extent the Quiteño, have rationalized the work situation: they pay the Negroes to dig trenches in
which they float logs to a bay after cutting them in the interior.
When a large number of logs have been rafted in a small sheltered
bay, the lumber buyer aids in the transportation by providing a
motorized launch.

Under the traditional system, the Negroes cut the more easily
accessible logs so that they would not have to dig trenches into the
interior (for there was no immediate profit in the long, hard trench-
digging task). In order to obtain good logs, the buyer was expected
to purchase everything the Negroes brought him. Deliveries of logs
were also smaller under the traditional system, because the Negroes
could not handle large rafts of logs that were not equipped with
motors. Finally, the idea of rafting logs until a large supply had
been built up did not appeal to a *minga* group bent on an immediate
profit. A new company that purchases raw timber for export to the
United States has greatly expanded and further rationalized the
lumbering operations.

The Italian and German sawmills deal with softwoods, chiefly
cuángare (dialyanthera gordoniaefolia, Acosta-Solis 1960: 55, known
in the United States as virola), a wood competitive with poplar and
gum. Since both mills deal with the same wood, and since both sell
to American and Ecuadorian buyers, a relatively controlled comparison is possible. The Italians, using their rationalized system of
wood cutting and transporting, are rapidly outdistancing the German mill, which obtains logs in the traditional way. The implications
for labor of the two different systems will be discussed in Chapter IV.
The third mill deals with tropical hardwood, locally called *chanul*
(humiria procera, Acosta-Solis 1960: 57), for which there has thus
far been only a domestic market.

San Lorenzo lumber mills compete with a very large sawmill in
Limones and another, smaller one in La Tola. These mills have
the advantage of being at the mouth of the Santiago River. From the

3. This is known as a *minga* organization and will be fully described in Chapter IV, pp.
69–74.

Santiago and Cayapas Rivers logs are easily and cheaply floated down to Limones and La Tola, where they are cut and sent by boat to Guayaquil and from there to Ecuador's interior or to the United States. In San Lorenzo wood can be shipped to the interior of Ecuador directly by rail, but the labor costs involved in getting logs to San Lorenzo are greater than they are for the mills at the mouth of the Santiago. Except for occasional shipments to the United States (the Italians made three in 1963, the German two), most of the lumber cut in San Lorenzo is sent to highland Ecuador by rail.

It costs 5,150 sucres (plus a 350-sucre municipal tax) to rent a 60,000-pound railroad car for a shipment from San Lorenzo to Quito. The hope of the sawmill owners and managers is for direct trade with the United States. Their hope is not unjustified; in 1963 alone, three teams of buyers from the United States came to San Lorenzo by chartered plane to inspect the operation of the sawmills and to find out whether or not they could meet certain specifications. However, selling raw timber may undercut San Lorenzo's lumber mills.

Raw Timber Exports

The export of raw timber direct to the United States began during the preparation of this study; its impact on the Negroes' social and economic life may become as important as that of the railroad. In March 1963 a Cuban, assisted by one Spaniard and one Ecuadorian, came to San Lorenzo to see if the northwest Ecuadorian forests were suited to the kind of exploitation already in effect in western Colombia. The forests seemed promising, the Bahía de Pailón could be used for shipments, and the Negroes provided an adequate labor force. The small company, with a sales representative in Miami, Florida, settled in San Lorenzo. It established an Ecuadorian office in the Hotel Pailón, contracted with a company in Mobile, Alabama, for the first shipment of cuángare, and set up a rational system of cutting, transporting, storing, and marketing raw timber. Some of the innovations made by the company are significant enough to warrant a detailed description of its activities and their implications for lower-class labor and social organization.

Briefly, the company accountant married a member of a middle-class family in San Lorenzo, becoming part of the social system of the town. Lower-class Negroes who frequently headed minga work groups were contacted, and through them other lower-class Negroes from San Lorenzo and the hinterland were hired as day laborers to set up a system of crude canals. The canals facilitated the movement of logs from island interiors to a bay or channel at high tide. Logs were cut only after preparations to move them had been made. Local middle-class men were hired to haul, check, and even politick. The new company brought in its own *calificador de madera* (lumber appraiser). The lumber appraiser is a man whose signature buyers in the United States accept at least tentatively as a guarantee of the quality of wood. Before this company there were no recognized calificadores de madera in San Lorenzo, and exporters had to make arrangements on a percentage basis with a man in Limones.

The operation of the lumber company resembles that of the Italian mill, but is more elaborate. It has involved men in all areas of community life. The company is becoming more firmly established and is an agent of change, especially in regard to labor. For the first time, an outside economic elite has begun to work on a fairly rational basis with local lower-class labor, with middle-class coastal Ecuadorians as intermediaries.

The timber export company has to function in a constantly shifting economic situation. Not only does the value of the sucre fluctuate, but, more important, the system of taxation is highly erratic. Since the Ecuadorian government will grant no long-term authorization for such large-scale export operations, the tax on each load of logs must be negotiated separately. At the end of June 1963, the following taxes were paid for a shipment of logs to Mobile, Alabama:

(1) 5 per cent of the total value of the shipment to the Banco Central del Ecuador (figured at 17 sucres to the dollar, a loss at the time of five sucres to the dollar);
(2) 20 sucres per log to the Ministry of Development;
(3) 15 sucres per log to the municipio;
(4) 7,500 sucres per ship on entry to the port and 7,500 sucres on departure to the customs authorities.

The Bank, the Ministry, the municipio, and the customs authorities are all free to set their own rates. These rates vary with the particular person making the assessment, the financial needs of the agency, and the ability of the company to pay. None of the sums were fixed until the day the loaded ship was to depart, which made it impossible for the company to predict what its profits on the shipment would be. Since United States prices are fairly stable, the company tries to compensate for fluctuating taxes by minimizing labor costs. It must pay enough to attract the workers it needs to secure good timber in sufficient quantity, but not so much that it risks operating at a loss. The pressures of rising taxes and unionized labor had forced the timber company to move from southern Colombia to San Lorenzo in the first place. The experience of the company is a revealing example of the pressures that must be faced by agents of change in San Lorenzo.

The Upper Class as a Social Unit

The upper class is notable for its self-awareness. Except for the clergy and the physician, it is composed of a small group of interdependent administrators and entrepreneurs in the lumber business. The former are dependent on the growth of San Lorenzo for their own advance; the latter contribute to economic growth, but in turn are dependent on the favors of government representatives. As members of a self-conscious class, how do these people live?

"San Lorenzo is the land of single men" was a favorite saying of the former head engineer of the Junta Autónoma. As members of the national rising *middle* class, the men have their families with them only a short part of the year—during their children's vacations from school. The real homes of the upper class are in the large cities, where the wives, children, and perhaps maids live for the school year, supported by funds the men send them from San Lorenzo. There are only two upper-class men who have their families with them: one is married to a middle-class mulatto with extensive commercial interests in San Lorenzo, and the other has recently married a highland woman and as yet has no children.

The life of the upper class is markedly different from that of the rest of the people in San Lorenzo. Junta Autónoma and government employees live in the Ciudadela. There are two exceptions: the radio operator lives in a workers' camp (where he has been allotted three sections) to be close to his radio; the man married to the mulatto lives with her in the center of town. The naval officers live at the base, the clergy on the church grounds. Sawmill owners have houses adjacent to their mills, and the head of the timber company lives with his higher-paid workers in the Hotel Pailón.

Most of the men in the upper class have running water in their homes, but only those who live in the Ciudadela have flush toilets. The others, however, do have private latrines, and all of them have beds with mattresses. While their wives are in the cities, the men eat at the Salón Ibarra, which is run by the wife of the Junta Autónoma's chief of supplies. They generally eat three large meals a day. Breakfast, consisting of fruit, coffee, bread, butter, and cheese (and fried meat with onions on Sunday), is eaten between six and eight A.M. The noon meal begins with potato, fish, peanut, or cow's-foot soup, followed by a small entrée of *empanada* (fried pie with leftovers inside), *llapingacho* (fried potato and cheese patty), or a vegetable, fish, or shellfish dish, then by a large plate of fried rice with one or two of the following on top: fried bananas, potatoes, eggs, beans, or a little meat or fowl. Seasonings—*ají* (hot pepper and onion sauce), salt, and catsup—are added at the table. A mixture of cane sugar and coconut is the usual dessert. Members of the upper class drink *fresco* (ground oatmeal in water or, more rarely, in milk), bottled water, or soft drinks with the meal, and often coffee after dessert. The evening meal is similar, with the addition of a piece of fried corvina, pargo, colorado, mullet, or other fish. Bread baked in San Lorenzo is eaten with every meal. Ordinarily, an upper-class man expects to pay 10 sucres a day for a very large amount of food, though he may pay as little as eight. Special food (e.g. extra meat or fish, or fresh vegetables from the Sierra) and extra coffee can raise the cost of three such meals to 18 sucres.

The upper class is expected occasionally to drink Ecuadorian beer, which costs seven sucres per half-liter. Beer drinking is a group activity; norms of drinking behavior stress friendship, conviviality, and generosity. A man is expected to insist on buying every friend a bottle of beer if he has one himself. The expectation is usually fulfilled, which makes beer drinking a rather expensive, and infrequent, social event.

When the upper-class families are in town, the cuisine does not change. The Salón Ibarra ordinarily prepares the food, and the family's maid, if there is one, or a young boy hired for the purpose, delivers it to the home of the family. No upper-class woman does

TABLE II
Middle-Class Occupations

Occupation	Base Income (Sucres)[a]	Occupation	Base Income (Sucres)[a]	Occupation	Base Income (Sucres)[a]
Junta Autónoma:		**Public Officials, continued:**		**Self-Employed:**	
Chief of mechanics	2,300	Secretary to comisario	300 + 2–300 graft	Carpenter	30/day
Doctor's helper	1,500	Teniente político	150 + 2–300 " [b]	Mechanic	20–30/day
Mechanic	1,200–1,500	Tax collector	10% of taxes + 1–500 graft	Sawmill foreman	20–30/day
Topographer	1,500	Postmaster	200	Pilot, boat and motor rental	ca. 1,500 (mode) [c]
Topographer's assistant	1,300	**Education:**		Hotel owner	500–2,000
Carpenter	1,300	Director of schools	1,600	Restaurant owner	500–2,000
Pilot	1,200–1,400	School inspector	1,500	Member of theater junta	400
Heavy equipment operator	1,300	Teachers	900–1,300	Mangrove buyer	?
Warehouse assistant	1,000	Sailors	700	Shellfish buyer	?
Chief of bridge maintenance	1,000	**Timber Company:**		Farm owner with cash crop	?
Station master	1,000	Accountant	unknown % of profits	Shoe repairman	20–40/day
Truck driver	950	Foreman	unknown % of profits	Saloon owner	500–2,000
Assistant station master	700	Lumber appraiser	unknown % of profits	Poolroom owner	500–2,000
Bridge maintenance man	700			Barber	200–400
Public Officials:				Liquor commissioner	1,000–2,000
SCISP head	2,300			Lumber appraiser	% of shipment
Comisario	900 + 1–3,000 graft			Cattleraisers	?
Police sgt.	1,000 + 3–400 "			Dentist (self-taught)	500–1,000
Customs agt.	800 + 800 "				

[a] Figures are monthly unless otherwise stated.
[b] Prior to the arrival of the comisario, the teniente político received 1,000–3,000 sucres per month in graft.
[c] Combined services.

her own cooking. Washing and ironing are also sent out to be done by Negro women. Most of the big social events attended by the upper class as a group take place between June and August, when the families are in town. Otherwise the group meets informally in the Salón Ibarra, unless a special social event or a political meeting brings them together. In San Lorenzo, upper-class wives stay at home, except for occasional walks to visit with friends.

The men of the upper class are in San Lorenzo to work, to accomplish something in a poor country that will make them a bit richer and give them a better life elsewhere in Eucador. Only the priests, and perhaps the one man with extensive commercial and social interests in the area, are not hoping to leave San Lorenzo.

Middle-Class Occupations

A middle-class household must have an average income of more than 1,000 sucres a month ($600 a year) in order to maintain its position, and as a rule members of the middle class must have more than one source of income. The exceptions are the men with the more lucrative and demanding Junta Autónoma jobs, the sailors, some public officials, and a few shopkeepers. Table II, therefore, lists middle-class occupations, but not necessarily the total income of any given person.

It is never easy, and often very difficult, to pursue enough economic activities to retain middle-class membership. From a purely economic standpoint, most people in the middle class are in a very tenuous position and find it difficult to maintain their economic standing by individual or family initiative alone. Those below them would appear to have very little chance of moving up into the middle class. Socioeconomic mobility, however, does exist in San Lorenzo, but it is contingent upon other factors (discussed in Chapters V and VI) besides the desire for economic betterment. Chapter VII, on kinship and socioeconomic mobility, shows how networks of kinsmen move into and maintain themselves in the middle class.

Junta Autónoma Employees

Middle-class Junta Autónoma employees are, for the most part, highland mestizos in dead-end positions. They lack the education, political contacts, and family ties necessary to improve their economic

standing. Their salaries, except those of the chief of mechanics, mechanics, topographer, and doctor's helper, are the minimum necessary for middle-class standing.

In 1961, there were no Negroes among the middle-class Junta
Autónoma employees. By 1963, one local Negro (the pilot) had
made a successful move from the lower to the middle class. He not
only is the Junta Autónoma's pilot, but also owns a cantina, which is
run by one wife, and the largest saloon in San Lorenzo, which is run
by another wife.

Most Junta Autónoma employees come from Ibarra. A few have
their homes in or around Quito or in Carchi province. Their families
live with them, for they have no money to maintain separate households. The possibility of losing one's job and not being able to find
another is a constant threat. Of the 130 workers discharged in 1961
when CIAVE withdrew, more than a dozen mestizo men remained
in San Lorenzo with their families. They have been reduced to a
meager lower-class existence, but they still look to the Junta Autónoma as a possible source of employment. They did not move on in
search of work because they could not; they simply did not have
sufficient funds.

The major hope for more than marginal participation in the
middle class lies in the establishment of labor unions (*sindicatos*).
Middle-class employees of the Junta Autónoma, along with a number of upper-class Junta employees, were very interested in organizing an effective union. The carrilanos' union, with its successful
strike, provided a model, but there are more carrilanos than Junta
Autónoma employees, and their union includes carrilanos from as
far away as Quito. In 1962, during the Junta Autónoma employees'
illegal strike, a union called the Sindicato de Obreros de San Lorenzo was formed. The union has no national affiliation as yet, but
it had national impact during its strike in the spring of 1962. The
structure of the Junta Autónoma union resembles that of a Communist organization. The governing body is a board of secretaries who
ostensibly share responsibility and divide functions, not authority.
There is no hierarchy of president, vice-president, and so forth. Actually the system of equal secretaries allows considerable maneuver-
ing for control once the secretaries are selected.

The problem of national affiliation for the local union is still un-
solved. In the early summer of 1963 the union almost joined the

national Communist union, known as the CTE (La Confederación de Trabajadores del Ecuador). The appeal to join the Communist union was based on the promise of immediate, tangible economic benefits. The merger was forestalled by a warning from members of the upper class that the political consequences might negate any benefits to the local union.

Public Officials

The teniente político in office in 1961 was officially paid 150 sucres a month, but was obliged to pay about 400 sucres a month to run his office. By taking graft he could earn as much as 2,000 sucres a month after expenses.[4] Though in 1963 the comisario nacional de policía and his secretary were usurping most of the teniente político's graft, he still earned enough to remain in office. The comisario received as much as 2,500–3,000 sucres a month in graft. Since graft is the all-important source of income for middle-class public servants, a brief digression on its nature and role is in order here.

El mame is an Ecuadorian neologism derived from the verb *mamar* (to suckle) to refer to the illegal solicitation of money for the performance of an action. El mame is a somewhat cruder term than *chupar* (to suck, to sip), which in polite highland society is also used to mean graft, but it is still the most popular Ecuadorian equivalent of the English "graft." *La teta* (the teat) is a cruder equivalent of el mame. A person who is taking graft is referred to in one of the following ways: *"El está en el mame"*; *"el tiene la teta"*; or *"el está con la teta."* In general, the idea of graft and the values associated with it are similar to those reported on *"la mordida"* (the bite) in Mexico (Erasmus 1961: 226–28).

Public officials make extra charges for every act they perform, whether it is ordering the arrest of a criminal, signing a legal docu-

4. Data on graft were not difficult to gather, since there was no particular stigma attached to the subject in San Lorenzo. People considered those in office to be within their rights to make what money they could. My data are drawn from long conversations with former occupants of the office of Tenencia Política and with people who had just been released from jail, who had some business to negotiate that necessitated a small bribe, or who had normal business with public officials (e.g. killing a pig, recording a birth, opening a cantina). Lumber dealers and Junta Autónoma officials were particularly helpful in supplying information. Some estimates of monthly earnings were made by noting the official's standard of living and comparing it with his legal salary. Finally, I have had many direct experiences with officials involving graft, ranging from being present when bribes were offered or extra charges requested by officials to being detained in 1961 by a policeman who was exceptionally eager for a bribe.

ment, letting a person out of jail, or keeping him in. Major crises, such as the apprehension of smugglers or the investigation of a murder, provide the best opportunities for graft. The higher the official the greater his opportunities: the comisario receives the lion's share and the policeman very little of any given bribe.

Taxation is another lucrative source of graft. The tax collector legally receives 10 per cent of all the taxes he collects. Unless the police accompany him, he may receive a far greater percentage. Obviously, the more he pays the comisario or teniente político, the less likely the police are to interfere with his activities. The taxes he collects are municipal taxes. All merchandise entering and leaving San Lorenzo is taxed at an unspecified rate; ordinarily traders pay the tax collector not to be taxed. The movie theater is taxed at a rate of 10 per cent a ticket. Here again, those running the theater prefer to pay the collector a lump sum. There is a tax on all butchered animals, usually amounting to 40 sucres per animal. Usually, since it is the lower class that is involved, the police go along to enforce payment, which has the side effect of limiting the collector's access to el mame. Only members of the upper class, and perhaps not even they, are affected by the graduated income tax that is supposed to be deducted from monthly salaries.

The policemen, the customs official, and the comisario come from outside San Lorenzo, but they are almost all from the southern coast. They do not represent the highland mestizo ethnic group as we have identified it. To date there have been no Negro policemen or comisarios in San Lorenzo. Personnel in these positions are transferred at least once a year and usually every four to six months. The teniente político, the secretary to the comisario, the tax collector, and the postmaster are San Lorenzeños. For at least twenty years, all the men who filled these posts for more than one month have been Negroes or mulattoes.

Education

Teachers, heads of schools, and the inspector are all appointed by the municipal council. The inspector resides in Limones, the capital of the canton. The boys' school is headed by a man, the girls' school by a woman; both are permanent San Lorenzo residents. The nine teachers come from San Lorenzo or other coastal areas. Teachers are required to have completed two-year's study in a *colegio*, but some teachers are granted temporary permits before they have met this requirement.[5] The teachers may be of any race, and although women predominate, sex is not a significant consideration. Ordinarily the teachers are Negro and mulatto women and light-skinned men. The colegio requirement, together with the social requirement that teachers dress well, restricts the teaching profession to people from middle-class families.

There are two schools in San Lorenzo; both the boys' and the girls' schools have been growing steadily since the coming of the railroad. There was a marked increase between 1961 and 1963 in both teachers and pupils. Table III, though inexact, is the official summary of pupil-attendance data for the school year ending in January 1963.

The school year runs for nine months, from April to January, and is divided into three trimesters, which end in June, September, and December with an examination. Classes are frequently interrupted by Ecuadorian and, occasionally, Colombian holidays, which last anywhere from one day to two weeks. A final public examination is given in late December or early January. There are six grades. A child is supposed to begin school when he is about six years old, though he may be as young as four and as old as 16. A few boys remain in school until they are 18. Most girls complete school by the age of 13–14, and almost all by 15–17. Ordinarily, a child's schooling is interrupted from time to time, even if the family is not traveling or living where there is no school. The usual reason given is that the parents do not have the money to buy the child clothes or school supplies. Sometimes, because of infrequent attendance, a student may claim to have been in school for eight years or more but still be enrolled in the first or second grade.

If students can pass the examination given at the completion of the sixth grade, they are free to attend a colegio. There are private and public colegios in Ibarra and Esmeraldas, and in Tumaco, Colombia. To attend even a public colegio, the student must have money for uniforms, food, and housing. The municipio of San Lorenzo does provide a few scholarships, which pay 200 sucres for the academic year, and there are some free dormitory facilities in Es-

5. Colegios are four-year institutions, some with technical, some with general, curricula.

TABLE III

San Lorenzo School Attendance

Students	Boys	Girls	Total
In school	280	297	577
Examined	223	244	467
Promoted	172	149	321
Not promoted	53	95	148
Dropped out	57	53	110
Per cent promoted[a]	72.5	69.2	70.8

Source: Acción Católica, Luz, No. 6, January 20, 1963, p. 6. San Lorenzo archives of the Catholic missionaries.

[a] These are the official figures. The corrected percentages are as follows. Per cent promoted of those in school: boys, 61%; girls, 50%; total, 55%. Per cent promoted of those examined: boys, 77%; girls, 61%; total, 69%.

meraldas and Ibarra. No one from San Lorenzo has completed more than four years in a colegio, i.e., no one has gone on to a university. There are, however, a handful of men from very small hinterland and coastal towns who have managed to obtain some university education.

Salary increases and promotions for teachers are contingent upon completion of four years in a colegio and some postgraduate work. Ordinarily the women teachers spend their January–April vacation away from San Lorenzo, ostensibly pursuing their education.

Military

The 19 sailors of the naval base and their families are marginal participants in the social life of San Lorenzo, but their economic participation is extensive. Furthermore, their social participation is no more marginal than that of most other middle-class mestizos. The sailors come from all over Ecuador. Most of them are not Negroes, but now and then one sees a Negro sailor in San Lorenzo.

Self-employed

To be a self-employed member of the middle class in San Lorenzo requires involvement in more than one of the occupations listed in Table II. In fact, since successful middle-class entrepreneurship is only partly an individual matter, detailed discussion of the middle-class self-employed must be postponed until essential information about social organization has been set forth. Except for those former Junta Autónoma employees who contrive to remain in the middle class, and a very few transient in-migrant highland merchants, the middle-class self-employed are Negroes and mulattoes from San Lorenzo or similar towns.[6]

The Middle Class as a Social Unit

The middle class is poor. Nationally it would fall into the upper-lower or lower class in income. Coastal Negroes and highland mestizos interpret their economic situation differently. The mestizos feel poor, depressed, and downtrodden. They see little hope for advancement and are ready to jump into any organization that promises to give them more money than they have. They are equally quick to leave an organization, and to act in a manner recently described as atomistic (Banfield 1958: 9–10) when economic returns are not rapidly forthcoming. It cannot be said that the Negroes and mulattoes in this class feel deprived. In fact, this ethnic group is at the crest of its development in San Lorenzo. The Negroes and mulattoes know this is true and say so; they act for the most part like people looking forward to a brighter economic future.

The staples of the middle-class diet are rice, fish, bananas, plantains, sweet manioc, coffee, and bread. From such foods the middle class does its best to prepare a three-course meal. For example, from one fish, a few potatoes, and some rice, a family might have a meal of fish and potato soup, a fried-potato-cake entrée, and a final dish of rice, potatoes, and fish. Members of the middle class live in houses without any plumbing (only a few have latrines). Many of the highlanders live in old camps built during the construction of the railroad. Some pay rent to the Junta Autónoma, but others live there on its courtesy. Others live in wooden houses, often with a tin roof but sometimes with a thatched roof. Most of the middle class lives in the center of town, in the old Section Number 1, or in the barrio Puerto de Manaos.

The woman of the house cooks for the family on an open fire built on a wooden platform. If she is absent, the man eats in the Salón Ibarra, or, more likely, in the Hotel Carchi or a small restaurant near the pier.

---

6. I have insufficient data to discuss the timber company's accountant, foreman, and lumber appraiser.

IV

Cash and Subsistence Economics: The Lower Class

The lower-class Negroes of San Lorenzo participate in both a cash and a subsistence economy. This chapter discusses both economic situations, and, along with them, the Negroes' reciprocal labor forms. The section on labor forms is particularly important because it introduces the concept of reciprocity, and its cultural patterning, which reappears in later chapters on status, kinship, mobility, and politics.

Before turning to the Negro lower class, a word about the lower-class highland mestizo element. Between 50 and 350 lower-class mestizos, mostly railroad workers, menial workers for the Junta Autónoma, or former railroad workers, can be found in San Lorenzo at a given time. Their participation in San Lorenzo economic life is marginal unless they join the Negroes by intermarriage or ritual kinship. This chapter is not concerned with them.

Should the Junta Autónoma leave San Lorenzo, life among the lower-class Negroes would not be seriously affected. With few exceptions, the Negroes in San Lorenzo and throughout the hinterland are still oriented toward a semisubsistence economy based on fishing, shifting agriculture, and the marketing of forest and sea products.

San Lorenzo contains elements of the three ecological zones of northern Esmeraldas described in Chapter I: inland rainforest, mangrove delta, and tropical island. And, within the limits indicated below, what is true of the lower-class Negroes of San Lorenzo is true of Negroes throughout the northern sector. In a sense, then, I am discussing the northwest Ecuadorian Negroes' economic order, not just the lower class in San Lorenzo.

The Cash Economy

The Junta Autónoma

The Junta Autónoma regularly employs between twenty and thirty Negroes to work with machetes at the rate of 15–18 sucres a day. Sometimes it hires Negroes to do a specific job for a set fee, or to work for only one or two days at 20 sucres a day. When hired to do a specific job, Negroes begin early—usually before dawn—and feel cheated if they cannot finish by 11 A.M. A job with the Junta Autónoma does not ordinarily last for more than three months. Occasionally the Junta Autónoma hires a few carpenters, masons, or other semiskilled laborers, but this is rare. On the whole, the Junta Autónoma is not a major source of employment for lower-class Negroes.

The Junta Autónoma supplies the lower class with water and electricity. When the electricity is turned on, i.e., from 5 to 7 A.M., 11 A.M. to noon, and 6 to 11 P.M., water is pumped into the tanks indicated on Map 3 (p. 210). Water, and public lighting in the form of crude street lights on corners, are free. To have electricity at home, one must pay 15 sucres a month for each bulb. This is cheaper electricity than in any other town in Esmeraldas province. Most people can afford this, and nearly 30 per cent of the Negro homes, except those in the barrio Las Tres Marías, have one electric bulb. However, public electricity has had little real effect on the Negroes' life. The bulbs do not provide much more light than kerosene lanterns, and they cost roughly the same. The saloons in San Lorenzo and throughout the province have their own gasoline-powered electric generators for use after 11 P.M.

Lower-class life is much less directly involved with the Junta Autónoma than the life of the middle and upper classes. But the income the upper and middle classes derive from the Junta Autónoma is indirectly diffused to the lower class.

Sawmills and the Timber Company

The three San Lorenzo sawmills and the mill in the Bahía de Pailón each employ three to eight Negroes at 15 sucres a day. Ideally the Negroes are paid monthly, but in practice the mills pay once every two to three months. In the meantime they arrange for local shops to extend credit to their employees. Indeed, many Negroes receive almost no cash on payday. The German mill once went nearly half a year without paying any cash. The owner offered free medical care, movie tickets, work clothes, rice, and a promise of money. His system of payment is really more typical of northwest Ecuador than the system of actually paying Negroes now in effect in the San Lorenzo mills.

The new timber company employs between fifty and sixty Negroes from San Lorenzo and the hinterland at 15–18 sucres a day. The company deducts for food, clothing, machetes, axes, and the like, but it does pay some cash whenever it concludes a sale. The Negroes who loaded the company's first shipment received 50 sucres a day for five days, an almost unheard-of wage in Ecuador.

Fifteen to 20 sucres a day, though a low wage by United States standards, is high in Ecuador. Day laborers in the highlands often earn only five to seven sucres a day. The wages paid by the Junta Autónoma, the timber company, and the sawmills compare very favorably with wages paid day laborers elsewhere in Ecuador.

General Day Labor

Negroes can earn about 20 sucres a day loading and unloading the ships that dock on most Sundays, some Thursdays, and whenever there is a special cargo. Eight to 12 sucres a day can be earned by stacking and weighing mangrove bark and dried fish on the pier, by carrying packages and doing odd jobs for restaurant owners and traders, by loading and unloading trains at the railroad station, and by carrying bananas and other foods from the station to the shops in town. Shrimp boats used to provide work for Negroes, but the high taxes in the canton Eloy Alfaro drove the industry to Guayas province, where it is not taxed.

An enterprising young Negro can occasionally earn a bit of money from tourists. With luck he can obtain five sucres or more for carrying a suitcase and promising to return when the visitor is ready to leave. Negroes may earn 20 sucres by hiring themselves out for a day to clean around a house, hotel, or restaurant. No highlander tends the grounds around his own house—he either hires a Negro or lets his grounds go untended. Saloons and restaurants occasionally hire a waitress or waiter. Only the Salón Ibarra has steady employees; the two young waitresses are paid 10–12 sucres a day, plus meals.

On rare occasions there is farm work for *peones*. When a cash crop of coconuts, bananas, or pineapples is harvested, a peón may be hired to load it on a canoe, paddle it to town, and unload it, for 15–18 sucres a day.

A Negro can usually earn 15–20 sucres in San Lorenzo by working for a day if he wants to. He cannot, however, pick the day he is to work. He must be known as a person always willing to work for others, he must be readily available, and he must in some way be known to upper- and middle-class potential employers.

Semiskilled Labor

Sewing, baking, carpentry, masonry, mechanical work, guiding, and outboard-motor maintenance are common occupations throughout the area, but there seem to be more people engaged in them in San Lorenzo than in other towns. The carpenters have their own shops and increasingly cater to lower-class and middle-class Negroes as well as to the better-off highlanders. Doors and hinged wooden shutters are becoming fashionable in San Lorenzo, along with more finished walls, floors, and the like. In 1963 the many carpenters who had been trained and employed by the Junta Autónoma were able to continue in their trade. Carpenters expect to earn about 30 sucres a day at the rate of four to five sucres an hour. Carpenters' wages are often used as a base in setting other wages. For example, when I was deciding on the wage to pay the teniente político for helping me with my census, everyone I spoke to agreed that the job was about as complicated as a carpenter's, and that the teniente político should be paid a wage equal to a carpenter's.

At least twenty women in San Lorenzo spend most of their day working at their sewing machines. They make, remake, mend, and patch clothes for upper-, middle-, and some lower-class men and women. Ideally, the women work only on women's clothes and tailors sew men's clothes, but in practice women sew for both men and women. Only women make clothes for funerals, special church services, and other important occasions, which may account for the greater number of seamstresses than tailors in San Lorenzo. The mechanics and motor-maintenance men, many of them trained by the Junta Autónoma, now have to take whatever work they can find. Usually one of the sawmills or the timber company can provide some work for them. To date, semiskilled laborers have not risen much above other members of the lower class who have some cash income. They are not inclined to hunt, fish, or garden, and their greater earning power is offset by their having to buy virtually everything. They are active participants in the cash economy, but their position in the market is not significantly different from that of other members of the lower class. However, their position is not a frozen one; their social mobility simply depends on more than individual initiative.

Proprietorship

Lower-class proprietors run small shops and cantinas on a sporadic, part-time basis. The proprietor opens his shop on a weekend when there is a surplus of food for sale and he is certain to make a profit. The shops are either in the home or in a little *kiosko,* no larger than a large broom closet, located in a propitious spot in town. A very small shop may consist of a small bin of oranges, a pile of coconuts, some rope, coils of home-rolled cigars, a pile of dried fish, a few clay pipes (*cachimbos*), canoe paddles, plaited fire fans, and dynamite. Other merchandise costs too much and is handled only by larger shops. Some Negroes serve meals costing from one to five sucres to railroad workers and others who are too poor to eat in restaurants but have no cooking facilities.

In 1961 there were only two cantinas in town. By 1963 there were more than thirty. A cantina is a small room in a person's home where *aguardiente* (cane liquor), or perhaps beer, is sold, and where a man can drink, play the guitar, and sing. Cantinas do not compete with saloons, which feature dancing. Cantinas are for men only; even prostitutes do not usually enter them. In 1961 there were four or five saloons in town. At any given time, only one saloon was frequented by large numbers of people interested in dancing and in seeking a partner for a brief sexual encounter. The others simply served as places for drinking and talking, as the cantinas do now. With the coming of the comisario, competition among saloonkeepers for permission to open (the one who paid the most graft was allowed to stay open the most) led to the closing of all but one saloon, which has expanded into what is now virtually a dance hall, catering chiefly to visitors.

By the end of August 1963, some cantinas were constructed as separate buildings, but their proprietors were members of the middle class. Lower-class proprietors do not have any more luxuries of life than other members of the lower class, but proprietorship itself plays a significant part in social mobility, which will be discussed in Chapter VII.

Other Occupations in the Cash Economy: Women

The major source of cash for women in San Lorenzo is gathering *conchas*, or shellfish—in this case mussels. *Ceviche de concha*, prepared with raw or cooked mussels, onions, *ají* (a hot pepper mixture), and lemon, is a national dish. The kind of concha used in ceviches grows in a symbiotic relationship with mangrove trees. Today, in Ecuador, such conchas are found only in Esmeraldas province, and they are particularly abundant in the northern sector. Since mangrove stripping, an important source of income in the region, destroys the trees, and eventually the conchas, Esmeraldas province, and especially the northern sector, is in danger of losing its mangrove and concha business in twenty years or so (Conforti 1962). In the province of El Oro, in southern Ecuador, the mangroves and conchas have already been destroyed.

The women who gather the conchas sell them to resident buyers from the highlands. Although there is some bidding and haggling, the price usually agreed on is five sucres per 100 conchas. The conchas are stored in large pens in the small inlets, where they are moistened twice a day by the tidal flow. They are shipped by rail to Quito in boxcars, soaked once a day with water. Cared for this way, the conchas apparently remain alive for a week or two after they have been gathered; once they die, they are toxic.

The concha business is growing almost daily. It began to thrive in 1960, when overland railroad trips between San Lorenzo and Quito became regular and relatively dependable. Before the railroad line to Quito was completed, conchas were shipped by cargo boats to Limones, Esmeraldas, Manta, Salinas, Playas, and Guayaquil. Until recently, ceviche de concha was a coastal specialty, but it is now found

in most Quito and other highland restaurants. Today almost all the
conchas shipped out of San Lorenzo are sent to Quito, where they
bring 15 sucres per 100. In Guayaquil the rate is 17 per 100. A good
Quito restaurant will charge as much as 30 sucres for a ceviche containing half a dozen conchas.

In 1961 there were no storing pens for the conchas and concha
gathering was a regular source of income for very few women. In
1963 there were nine large pens in the town, and more were being
planned. At least half the able-bodied Negro women are regularly
engaged in concha gathering. Women gather the conchas in groups
of three to six *concheras* to a canoe. The concheras working in the
same canoe are always relatives, and they always live in the same or
adjacent barrios—often in the same household. Mothers take their
young daughters to teach them to gather. There is no head conchera;
profits are divided equally among the women in a canoe, and they
all enter into the bargaining with the buyers.

Gathering conchas is hard and sometimes treacherous work. The
women must paddle a canoe an hour or two to find a choice spot, and
then they must keep it a secret from other concheras. Working nude
or half-nude, the women either dive for the conchas or walk along
the mangrove swamp feeling for them with their feet. In their search
they may step on a stingray, a Portuguese man-of-war, or one of several varieties of fish with sharp dorsal fins. At the end of the day,
they face the long return trip to San Lorenzo. For a day's work, however, good concheras can expect to share 20–60 sucres per canoe.

Lower-class women can also enter the cash economy by washing,
cooking, and ironing for upper- and middle-class families. They may
also help their husband with cash crops and with raising animals.
Like men, they make charcoal to sell. Half a dozen women in Old
Section 2 occasionally pan archaeological gold, sold at 40 sucres per
gram, from the little inlet northeast of the Casa de la Marimba (see
Map 3, p. 210). The women earn about as much as they would in
an equal amount of time spent gathering conchas.

Finally, some women support themselves by prostitution. Some
thirty women between 25 and 40 years of age in San Lorenzo are
now prostitutes or have been prostitutes at some time in their lives.
Prostitutes charge as much as their clients are willing to pay, the
minimum being five sucres. With luck and a generous patron, a pros-

titute may earn enough to enter the middle class. The most attractive and skillful prostitutes aim for long-term relationships with single middle-class men, especially mestizos. If they succeed, they become members of the middle class themselves. Lower-class prostitutes usually live with and support a man, known locally by the derogatory term *cabrón*. Except for the woman's occupation, and the relative freedom from economic cares it brings the man, the life of such a couple in San Lorenzo is more or less typical.

Other Occupations in the Cash Economy: Men

In San Lorenzo men cut timber, strip mangrove bark, raise animals and crops, and make charcoal, canoes, paddles, wooden washing bowls (*bateas*), and other utensils. All these occupations, except mangrove stripping and some types of timber cutting, are only marginally part of the cash economy, since they are also the basis of the subsistence economy. (When men cut timber to use in building their own house, this, too, is a subsistence activity.)

Mangrove bark is used in the Quito tanning industry. The man who cuts the bark, often with the aid of his son or brother, sells it to a local buyer. He, in turn, stores the bark until a loaded boxcar can be shipped to Quito, or a boatload, or partial boatload, to Guayaquil. By working very hard a pair of men can match, but not exceed, the daily income of two or three concheras. Mangrove stripping is an individual occupation and no reciprocal-labor rules govern it. Lumbering, however, is based on reciprocal labor forms, and will be taken up in the following discussion of these forms.

Reciprocal Labor Forms

Minga labor, as it is practiced today by lower-class Negroes in northwest Ecuador, is a system of exchange labor combined with elements of festive labor. Erasmus (1956: 445) reports the designation *minga bailada* for the system prevailing in northwest Ecuador, but I have never heard the term used in or around San Lorenzo. Erasmus (1956: 445) distinguishes between exchange and festive labor according to "the degree of obligation to reciprocate labor as well as the quantity and quality of the food and/or drink served the workers." There is no such practical distinction made in San Lorenzo, nor in the immediate hinterland, and the conceptual distinction is inapplicable to San Lorenzo for two reasons. First, in San Lorenzo and the surrounding hinterland, the system of reciprocity among members of the lower class extends beyond the minga relationship, and therefore obligations of minga workers and host are linked to a broader network of relations. Second, norms of reciprocity are influenced by the class hierarchy in such a manner that asymmetrical obligations, obligations of different kinds (Foster 1961: 1174; 1964: 1280–93), obfuscate the conceptual distinction between festive and exchange labor.

West (1957: 131) traces the origin of the term minga to a highland Quechua forced-work group, and discusses the possible African provenience of the form of minga practiced among the Negroes in the Colombian Pacific lowlands.[1] The concept behind minga labor, as the Negroes express it, is equal, mutual aid. Everyone helps one man, who is then equally obligated to all the others. The only qualifying factor admitted is the festive exchange, through which the generous host partially discharges his obligation. A corporate group of rotating hosts should exist, with an option of festive exchange decreasing the obligation of a generous host. Whether such a system ever existed among Negroes of northwest Ecuador, I do not know. Erasmus (1956: 449) was told of a permanent rotating minga committee during a short stay in a Negro village on the Cayapas River, but he questions the accuracy of the report.

The *idea* of mutual aid in the minga may be considered an extension of an existing cultural pattern: Negroes do not like to work alone and avoid traveling without a partner. Partners are social and economic equals. They do the same amount of work and share profits and losses equally. In their conversation and folklore, too, Negroes idealize work in pairs.

All Negroes interviewed about the minga immediately told me that it is based on the ideal that work time given should be repaid with an identical amount of time. Those who speak of the minga among themselves, or to sawmill managers, express the same notion. Since I have never seen minga labor function in accordance with this

1. For a discussion of African parallels, see Herskovits (1958: 161–67). Guevara (1957) gives a full description of highland Ecuadorian mingas. Similar organizations exist among Colombian coastal Negroes but sometimes carry a different name. One good example is the *winúl* group, which exists north of Gallo Island, in and near the town of Salahonda (author's observations).

ideal, I think that the anthropologist must describe in terms of cultural patterns the reciprocity that the Negroes express in terms of time worked. Before giving such an analytical description, I will describe the minga as it is now organized.

Crucial to an understanding of the minga as it actually exists is the role of *jefe de la minga* (head of the minga). Essentially, the jefe de la minga is a man who *always* organizes a minga committee to cut and transport lumber to a sawmill, and who receives *all* of the profits. I will return to the jefe de la minga shortly.

In 1961, and to a lesser extent in 1963, minga labor functioned primarily in the lumber industry. The head of the minga initiates negotiations with the owner or manager of a sawmill, and agrees to supply a certain amount of timber in return for a cash advance with which to buy food and drink for a crew of workmen. He then asks a number of able-bodied men to travel with him into the forest, cut timber, and bring it to the sawmill. While in the forest, the head of the minga feeds his workers and the women they have brought along to cook. The minga lasts from three to seven days; when the logs are delivered, the head of the minga is paid. The profit is his to keep, but, ideally, he owes every man who worked for him an equal amount of time—at the man's convenience.

In San Lorenzo, the position of jefe de la minga has a definite social status in a wide pattern of interacting lower- and middle-class networks. Leadership does not rotate among the members of a timber party. The same men tend to organize and head mingas again and again. Why, then, do Negroes who constantly work in minga groups but never head a minga themselves insist that their motive in participating is the guarantee of reciprocal aid? Because every member of a minga does receive aid when he needs it, but not in the form of work time equal to the time he has given. The head of the minga repays each man according to the man's economic position and status in the community. He is always ready to lend money to men who have worked for him. When drinking, he is generous with his aguardiente and beer. He speaks well of those who work with him, and he gladly lies for them, even before the law.

The minga head is characterized by his *conspicuous giving* (Erasmus 1961: 101–34), which keeps him solidly in the lower class despite his earnings. He converts his economic resources into power and prestige over those who work on the mingas he organizes. He is the center of an interacting group functioning in an economic context. The highest expressions of group interactions are the occasional money-earning mingas. The head of the minga does not always take the initiative in recruiting workers. Many young men borrow money or goods with no intention of repaying in kind. They are only too glad to borrow repeatedly from the same man and then wipe out their debt by working for him for a few days.

We can now analyze the cultural pattern of the minga, with the aid of technical constructs. Initially, minga work groups are based on "dyadic contracts," which according to George Foster (1961: 1174) are "informal, or implicit, since they lack ritual or legal basis."

They are not based on any idea of law, and they are unenforceable through authority; they exist only at the pleasure of the contractants. The contracts are dyadic in that they occur only between two individuals . . . the contracts are noncorporate, since social units such as villages, barrios, or extended families are never bound.

When two Negroes establish a dyadic contract, they continue to reciprocate for an indeterminate period. Radcliffe-Brown (1957: 133–37) noted that this was a universal aspect of reciprocity, and explained it in terms of the desire to always return a little more than what one had received. Such an explanation accords with my observations.

For a full understanding of the minga organization, Foster's concept must be expanded to include the idea of *serial* dyadic contracts. In San Lorenzo, if a man cannot repay a debt when his assistance is needed, he usually asks others to help. If they agree, all parties to the agreement enter into a relationship that amounts to a series of long-term contracts. The jefe de la minga is the central figure in all the serial dyadic contracts and as such is responsible for seeing that all of them are fulfilled. Mingas in San Lorenzo, particularly the lumber mingas described above, bring the jefe de la minga an immediate economic gain, and the workers (and their families) gain a large measure of long-term security. The relations between minga structure and the kinship system will be analyzed in Chapters VI and VII.

The term minga may also be used for a cooperative effort such as a neighborhood clean-up party, initiated by a prominent man. Also, with the addition of appropriate modifying phrases it may refer to any collective enterprise of short duration. A cemetery clean-up party, for example, is known as a *minga para los muertos*—minga for the dead. In July 1963, San Lorenzo's school teachers put all the little boys to work cleaning the grounds around the school, and referred to the project as *minga por los niños*—minga by the children. This broad application of the term minga seems to reflect a highland influence among the Negroes of the coast, since it occurs only where there has been fairly extensive contact with highland mestizos and Indians.

The effect of the new methods of the timber company and two sawmills has not been the complete breakdown of the minga system. The sawmill owners and the timber company recruit workmen through the minga heads. Workmen are paid at the same daily rate as the minga head. He is responsible for seeing that a certain number of Negroes work on a given job each day. He may ask Negroes in his debt to work for a few days in order to give others time off to tend gardens, fish, or perform some other task. The jefe de la minga is actually the only full-time employee; it is he who divides up the work to be done and assigns specific men to specific tasks. In 1963, five men held such positions, each one working in a different location. In this new context, the jefe de la minga is again the center of an interacting network, in which all the workers owe their jobs to him and he is obliged only to allow them to work when they wish. Only when he asks them to work does he place himself in their debt. In the new context he gains a favorable balance of reciprocity; all are indebted to him for the opportunity to earn cash, and he no longer need sacrifice his economic gain for power and prestige. However, his new gains are offset somewhat by his increased managerial responsibilities and his obligation to learn new techniques.

Minga heads are now found in two contexts, the traditional lumber minga and the new wage-labor lumber system. They are, then, key figures in the transition from traditional to rational labor. More will be said about their position vis-à-vis the middle class in Chapters VII and VIII. It should be noted, however, that the paying of steady day wages for labor in the forest has already led some Negroes to ask for work directly of the head of the timber company, instead of trying to establish a dyadic contract with a minga head. As more workers perceive a distinct advantage in this rational form of employment, as opposed to the traditional reciprocal exchange system, more of them may sever bonds with the minga head. However, the position of jefe de la minga ramifies into other areas of sociocultural activity and, for the present, the system of serial dyadic contracts, which functions alongside cash labor, still seems to be congruent with other aspects of the culture of the northern coast. Rational day labor will not wholly supplant reciprocal labor until it brings the worker distinctly higher returns than the older system. At a daily wage of 15–20 sucres, there is not yet such an advantage.

Subsistence Occupations

As the accompanying list indicates, lower-class Negroes tend to divide the major day-to-day tasks between the sexes, although some important tasks and responsibilities are shared more or less equally by men and women.

Men's work	Women's work
Build house	Clean house, clothes, children, food
Tend house grounds	
Make canoes, bateas, paddles, sails, anchors, utensils	Cook
Cut and transport timber	Sew women's clothes
Slash out area for planting	Gather conchas
Plant and harvest large crops (plantains, bananas, pineapples)	Fetch water
	Kill chickens and turkeys, gather eggs
Fish and hunt	Gather daily food (*rascadera*, sweet manioc, papaya)
Gather crabs and shrimp	
Sew men's clothes	Make hammocks and straw sleeping mats
Make bark mats	Make and keep fire in home
Paddle back of canoe (standing)	Paddle front of canoe (sitting)

Shared tasks
Plant small crops
Make charcoal
Plait fire fans and baskets
Slaughter pigs and cows
Take responsibility for children

Fishing, agriculture, and animal husbandry are the main subsistence sources for the Costeños from northern Esmeraldas. Hunting and gathering are less important for survival, though shellfish and wild animals are favorite foods.[2]

Fishing Techniques

Fish are caught with screens, nets, hooks, traps, harpoons, and dynamite. Poison is not used, although I have heard reports of Negroes' poisoning fish on the Mataje River.

1. Screen fishing involves placing a large bamboo screen across a tidal inlet at high tide and gathering the trapped fish at low tide. The men who make, mend, and set the screen share the catch equally. No one man heads the operation.

2. There are two types of net fishing. In one, a man, working with a partner (often a son or young relative), casts the round *atarraya*, a net with a radius of about five feet weighted all around the edge. The second type involves a group of men (*chinchorreros*) who use the *chinchorro*, a long net that they all make, own, repair, and use. The chinchorreros share the catch equally. The uneven ocean bottom and the many mangrove roots make chinchorro fishing impractical in and around San Lorenzo and it is not found there. It is used extensively on the sandy coast and beaches of the outlying islands, and at the mouth of the Santiago River.

3. In one type of hook fishing, a hook is tied to a line, baited, and set on a stick with a balsa float. The fisherman sets several such lines, and waits in his canoe for a fish to bite. The hooked fish is then pulled into the canoe. Another form of hook fishing consists of setting a series of hooks (or trot line), called *calandra* (West 1957: 161 calls it *belandra*), baited or unbaited, across a channel to catch fish as they run with the tide. The calandra is also used for larger fish in the open sea.

4. Small, rectangular bamboo traps, with a sliding door, are used on the tidal rivers but never on the coast or in the mangrove swamps. Fish enter at high tide and the door is shut before low tide. Traps were common when shad were plentiful, but they are less widely used now because extensive dynamiting has curtailed the shad runs in recent years.

5. Harpoons are used to catch manta rays (*raya*) and sawfish (*guacapa*). The raya is harpooned as he drifts toward the surface.

2. For a more detailed description of Negro material culture and subsistence techniques, see West (1957: 82–254).

The guacapa is ordinarily hooked on a line first and then harpooned as he is brought near to the canoe. Harpooning such large fish (the guacapa may weigh as much as 800 pounds) requires the cooperative efforts of two to six fishermen, who divide the catch equally. Unlike the Cayapa Indians, Negroes do not harpoon smaller river fish.

6. Dynamiting is now the favorite method of catching small fish to be eaten or used as bait for bigger fish. Dynamite is slowly replacing the atarraya, though the latter is still used extensively. Although dynamiting is illegal, there has been no effort to curb it. Very serious accidents occur at least four or five times a year, usually because of the Negroes' habit of blowing on the ignited fuse while watching the movements of a school of fish.

Either fish are fried the day they are caught or the next day, or they are dried under the sun on a simple wood and bamboo platform (called *barbacoa*). No fire is used in drying. Fish is a major food staple in San Lorenzo as it is elsewhere along the coast and mangrove estuaries and channels.

Agriculture and Animal Husbandry

The fruits grown and used in and around San Lorenzo include: sapote, white sapote, star-apple, mango, Asiatic breadfruit (locally called *pepepan*), papaya, white pineapple, New World peach palm, avocado, cacao, banana (called *guineo,* including the little *chileño,* larger *manzano,* and large *mata serrano* and *guineo de cruz*), orange, lemon, lime, grapefruit, fig, three varieties of guava, known as *guayaba, guayaba de mono,* and *guayaba agria,* plum, coconut (two varieties), plantain, soursop or custard apple, cherimoya, *guama* (locally called *guava*), *pepino,* and *mamey.* Among the vegetables raised locally are: sweet manioc, sweet potato, potato, sugarcane, onion, tomato, pepper, rice, *chilma, papachina,* and *rascadera,* which is a tuber resembling taro (West 1957: 139).

The staples of subsistence agriculture are sweet manioc, plantains, sugarcane, rascadera, and sweet potato. Bananas, coconuts, oranges, and lemons are raised both as cash crops and for personal consumption, as is rice, which is more often purchased than raised in or near San Lorenzo.

These staples are usually beaten and fried with meat or fish. Common dishes include: *tapado,* plantains with fish; *sancocho,* meat, plantains, sweet manioc, and rascadera; *seco*, concha with coconut; *seco de pescado*, fish with coconut; and *locro de yuca*, meat with sweet manioc. Green boiled plantains (*peán piado*) are eaten at every meal in place of bread. *Guarapo*, a sugarcane beer, is made and consumed in the outlying islands, but not in San Lorenzo.

Little work is involved in raising the local fruits and vegetables. First, seeds are broadcast directly into the bush and cuttings and shoots planted before the bush is cut. Then men slash out the area that has been planted, but they do not burn it. The brush rapidly decays to mulch, and fertilizes the growing crop. West (1957: 129) aptly calls this the "slash-mulch system." Once the crop rises above the weeds, it is tended only sporadically. Bananas and plantains are not pruned, and hence after the first few years, they become so thick and the soil so depleted that they cease to bear fruit. Then they are all cut down or the site is abandoned. Crops are harvested during a "waning moon," called *menguate* (more properly, *menguante*) when the sap is supposedly in the roots. Negroes in San Lorenzo, as elsewhere in northwestern South America, plant and raise onions, small peppers, and medicinal herbs in raised platform gardens (*azoteas*), which are often made of discarded, rotting canoes.

Animal husbandry involves little more than acquiring a pig, cow, turkeys, or chickens. Only on the rivers are the pigs penned, and until June 1963, cows and pigs roamed freely in the streets of San Lorenzo. (The manner in which the animals were removed from the town will be discussed in Chapter VIII.) Animals are not ordinarily fed; they eat what they can find. Cows and pigs are used for their meat; cows usually are not milked. Turkeys are ordinarily sold, not eaten. Hens are used for egg production until they are very old. Roosters are not killed for food until they are very old, and then they may be sold rather than eaten.

Hunting and Gathering

Men hunt wild peccary (*tatabro*), paca (*guagua*), agouti (*guatín*), and wild pig (*saíno*). They occasionally kill wild fowl and squirrels or more rarely a rabbit for food. Negroes kill grown monkeys, sloths, jaguars, ocelots, and snakes if they happen upon them. Their pelts are often marketed; the carcasses are not eaten. Young monkeys, sloths, kinkajous, ocelots, anteaters, parrots, and toucans are captured and kept as pets or sold to tourists. I am told that caymans used to abound, but they are nearly extinct. Conchas are an important part of the Negroes' diet. Crab and shrimp are considered delicacies, but they are gathered infrequently. Iguanas and tortoises are captured, kept alive for awhile, and eventually made into a stew.

Men hunt with muzzle-loading shotguns of 20 gauge or smaller. Success with this crude firearm requires the ability to approach game to within ten to fifteen feet. Few men in San Lorenzo travel to the forest for the sole purpose of hunting. Men on mingas or traveling in the forest for another reason usually carry a gun in case they see something to shoot.

Crafts

The following items are made for personal use: brooms, calabash and coconut bowls, bateas, canoes, canoe paddles, anchors, stools and tables, axe handles, fire fans, baskets, rush and bark sleeping mats, hammocks, fishing nets, traps and screens, drums, marimbas, pipes, sails, rope, floats, wood and clay hearths, houses, and pens.

Though some people become especially proficient at making a particular item and market it on a small scale, most people make their own household belongings. Major purchases include machetes, axe heads, fish hooks, dynamite and caps, cloth, and pots and pans.

Part-Time Specialists

Singers and Musicians

Cantadoras are women singers who sing at *arrullos* (wakes for children) and *alavados* (wakes for adults), and serve as *respondedoras* during the marimba dance. In the marimba dance there are two respondedora roles: the *solista* sings the melodic response, and the *bajonera* harmonizes with her. Cantadoras make their own maracas, used at arrullos, and *guasás*, which are shaken in the marimba dance. There are eight recognized cantadoras in San Lorenzo, although from time to time other women may temporarily assume the role.

Marimberos are male musicians in the marimba orchestra. The most important is the *glosador*, who leads the singing, gives the *gritos* (shouts), and indicates to the respondedoras what they should be singing at any given time. Two musicians play the marimba, the *bordonero* who plays the melody on the lower half of the instrument and the *tiplero* who plays harmony and counterpoint on the upper half. Other musicians for the marimba, less specialized, include the *bombero*, who plays the *bombo*, which is similar to a bass drum, and the *cununero*, who plays the cone-shaped *cununo*, which resembles the Cuban conga drum. In any Negro community in the northern sector, there are one to three glosadores, six or ten marimba players, and up to twenty bomberos and cununeros.

The guitar is the most popular instrument among younger people, and two dozen young men in San Lorenzo can play it. Bongo drums are also favored by young men, though to date very few can play them.

Midwives

There are 12 recognized midwives (*parteras*) in San Lorenzo, all of them over 40. Another twenty women claim at times to be midwives, but their competence is not generally recognized. Midwives aid in delivery by using traditional "direct coping techniques," for example by administering herbal concoctions to increase contraction pain, and "indirect coping methods," such as diagnosing magical causality for difficulties in delivery. Although the Junta Autónoma doctor in San Lorenzo gave the midwives four months of instruction and has good working relations with them, they continue to use their traditional methods along with those they learned from him. During birth the midwife serves as witchfinder; she detects the presence of men with *mala espalda* (bad back), a condition said to hinder delivery, and keeps an eye out for the ever-elusive bird or vampire bat-like *brujas* (witches), who might wish to bite the child while it is still in the womb, giving it a hair lip. Midwives also issue post-partum taboos, restricting the new mothers' food, movements, etc. Their injunctions are rarely, if ever, heeded.

The basic equipment of a midwife costs between 30 and 40 sucres. It includes sterile gauze, antiseptics, and scissors. For a successful delivery she receives 50–80 sucres, or the equivalent in kind. She receives no payment for a delivery in which the child dies.

Folk Healers

Folk medicine is practiced throughout Esmeraldas province, with considerable local variation and embellishment. Paredes Borja

(1963a: 281–96; 1963b: 47) claims that the Negro slaves who escaped in the sixteenth century introduced the dominant medical concepts and practices to the northern coast. Whether or not this is true, there is a rich store of folk medicine among the Negroes in Esmeraldas province. In San Lorenzo there are two classes of folk doctors, the *sabador* (chiropractor) and the *curandero* (herb doctor). The sabador corrects dislocations and fixes fractures and sprains. There are six or eight sabadores in San Lorenzo at any given time, some far better than others. In order to be successful, the sabador must be able to distinguish a sprain or dislocation from a fracture. The former are treated with extensive manipulations, the latter with splints, once the bone has been set. Sabadores work with both people and animals.

There are six or eight curanderos in San Lorenzo, although only three or four are really active. They use herbal concoctions and incantations to God, Jesus, and Mary. They cure ordinary fevers, infections, and the like, but they assign them supernatural causes, notably *pasmo, mal aire, mal de ojo,* and *espanto* or *susto.*

Some curanderos choose to specialize further. In San Lorenzo there are two who specialize in curing snake bites. Since many people who are bitten by nonpoisonous snakes run to the curandero, his treatments are often successful. Sabadores and curanderos receive five sucres or more for cures. It is difficult to estimate their income, for they are often paid in commodities rather than cash.

A few other men, usually transients in San Lorenzo, cure ills with commercial tonics, sulfa, penicillin, and vitamin shots. San Lorenzo is also beginning to be subjected to traveling quacks, who spend a day or two in town selling amulets, tonics, and other cure-alls, with a spiel reminiscent of the old-time "Indian curers" in the United States. To date they have made little impression on lower-class Negroes, but the middle-class mestizos and Negroes are quite taken with them.

Sorcery and Witchcraft

Brujos and *guardas espaldas* visit San Lorenzo from time to time. They are Negroes who come for a few days to remove malign spells believed to be the result of witchcraft from an unknown source. The brujo is the active sorcerer and witch finder. The guarda espalda protects the brujo from rebounding spells and the spells of other brujos. A brujo's fee runs from 50 to 200 sucres. However, there is very little call for a brujo in San Lorenzo. The few times one visited while I was there, he had only about eight patients. Most of them suspected "someone" (always unspecified) from another town or a dead, unknown, and unspecified relative, and not someone living in San Lorenzo, of working witchcraft.

There are no *pildé* eaters in San Lorenzo, but many Negroes know of them. Pildé is a vine (*el bejuco bravo*) that is said to have a narcotic effect when beaten and drunk with aguardiente. Though pildé is known to grow in the forests as close to San Lorenzo as Najurungo and Molina, it reportedly is not used there. It is used on the Cayapas River and the Ónzole River, according to reports from both Negroes and Cayapa Indians. The pildé-aguardiente mixture supposedly is drunk daily by devoted brujos who wish to see the future and perceive events beyond the range of their normal senses. Negroes will not experiment with pildé, since they claim that to do so without having established a tolerance for the drug induces severe psychotic states, punctuated by tremendous "frights."

Markets and Marketing

Any commodity mentioned above as having a role in the subsistence economy can be and is marketed. At any given time, most members of San Lorenzo's lower class seem to have more than enough of one thing and not enough of another. There is a constant daily interchange of goods in town and between San Lorenzo and nearby farms and smaller villages.

There is no central market in San Lorenzo. In 1961 there was an incipient centralized market in the area around the dock where the train met the ships, but Junta Autónoma planners moved the trainstop to the other end of town (nearer the New Town). By 1963, with the completion of the train station, there were two centers of trade, one near the wharf and the other at the station. Members of the lower class as well as middle-class shopkeepers purchase incoming goods directly at these two outlets.

Home-grown goods that are not sold to a lower-class proprietor are marketed by men and women crying out their wares through the streets and pathways of the town. For fish, fowl, and meat, fulcrum scales made from coconut or calabash halves are used. The meat or fish is placed in one side and a stone of agreed weight in the other.

People ordinarily keep their own stones. The following prices are fairly stable, and serve to illustrate the current cash exchange among members of San Lorenzo's lower class:

Item	Price (sucres)	Item	Price
Large fish (8 to 10 lbs.)	6–7	Papaya	2–3
Large dried fish	8–10	10 Bananas	1
1 doz. Small fish		8–12 Plantains	1
(6–12 in.)	5–10		
25–30 Conchas	1	Dugout canoe	200–800
5 Crabs	1	Canoe paddle	6–8
Coconut	1	Batea	3–7
Pineapple	1	Basket	2–5

Sweet manioc, rascadera and the most common fruits are seldom bought or sold. Most rice is imported from the south at very small expense. A few sucres will buy enough rice to feed ten people for a day or two.

A Typical Day

For a picture of subsistence life on the edge of the cash economy, let us consider a day in a typical household, a household in which neither the man nor his wife holds a job, but in which both would like to raise their standard of living above the subsistence level by marketing the fruit of their labors.

Let us say that they live in San Lorenzo, where they raise sweet manioc, rascadera, and papaya, and keep a pig and some chickens. They have a small farm on the edge of the sea, an hour's journey from San Lorenzo by canoe, where they grow more coconuts, bananas (or pineapples), and plantains than they can consume. These cash crops rim the sea, in front and to each side of the house. Sweet manioc is grown in among the cash crops. Around the house, behind the coconuts and plaintains, grow cacao, papaya, and other fruits. A calabash tree supplies the family with water-carrying vessels.

In the morning the woman decides to gather conchas near the farm, instead of washing clothes. She leaves San Lorenzo on the ebb tide, taking her children and a younger sister with her. While the woman gathers conchas with friends, her sister and children play, and gather yuca, bananas, plantains, and other ripening fruit from the farm. The woman keeps four dozen conchas for the family's supper; her share of the proceeds from selling the remainder of the conchas comes to eight sucres.

In his turn, the man decides to go fishing with his cousin who also shares his household, instead of stripping mangrove bark, making charcoal, bringing in a load of bananas from the farm, or joining a minga. He purchases three four-inch sticks of dynamite, including caps, for five sucres. After paddling along the mangrove channel for half an hour, he locates a school of mullet and tosses his first stick of dynamite. He is skillful and hits the school. He now has more than thirty mullet, only a few of which he will use for bait, and he can save the remaining two pieces of dynamite for another day.

He sets three lines in a mangrove channel, each baited with half a mullet, and sits down to await some action. He may also work, or visit, with a man who has come to the same spot. In the course of the day, he catches three large fish, two corvina and one colorado. He erects a small spritsail on his canoe and comes into San Lorenzo with the evening breeze that always blows down the Bahía de Pailón.

The household makes its evening meal from the conchas the woman brought home and the mullet the man caught, combined with plantains, rascadera, papaya, and rice. Coconut or banana is mixed with the other foods which are cooked in the coconut or banana oil. There are enough plantains, papaya, rascadera, and sweet manioc for three or four more days. What is left can be sold. How much do the members of the household earn, in sucres, by marketing their surplus food?

Income:

Bunch of bananas	5	
Three large fish	20	
Conchas	8	
Total		33

Expenditures:

Dynamite	5	
Rice	2	
Total		7
Net Income		26

This net intake is not unusual, although it is not duplicated every day by every family. When a full crop of pineapples or bananas is harvested, the profit is of course much greater. It is not impossible to earn as much as 50 sucres in one day. Averaged over a month, the daily net income of a lower-class family may amount to 15 sucres. The significant point here is that by marketing essentially subsistence products, a lower-class household may earn as much money as it could by working regularly for wages. It is not economic factors, alone, then, that determine what tasks lower-class families set themselves. The social factors affecting the way in which a family supports itself will be discussed in later chapters.

The Style of Life of the Lower Class

The typical Negro house is made of wood or bamboo; it stands on piles and is covered with a thatched palm roof. The kitchen is first built and enclosed, and then the floor of the larger structure; often all but the kitchen remains unwalled for two years or more. Very few lower-class families have any sanitary facilities. A few families have erected outhouses over one of the little inlets; they usually bathe in the same area. The area behind the kitchen where the rascadera grows is the standard spot in which to urinate. The interior of the house may be one large room or partitioned into many rooms, depending on the number of people in the household (there may be as many as twelve) and on kinship factors to be discussed later. The furniture is sparse: a homemade table and stools, crude hammocks for resting during the day (never slept in at night); bark and straw sleeping mats, one or two mosquito nets for the older members of the family, and occasionally a sleeping platform or bedstead. Pots and pans are hung in the separate kitchen where a charcoal fire, which is built on a raised platform, is kept smouldering on a clay bed.

Two meals a day are usual, and there is sometimes a third. In the morning—or, more accurately, when people set out for work, which may be any time between 1 and 10 A.M.—people generally have *culada*, which consists of a pounded and fried fish and plantain mixture, and coffee. In the middle of the work day, or sometime between 10 A.M. and 5 P.M., they may eat a light meal of fried mullet (often fried in the canoe), or a piece of boiled plantain or bread, or soup made from any combination of fish, shellfish and vegetables, and sometimes packaged macaroni. Less frequently a can of tuna fish or large sardines, costing two sucres, is eaten with the soup. Dried fish is the most popular mid-day meal. It is either eaten alone, or pounded into a paste with yuca, plantains, and rascadera, and fried. Fresh fruit is eaten throughout the day, as appetite and availability allows.

The main meal, locally called *la merienda,* is generally eaten between 6 and 8 in the evening, though it may be taken as late as midnight. The merienda consists of fish, rice, sweet manioc, rascadera, and plantains, and may also include game, pork, conchas, canned sardines, canned tuna fish, and fresh fruit. People do not ordinarily eat in large groups. The women and children eat whenever the food is ready, and the men eat whenever they happen to come home. People gobble down their food and go on to something else; no one lingers around the table or remarks on the quality of the food.

Negro women ordinarily have one or two clean work dresses, and one good dress for church affairs, wakes, and other social events. The men wear tattered clothes to work in, often little more than improvised shorts and no shirt. Besides these work clothes, they usually own one or two shirts and one or two pairs of trousers. To the saloon and to church, men are likely to wear a white shirt, white trousers, and, increasingly, black shoes.

Many more Negroes owned shoes in 1963 than in 1961. In the summer of 1961 one rarely saw a lower-class Negro with shoes, but in 1963 I estimated that a little more than 40 per cent of the Negroes between 18 and 50 had shoes to wear on special occasions. More women than men owned shoes, thanks to the appearance on the market of very inexpensive Japanese rubber sandals. There was a similar striking increase in the number of radios in town. In 1961 there were only three radios in San Lorenzo, but by 1963 one out of eight lower-class households had purchased Japanese transistor radios. Comic books, too, made an appearance in 1963, although few of them were sold.

The lower-class Negroes of San Lorenzo do not strike one as oppressed, poverty-stricken people. Rather, they seem to be robust and relatively fulfilled people, who are just becoming aware that they do not have all that they might out of life.

Time and the Subsistence and Cash Economies

To understand the Negroes' attitude toward work and the reasons for their choice of economic activities, one must know something about concepts of time in San Lorenzo. Negro lower-class life is governed by two concepts of time: one is based on the national system, which follows United States eastern standard time; the other is based on the lunar day, that is, on the rise and fall of the tides. Everything that has not been introduced to San Lorenzo from the outside operates according to the rise and fall of the tides. High and low tide each occur twice every 24 hours and 51 minutes. People leave San Lorenzo on the ebb tide and enter on the flood tide; the tides govern where and when one fishes and gathers sea products. The average difference in water level between high and low tide is about 12 feet. It would be foolhardy, to say the least, to try to bring in several tons of timber against the tide, with no more than large oars for propulsion. Nor can a canoe be moved easily against the flow; even a canoe with a motor can enter many areas of the mangrove swamp only when the tide is flowing in (at low tide the channel is dry) or flowing out (at high tide the mangrove roots form a solid wall at water level).

The need to move with, not against, the tide has an influence on Negro life that extends beyond such immediate, practical considerations. The lowest tidal flows (the spring tides) occur during the waning moon. Negroes emphasize that an enterprise that involves cutting, altering, or making something is best undertaken during the "waning moon." It is then that Negroes prefer to make canoes, kill animals, cut timber, and harvest crops.

Although San Lorenzo employers have relatively flexible time standards, they expect the Negroes to work according to the national time system. Their principal complaint is that the Negroes cannot be relied upon to arrive at work on time or to have enough energy to do the work when they come. The Negroes' apparent indolence usually can be traced to two factors. First, Negroes have often been working for eight to ten hours by the time their workday officially begins. They cannot simply go fish for an hour or two in the evening, because the tide may not be right. Second, Negroes seem to have internalized a time sense based on the lunar day, not on the clock.

Time and again I have seen indications that Negroes are actually functioning on lunar time; for example, they may ask for breakfast at lunch or dinner time, or greet a friend in the afternoon with "good morning," and then become very confused when a highlander points out, or makes a joke about, their "error."

For many San Lorenzo Negroes, mechanistic time is replacing the lunar day. But many other Negroes in San Lorenzo and even more in the hinterland still operate on the lunar day. The timber company lends itself most easily to a lunar-day orientation because of the nature of the work itself. Logs are simply moved in with the tide and anchored as the tide recedes. Under the new lumbering system, shallow ditches have been cut by Negroes through the islands; the tide fills the ditch at high tide and floats the logs out into a channel. Thus the Negroes' time orientation is the one best suited to efficient job performance. It is probably for this reason that the men in charge of timber operations, unlike other local employers, have not complained about the Negroes' indolence; in fact, they consider the Negroes excellent workers.

When a Negro accepts a job with the Junta Autónoma or a sawmill, either he must put all his faith in his employer's ability to pay, and rely on credit until payday, or he must have the stamina for subsistence work in his spare time. Even if he has the strength, optimal tidal conditions may not coincide with his hours off. The majority of lower-class Negroes do not see any great advantage in steady day labor. To exploit their natural environment they must live close to it. They must make careful note of fish runs, the peculiar characteristics of each channel, and promising spots for future utilization. They cannot do this if they are tied to a full-time job, and they are fully aware that they cannot. On the whole, a man who lives by selling his surplus subsistence products can expect an income comparable to that earned by a day laborer, with no greater risk. In fact, it is not unusual for a man who is working by the day to become so overdrawn in credit that he never has any ready cash. If a man is not tied to a full-time job, he can take advantage of opportunities for a quick gain. Many fishermen point out that they can earn more by selling three fish than by working in a sawmill for a day. Most lower-class Negroes in San Lorenzo see a distinct advantage in working for the new timber company. The time factor is right, the economic gain obvious. Workers are paid every two or three weeks, and when a shipload of timber leaves San Lorenzo their pay is more than doubled. Furthermore, the work is conducted in a traditional context, through minga heads with personal ties with the participants.

In general, then, lower-class Negroes are interested in improving their material position, but they are not terribly dissatisfied with the way they now live. They see advantages and disadvantages in both day labor and subsistence pursuits. Neither is considered to have a clear-cut advantage by the Negroes as a class, but they are agreed that one cannot both work by the day and engage in more traditional economic pursuits.

Some twenty young men prefer to work exclusively in town, performing menial chores such as loading and unloading ships and railroad cars on a catch-as-catch-can basis. Their success depends entirely on their strength and endurance and on making their availability known. Except for these men, the Negroes prefer to support themselves by marketing surplus subsistence commodities until they see a clear economic advantage in abandoning a relatively secure way of life.

Negroes do move from the lower to the middle class, and to do so is becoming increasingly possible. Upward mobility is not dependent on saving money gained by working as a day laborer or by marketing surplus goods. In San Lorenzo mobility depends on a complex of social factors to be set forth in the following chapters.

V

Ethnic and Status Groupings

In this chapter the objective class situation presented in earlier chapters is modified by the addition of noneconomic aspects of social structure: ethnic and status divisions. Ethnic divisions themselves in San Lorenzo may be considered, at least in part, to be status divisions. Weber (1958: 185) noted that " 'status groups' hinder the strict carrying through of the sheer market principle." Ethnic and status lines divide classes in San Lorenzo; they influence the manner of participation in the economic order and figure prominently in the dynamics of socioeconomic mobility. Before we consider the major aspects of social status in San Lorenzo and their relation to class structure, the ethnic divisions must be fully explicated. After noting all terminologically recognized ethnic categories, I will set forth the broader status categories and groupings, which have the greatest impact in socioeconomic activities.

Ethnic Groupings in San Lorenzo

According to Ashley Montagu (1960: 698–99), the term ethnic group "may be applied to any group concerning which physical and cultural traits are so identified that it is given a certain distinctiveness which appears to separate it from other groups."

The phrase may also be used as embracing the definition of race in the biological sense, and particularly groups which are less clearly defined, which may or may not be races and hence should not be called races in the absence of the necessary scientific demonstration. All that we say when we use the phrase "ethnic group" is that here is a group of people who physically, and perhaps in other additional ways, may be regarded as a more or less distinct group.

Ecuador is an ethnically plural society, and San Lorenzo's ethnic situation seems to be even more heterogeneous than is usual for any particular area of the country. There is little clear-cut consensus in San Lorenzo about ethnic groupings. The ensuing discussion of the ethnic situation is based on apparent tendencies and social relations.

In previous chapters I distinguished between only two ethnic types—the highland and foreign white and mestizo, and the coastal Negro. This distinction, adequate for a discussion of economics in San Lorenzo, must now be further refined. We shall leave aside for the moment the highland whites and mestizos and concentrate on the varieties of racial distribution in Esmeraldas province and the coastal designations for them. It is mainly in the eyes of the mestizo, however, that this racial variation assumes an ethnic character.

The following tendencies prevail in northwest Ecuador, although there are striking exceptions to each of them:

(1) The higher the class the lighter the color.

(2) The closer to the coast the greater the variation in skin color, hair form, lip form, nasal index, and so forth. Riverine peoples tend to be either "true" Negro or Indian.

(3) The greater the urbanization in a town the higher the percentage of non-Negroid features.

(4) The nearer the center of town, the less Negroid racial features become; the fringe of the town is likely to be "true" Negro. San Lorenzo offers a unique exception to this because of the number of highland mestizos who have settled along the railroad tracks.

(5) In the large towns, where race lines are stiffening, Negroid features have a negative value.

The following ethnic terminology is in current use among the coastal people (as opposed to the highlanders) of northern Esmeraldas:

Costeño. A man from the coast. This is the major identity referent, regardless of physical features, for all those who have a coastal way of life.

Moreno. The name favored by Negroes, zambos, and dark mulattoes in referring to themselves. One is first a Costeño and second a moreno. Very dark people tend to regard almost everyone except the very light as morenos, but the lighter-skinned people themselves have other categories, listed below.

Negro. A derogatory term for a Negro, zambo, or mulatto when used by a non-Negro. Negroes, however, refer to one another as "negro" just as lower-class Negroes in the United States may call one another "nigger." In San Lorenzo "negro" can be an insult or a sign of affection, depending on the context.

Mulato or *mulât.* A very light-skinned Costeño. Often racial affinity to Negroes can be established only by reference to genealogy.

Cholo. A generally dark Costeño with straight hair. Only when the straight hair is manifest does this Indian-Negro admixture (zambo) have ethnic significance; color does not ordinarily enter into the designation "cholo." Some cholos appear to be coastal Indians without tribal or linguistic identity. Both Indians and Negroes believe cholos to be stronger and braver than either Indians or Negroes.

Blanco. Any middle- or upper-class mestizo, Caucasian, or mulatto who is held in some degree of respect.

Montuvio. There are three overlapping meanings for this term in northwest Ecuador. (1) A monolingual Spanish-speaking Indian native to the coast. (2) A person who is uncivilized, inherently dirty, slovenly, and dangerous, and who does not respect others. Regardless of race, a person who commits murder, or a person who at the same time has a rural style of life and is distinctly antisocial, is montuvio. (3) Any lower- or middle-class, light-skinned person from Manabí or Guayas province is also called montuvio. The ordinary connotations of this term in San Lorenzo resemble those of "poor white trash" in the southern United States. Farther south, montuvio is used only in the first sense.

Indio. Cayapa, Colorado, Otavalo, Putumayo, or any other Indians in native dress.

Serrano. Anyone from the Sierra, regardless of race. This category includes highland Negroes who occasionally visit San Lorenzo.

Gringo. Any stranger, including Argentines, Mexicans, and other Latin Americans, as well as North Americans and Europeans.

The highland mestizos distinguish among the ethnic types listed below. Their terminology does not always coincide, and may contrast, with that of the Costeños.

Serrano. A person from the Sierra.

Costeño. A person from the coast.

Negro. Any Costeño with dark skin. It is also a term of endearment when applied to a Serrano.

Cholo. Used both to designate a poor phenotypically Indian highlander and as a term of endearment for children, close friends, and spouses. A derogatory term when used to mean a lower-class mestizo.

Mestizo. A seldom-used racial term meaning mixed blood.

Blanco. A middle- or upper-class highlander; any highlander to whom respect is given.

Montuvio. A light-skinned Costeño with no striking Negro features, especially one from Manabí or Guayas province.

Mulato. A mulatto in the United States meaning of the term. The distinction between *negro* and *mulato* is far more important to highland Eucadorians than to Costeños. Some Serranos adopt the north coast terminology but only if they are in close contact with the darker-skinned Costeños.

It is the use of the term *negro* and, less frequently, *montuvio* in what may be taken as a derogatory sense that creates social cleavage between many Costeños and Serranos in San Lorenzo. The influx of highlanders to San Lorenzo has heightened ethnic awareness by putting the lighter-skinned Costeños in a favored position. Whether or not the light-skinned Costeños (*mulatos* and *blancos*) formed a distinct ethnic category prior to sustained contact with the Serranos cannot be determined. Now they most certainly form what Bott (1957: 167–68) refers to as a "constructed reference group," i.e., a social category, in the eyes of both highlanders and—to a lesser extent—Costeños. The significance of this is that the light-skinned Costeños, who share coastal identity with the darker morenos, are increasingly seen as cultural mediators between highland mestizos and coastal Negroes in northwest Ecuador. Henceforth, I will refer to this constructed reference group as "light Costeño."

Although there is a tendency for lighter-skinned people to be favored socially, economically, and perhaps politically, and to serve as mediators, there are too many other factors at work in San Lorenzo's social relations to give a disproportionate emphasis to race or ethnic relations. Figure 2 illustrates the significant ethnic divisions in San Lorenzo. Other ethnic designations, which may occur anywhere in the structure, will be presented as they seem relevant to the discussion of status and status groupings.

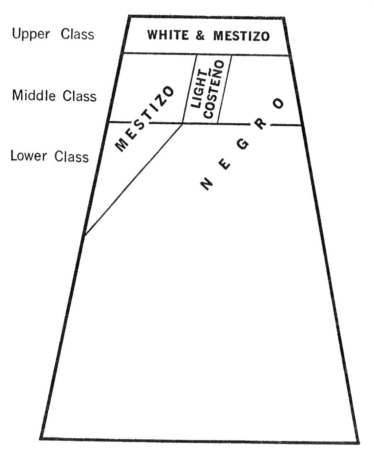

Figure 2. Major Ethnic Divisions

Status Groupings in San Lorenzo

The concept of social status, unlike the concept of social class, refers to a subjective category arising from notions of "social honor." "In contrast to the purely economically determined 'class situation' we wish to designate as 'status situation' every typical component of the life fate of men that is determined by a specific, positive or negative, social estimation of *honor*." (Weber 1958: 186–87.) To some extent concepts of social honor relate to class and ethnic situations, but they also cut across such lines. Except for a few idiosyncratic men and women, people hold and live by values that are supported by rela-

tively intense interpersonal or associational networks. I will set forth
the various status situations by discussing values and group affilia-
tions as they relate to the objective class situation.

In the upper class, class and ethnic boundaries coincide to a considerable extent. A member of this class is ethnically "white"; he
controls some tangible aspect of the social order of the town (re-
ligion, economics, medicine), and shares with the other members of
his class a distinctive style of life. In this sense class consciousness is
stronger in the upper class than in the other classes. But in the upper
class, as in the rest of the community, there is a basic bifurcation
in values. This bifurcation is between those who are "community-
oriented" and those who are not.

Community Orientation in the Upper Class

High social status is accorded to all members of the upper class, but
some of them are distinguished by their community orientation, i.e.,
by their desire for community approval of their actions. If community approval of his actions is of major importance to a person in
maintaining his "status image," he is "community-oriented." "Status
image" refers to "that hierarchy of values according to which [one]
judges himself and his place in society" (Eisenstadt 1954: 180).
Values are defined in Kluckhohn's (1951: 395) manner: "A value
is a conception, explicit or implicit, distinctive of an individual or
characteristic of a group, of the desirable which influences the selec-
tion from available modes, means, and ends of action."

Community-oriented members of the upper class differ from the
rest of the upper class in some of their actions, in their concepts of
the desirable, and in their treatment of those in lower classes and
different ethnic situations. Community-oriented highlanders ask
native townsmen more questions about the coast, try to use coastal
ethnic terminology in dealing with San Lorenzeños, use formal
titles when dealing with members of the middle class, join voluntary
associations in which close interaction with members of the middle
and lower classes is necessary, and take an interest in local customs.
The community-oriented members of the upper class form an interacting group of people who share a major status referent in community approval, or what they take to be community approval.

Other members of the upper class, whom I will call the "non-community-oriented," do not share this status referent. Their status image comes from divers sources. In San Lorenzo they are very conscious of ethnic differences. Frequently, though not always, they look to absentee friends and tourists for support of their status image.

From the resident highlanders' viewpoint, all members of the upper class have less social status in Ecuadorian society than the many highlanders who visit San Lorenzo briefly but with increasing frequency. There are two main reasons for this. First, most of the visitors are wealthier than the local upper class, and show obvious signs of leading a more enviable way of life. They dress better, drink more beer, name-drop. Second, visitors to San Lorenzo may stand higher in the government bureaucracy that has control of the means of developing San Lorenzo. A visit by a government official may mean a change in policy, in personnel, or in both.

The one manifest attitude shared by all the non-community-oriented members of the upper class is one of contempt for San Lorenzo, the coast, and the Negroes. Usually this contempt is not overt or public, but occasionally it is. There is no direct relation between a person's attitude toward San Lorenzo and the length of time he has spent there.

Community Orientation in the Middle and Lower Classes

The same bifurcation of values can be seen in the middle and lower classes, and it cuts across ethnic lines as well. A person striving for recognition in San Lorenzo, then, has two possible patterns of emulation open to him; he may either ignore community approval and look elsewhere for support or seek recognition based upon community approval. In the latter case community approval is in reality the approval of the inter-class network of community-oriented persons. The generally recognized way to demonstrate a community-oriented status image is to participate in formal voluntary associations.

I checked membership lists for all the voluntary associations, however ephemeral, in existence between 1958 and 1963, and found that the same people, or members of the same families, appeared over and over again. I then asked those I had designated as community-oriented members of the upper class to name the middle- and lower-class people they associated with fairly frequently or would

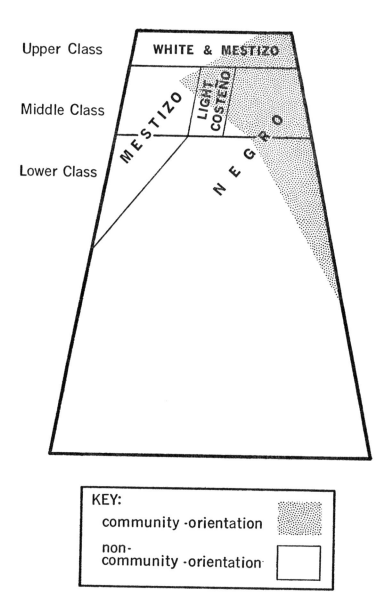

Upper Class

Middle Class

Lower Class

WHITE & MESTIZO

MESTIZO

LIGHT COSTEÑO

NEGRO

KEY:

community -orientation

non-
community -orientation

Figure 3. Bifurcation of Values

associate with. I found a high degree of correspondence between the joiners and those favored by the upper class. From the standpoint of the middle and lower classes, the community-oriented members of the upper class are unquestionably the favored patrons for whatever activities the middle and lower classes may engage in.

Approximately 40 per cent of the upper class, 50 per cent of the middle class, and 20 per cent of the lower class set themselves off as community-oriented, and expect eventual rewards for their behavior in the form of economic and social advancement or vertical and horizontal mobility. The non-community-oriented are more conscious of class position, and scorn group endeavors that do not offer obvious material gain. Their concept of mobility is strictly vertical (i.e., economic) mobility. This does not mean that there is hostility or conflict between the community-oriented and the non-community-oriented, or that the non-community-oriented are necessarily "outsiders." There is no more likelihood of conflict between these two status groups than within them, and perhaps less.

The major significance of these status groupings is that socio-economic mobility is easier for the community-oriented. Furthermore, those who have been able to better their life chances commonly gravitate toward community orientation. Figure 3 illustrates the relations between class, ethnic, and status divisions in San Lorenzo.

Formal Associations

Formal organizations apparently began to flourish in 1958; their number increased from 1961 to 1963. Most of these organizations are religious or quasi-religious in character.[1] They are supported by men of all classes, but only a few upper- and middle-class men are active participants. Their active membership is composed mainly of middle- and lower-class women.

In one way or another, all the religious associations stem from a voluntary association of members of the Catholic Church in San Lorenzo, known as Acción Católica. Members meet once a week to discuss religious and social questions and to take action on social and moral issues. There are separate men's and women's branches of

---

1. Organizations of a purely political nature—e.g., the Junta Parroquial—will be discussed in Chapter VIII, "The Political Order."

Acción Católica, and although there are many men's names on the roster, only the women are active participants. In the last two years the organization has sponsored a monthly dittoed newsletter, which contains information on religious, moral, and social subjects. It distributes powdered milk and other charitable gifts received through CARE and CARITAS, and it has founded a bank (not yet functioning) where it is hoped people will establish savings accounts and take out loans. Acción Católica also sponsors many sporting events (e.g., volleyball tournaments between the town and the naval base) and organizes fiestas for such occasions as May Day, Easter, and Independence Day. It also sponsors a drum-and-bugle corps, a drama club, and a volleyball team.

Membership in Acción Católica symbolizes community orientation to both those who seek identity as community-oriented and those who do not. Acción Católica is not supported by non-community-oriented mestizos in the upper and middle classes, even though these mestizos may attend church far more regularly than, for example, the middle-class Negro supporters of the organization. No correlation can be drawn between religious piety and membership in Acción Católica. It was through the general agency of Acción Católica that the Junta Patriótica was founded. The establishment of the Junta Patriótica marked the first real formalization of the schism between community-oriented and non-community-oriented persons in the middle and upper classes.

In the sphere of education, there is an organization known as "Comité de Padres de la Familia" (resembling the American P.T.A.) that supposedly keeps a check on the teachers and makes sure that children are getting a good education. More than anything else, this organization allows its members to demonstrate their interest in education. For the most part, its membership coincides with that of the religious organizations. However, there are no upper-class members, because there are no upper-class children in the local school.

A few active members of Acción Católica have attempted to formalize aspects of San Lorenzo's barrio system. Two striking efforts include the formation of the barrio Puerto de Manaos, to symbolize the dependence of that barrio on the opening of San Lorenzo as a free port to Brazil, and the recent founding of the barrio Las Tres

Marías. In both cases a president and a committee were elected to direct the cleaning of the barrio. The barrio leaders chosen thus far have all been aggressively community-oriented; they expend a great deal of energy for the welfare of the barrio and the community without any tangible reward.

The present president of the barrio Las Tres Marías is a Negro, a common laborer who gained a position with the Junta Autónoma in 1962. Between 1961 and 1963 he became one of the most respected members of the lower class, in the eyes of the upper, middle, and lower classes. In fact, members of the upper class are surprised to learn that he has no more money than anyone else in the lower class. His employers frequently speak of promoting him, although to do so would be an exceptional act. Relatively uninvolved in community life in 1961, by 1963 he was attending all meetings relating to community affairs, and was a member of every formal organization. He has stopped going to saloons and joining in folk dances. When he became president of the barrio he married his consensual spouse. The last three modifications in behavior are not manifestations of community orientation per se. They are what I call "respectability symbols" (described below), and coincide to a great degree with community orientation, especially among mobile middle- and lower-class Negroes. The new barrio president is a striking example of status mobility without economic advancement; he has, however, an excellent chance of economic mobility in the near future.

Forming *clubs* has become popular in San Lorenzo. All clubs have been formed by non-community-oriented, middle-class Negro and light-Costeño men. They may represent an attempt to compete for prestige with horizontally mobile, community-oriented Negroes and light Costeños. In any case, they are short-lived, popular, and merge into one another as disputes arise over presidencies and similar issues. The most significant features of club formation seem to lie in their political role, a subject reserved for Chapter VIII.

Informal Associations

Members of the upper class have few informal associations, for, except for community-oriented work, the entire class forms a socially interacting group. The members of the middle and lower classes who are not oriented toward community referents in their day-to-day image of themselves form associations freely, but they prefer not to have formal ties. Among the many relatively long-lived informal groupings are cliques within non-minga work groups such as dock gangs and Junta Autónoma workers, who tend to continue work group interaction in other contexts. To some extent the barrio divisions described in the appendix demarcate informal groupings. Performing tasks such as going to the river to wash clothes together seems to encourage more women than men to form barrio-based informal groups.

Associations formed through such minor interests as drinking and dancing may lead to solid ties that survive in a variety of contexts. Dyadic contracts and their tendency to take on a serial nature encourage essentially economic associations to carry over to other contexts. For example, if Edelberto owes Neri the equivalent of two hours' work, he may reciprocate in a social context: when drinking in a cantina with three friends who are paying for the drinks, he may call Neri over to drink with them at his friends' expense, without asking his friends. He thus discharges his debt to Neri and becomes indebted to the three friends. At a later date he may ask Neri, or a person Neri is obligated to, to help his three friends. In this way a variety of informal clique groupings cuts across contexts of associations and binds non-community-oriented persons in a solid network of interpersonal relationships.

Asymmetrical Dyadic Contracts

While on the subject of dyadic contracts and their significance in the social system of San Lorenzo, I must return to the class hierarchy, within which status considerations operate. In the previous discussion I referred only to dyadic contracts between persons sharing the same life chances. These can be called symmetrical since the contractants owe the same kind of things. Professor Foster sets forth a second type of dyadic contract, the asymmetrical, which is based on non-complementary role relationships (Bott 1957: 3) between people of different socioeconomic positions. In asymmetrical dyadic contracts, the contractants owe different kinds of things (Foster 1961: 1174). More recently, Foster (1963: 1281) has referred to such contracts as "patron-client" relationships:

Depending on the relative positions of the partners, and on the kinds of things they exchange, two basic types of dyadic contract may be recognized. *Colleague* contracts tie people of equal or approximately equal socioeconomic status, who exchange the same kinds of goods and services. Colleague contracts are phrased horizontally, and they can be thought of as symmetrical, since each partner, in position and obligations, mirrors the other. *Patron-client* contracts tie people ... of significantly different socioeconomic status (or order of power), who exchange different kinds of goods and services. Patron-client contracts are phrased vertically, and they can be thought of as asymmetrical since each partner is quite different from the other in position and obligations.

To the Negroes and other Costeños of San Lorenzo, it is a matter of social honor that contracts operate asymmetrically between persons of different classes. Since a lower-class Costeño can discharge his obligation to a middle-class man who has done him a favor simply by thanking him profusely, he will generally withhold his thanks, and in so doing implicitly contract to reciprocate on an asymmetrical basis. Negroes expect one another to reciprocate according to their *apparent* means. A man who has more is supposed to give proportionately more than a man who has less. Hence, conspicuous display of material possessions by the upward-mobile or middle-class man may well lead to heavy obligations that will result in economic leveling. It is probably for this reason that successful middle-class Negroes avoid any overt display of wealth. The way in which socioeconomic mobility takes place in spite of the potential leveling effect of the asymmetrical ethic will be discussed in Chapter VII, "Kinship and Socioeconomic Mobility."

The nature of asymmetrical dyadic contracts in San Lorenzo leads to two interesting features of social honor and class participation. First, Serranos in the middle and upper classes interpret the lower-class Negroes' reluctance to express thanks as an insult. They feel that the Negroes wish only to exploit them and do not appreciate what is done for them. Second, there is a strong tendency to conceal real income on the part of the Negroes and light Costeños for fear of incurring an imbalance of reciprocal obligations.

Although both symmetrical and asymmetrical dyadic contracts are more often formed within status categories than between them, there are, nevertheless, many cases of dyadic contracts between community-oriented and non-community-oriented persons. In this sense the status categories do not seriously hinder economic activities. But status groupings do impinge on the strict operation of the market principle in San Lorenzo precisely because the community-oriented formalize their associations more frequently than the non-community-oriented, who act more strictly according to the market principle.

Compadrazgo Relations in San Lorenzo

The *compadrazgo* system, a system of ritual kinship, solidifies informal and formal status groupings in San Lorenzo and binds them to the class and status structure.

Compadrazgo is the structured social relationship between the parents and godparents of a child which exists throughout Latin America (cf. Foster 1948; Mintz and Wolf 1950). Highland and coastal forms of compadrazgo in Ecuador are not identical, and the discussion here of compadrazgo in San Lorenzo refers only to the coastal system; it cannot be applied to all of Ecuador. *Padrinazgo* refers to the relation between godparent and godchild; in San Lorenzo it is also used to denote the relationship between high-status sponsors and the rest of the community on special occasions.

Formally, compadrazgo refers to the spiritual relationship between two Catholics who are bound by shared responsibility for a child of one of them. Godparents as well as parents may participate in every major religious event in a child's life—baptism, confirmation, first communion, marriage. In practice baptism is the most important rite involving godparents in San Lorenzo. The godparent calls the godchild *ahijado* or *ahijada,* and the child calls the godparent *padrino* or *madrina.* The parents and godparents are *compadre* and *comadre* to one another, and it is this relationship that carries the greater social significance. This terminology is part of the social system, not of the Catholic terminology of baptism. First used during and after the baptism ceremony, it is ideally maintained for life and supersedes other kinship and status terms.

According to the Catholic Church, there must be a madrina for a girl and a padrino for a boy, and there may be both for either. In San Lorenzo the appropriate godparent takes the child to be baptized, accompanied by the father if he is present. The mother waits either at home or outside the church. Although the Church says that a child must be baptized by the time he is eight days old, children in San Lorenzo are baptized at any age between a few weeks and one year. Costeños in San Lorenzo call an unbaptized child *moro* (Moor). Until 1958 all baptisms were administered by visiting priests.

Estimates of the number of children baptized in San Lorenzo from 1953 to 1962, including children from other areas who were brought to San Lorenzo for baptism, are as follows:[2]

1953	 28	1958	 236
1954	 330	1959	 170
1955	 219	1960	 220
1956	 454	1961	 368
1957	 342	1962	 221

The figures are probably low except for the 1960–62 estimates.

Children are confirmed any time after the seventh year, but the ceremony is not considered as important as baptism and is performed only when a bishop visits San Lorenzo. Fewer people have their children confirmed than baptized, and the social relationships involved are much less formal and have far less social importance. During and after confirmation, the padrinazgo relationship—between godparent and godchild—is the only one with any social significance, and even that is weak and unimportant. The padrinazgo relationship is again established at the first communion, which occurs any time after confirmation, but here it is very weak and socially insignificant. Frequently the godparents for baptism serve in the later ceremonies of confirmation and first communion. I know of no Costeño who has had an honorary padrino or madrina as a wedding attendant.

Intra-Class, Intra-Status Compadrazgo Relationships

Within class and status boundaries, compadrazgo relationships formalize existing friendships, dyadic contracts, and kinship ties, and ensure their continuance. They also function as a curb on sexual relations. Sexual relations between parents and godparents are taboo, as are relations between godparent and godchild. No such taboo exists

2. Archives of the Comboniano missionaries, San Lorenzo.

between the godparents themselves. The taboo is expressed in terms of respect, not avoidance, but sexual intercourse with a godparent is considered worse than intercourse with a brother or sister, and as bad as intercourse between father and daughter. A man must never agree to be the padrino of his own child. In cases of doubtful parenthood, the mother or her husband may ask the suspected man to be padrino of the child. His refusal is taken as an admission of fatherhood, and his acceptance as a disclaimer. Occasionally a man asks to be godparent to a child to demonstrate to his own spouse that he has not had sexual relations with the child's mother. Also, a woman with a child but no husband may curb the sexual advances of another man by asking him to be her child's godparent.

Compadrazgo also serves as a check on polyandry, and to a lesser extent on polygyny. When two brothers share a house and one marries, he often moves his wife into his existing household. At the birth of their first child he will usually ask his brother to serve as padrino, thereby publicly asserting that he, not his brother, is the father and ruling out the possibility of shared sexual relations in the future. Since two brothers may frequently travel together and take the wife of one to do the cooking for them, compadrazgo bonds between the brothers help establish the absolute sexual rights of the husband. The same holds true when two cousins, or even two unrelated men, work, live, or travel together with the wife of one of the men.

In San Lorenzo, godparents do not buy clothes for the child or give a party or a gift of money at the time of baptism, as they would in much of Latin America. Only in the middle class do godparents pay the priest's fee of 10 sucres. They accept no responsibility for the child's moral or religious upbringing. In practice the godparents' attentions to the child last only two to three years, although the Church considers the relationship a permanent one. The only obligation to the child is to aid with medical expenses if necessary. Such aid, of course, helps the parents as much as the child. Should the child die, the godparents are expected to help with the simple arrangements for wake and burial.

Relationships between compadres are stronger. Compadres drink together and work together. Comadres perform household tasks (e.g., wash clothes) together and gather conchas together. Such a relationship is made much of for several years, even after nominal responsibility for the child disappears, and sometimes the bond is a lifelong one.

Compadre and comadre, ahijado and ahijada, padrino and madrina supersede all other terminology relating to kinship and status. For example, when a paternal grandfather is made godfather of a child, the child refers to him as "godfather," not "grandfather," and the father of the child refers to his own father as "compadre," not by one of the terms for father.

A person is asked to act as godparent in a brief and fairly formalized request. The parent goes to the prospective godparent's home and says, "Quiere usted ayudarme acristianando mi hijito?" (Do you want to help me baptize my little son?) Acceptance or refusal is immediate. Acceptance is signified by a simple "sí," but refusal is never indicated by a flat "no." The unwilling prospective godparent usually asks for time to think, or for a postponement. More rarely, he will say he is not a Catholic or he does not like the priest. Refusals, however, are almost nonexistent among peers.

Inter-Class, Inter-Status Compadrazgo Relationships

Compadrazgo relationships between persons sharing different life chances or different styles of life always initiate with the one who is in the lower class or has less social honor. Ordinarily, the establishment of a compadrazgo relationship formalizes an existing asymmetrical dyadic contract. A man is not supposed to ask someone of higher prestige or class standing to be his compadre unless a mutually satisfying relationship has already been established.

The most important factor in inter-class compadrazgo relationships is the social status of the patron. A person rarely selects a compadre on purely economic grounds. Consider the typical case of a lower-class Negro for whom a middle-class Costeño has done a few favors and to whom the Negro is therefore obligated. The Negro asks the Costeño to become godfather of his child. Since the request is an honor, the father of the child absolves his responsibility to the patron, and the patron in turn is obligated to him. The middle-class Costeño can return the obligation to the lower-class Negro either by accepting the role of compadre, or by refusing and later helping him in some other way. Either way, the request ensures some measure of continuance of an asymmetrical contract. In a sense compadrazgo is its own answer to asymmetrical contracts because the higher the status of X the greater the honor conferred on Y when X accepts a compadrazgo relationship. Conversely, Y adds to the social honor of X by initiating the relationship.

Inter-class compadrazgo between the middle class and the lower class is based on status, not economic, considerations. The patron's only financial obligation is to pay for the child's medical care, although if the economic difference between him and the father is great, he may assist the father in other ways. Ideally, however, such assistance is not the principal reason for initiating an inter-class compadrazgo relationship, and the ideal is realized in practice. Should the patron feel that he is being exploited, he may flatly decline to serve as godfather with the words *"No puedo"* ("I cannot"). In inter-status, intra-class compadrazgo relationships, social honor is obviously all-important.

Compadrazgo relationships between the middle and the upper class have more complex social ramifications. The middle-class Costeños who seek to extend ritual kinship into the upper class enter a a system in which mutual obligations are seen from both highland and coastal perspectives. In general, middle-class San Lorenzeños ask members of the upper class to be their children's godparents in order to secure social honor, economic advantage, or a political favor. Since the upper class is far better off economically, and since its members seem to control some aspect of the life chances of others in San Lorenzo, middle-class Costeños who achieve a compadrazgo relationship with a member of the upper class are, from their own frame of reference, in a highly advantageous position with regard to asymmetrical reciprocity.

Members of the upper class all perceive the advantage a middle-class Costeño derives from establishing compadrazgo relations with them, but they do not all see any advantage to themselves in such relationships. Many members of the upper class see only that they will be on the losing end of an asymmetrical relationship and refuse all compadrazgo requests from members of the middle class. Some people in the upper class, however, believe they will benefit by gaining increased community prestige and further integration into San Lorenzo's social system *if* the middle-class Costeño making the request seems to them to manifest a high degree of social honor. Whether or not a member of the upper class is willing to accept middle-class Costeño children as ahijados and their parents as compadres is dependent on whether or not he is community-oriented. I compared participation in voluntary associations by members of the upper class with middle- and lower-class Compadrazgo ties to participation by those without such ties, and found that those who are joiners and manifest an interest in the community are also those who accept compadrazgo relations with middle-class Costeños. Community-oriented members of the upper class accept compadrazgo relationships with middle- and occasionally lower-class Costeños despite the obvious economic disadvantage, whereas non-community-oriented members of the upper class absolutely refuse such relationships.

How much social honor he attributes to the person making the request is the crucial factor in the community-oriented upper-class man's decision. He will ordinarily accept a compadrazgo relationship with members of the community who belong to the same voluntary associations he does. However, membership alone is usually not enough, especially when the person seeking to initiate the relationship is a member of the lower class. For community-oriented members of the upper class, certain critical symbols of respectability distinguish the acceptable from the opportunist. The following section presents status terminology and then describes prominent status symbols.

Status Symbols and Class Latitudes

In the lower class, people call one another by their first name or by a nickname; men are addressed and referred to as "hombre" (man), and women are referred to but not often addressed as "hembra" (female). One lower-class man would refer to another of equal status, in all respect, as "el hombre Rosendo." A middle-class Costeño informally refers to someone in the lower class by his name or nickname or as "el hombre." To show greater respect, a person in the lower or middle class may refer to a member of the lower class by his occupation sometimes followed by his first name or nickname. e.g., "el carpintero Chicao," or even "el pescador Cholongo," or simply "el carbonero." In the cases of the fisherman and the charcoal maker, referring to his occupation is a sign of respect even though the occupation itself has no prestige whatsoever. In respectful address a semiskilled or skilled worker is called "maestro" regardless of the class to which he or the speaker belongs. Military and official or quasi-official terms, e.g. "lieutenant," "president," are used across all class and status lines.

To show respect for a woman one can say "la hembra de Rosendo" (Rosendo's female), or better, "La mujer de Rosendo" (Rosendo's wife). Within the lower class the former is more often used. People in the upper class frequently refer to a man in the lower class as "el negro," or "el negro" followed by his first name. More politely they may say "el moreno" (the dark one). They usually use the ethnic terminology as given earlier in this chapter (pp. 90–92), whereas lower- and middle-class Costeños ordinarily do not use ethnic terminology except when referring to the highlanders (as Serranos).

Members of the upper class are addressed and referred to by everyone else either by occupation ("doctor," "engineer"), by nationality, or by a more general category ("gringo," "mister," "montuvio"). In address, "señor" and "señora" are used unless they are superseded by the occupational title. "Señor" is followed by the man's first name, "señora" is used alone. A man in the upper class who is liked and respected or has economic power is addressed and referred to as "Don" followed by his first name. The Costeños almost never refer to or address anyone in the upper class or an employer as "patrón." In fact, to do so is to call forth severe criticism or laughter. A few children and at least one adult in San Lorenzo have picked up the use of the term from highlanders.

In the middle class, the terminology varies. A man whose prestige is high may be referred to and addressed as "señor" (and his wife as "señora") even by someone in the same economic position. Those in the community-oriented group are much more frequently referred to as señor or señora. A few greatly respected middle-class men may be addressed as "Don." Non-community-oriented middle-class men may be called "Don" if it seems as if their prestige or class situation is about to improve or if they wield considerable political power.

Compadrazgo terminology supersedes all status terminology. Hence if a man agrees to become another's compadre, it demonstrates a working association to everyone. A man must be careful about who calls him compadre as there is a tendency to attribute the faults and debts of a person to those in compadrazgo relationship with him.

Upper-Class Status Criteria and Symbols

For members of the upper class, the pre-eminent status criteria are economic situation, educational preparation for an occupation, and a highland style of life. To these status criteria community-oriented members of the upper class add public service, and consider themselves superior on this count to the non-community-oriented. They also add certain status symbols, or what might more appropriately be called respectability symbols. Respectability symbols in San Lorenzo refer to a complex of sobriety, chastity, political moderation, and gracious manners more or less like that esteemed in the typical, white, middle-class, urban-suburban United States community.

Community-oriented members of the upper class talk more about respect, and what symbols represent respect. But in their behavior, for the most part, the community-oriented manifest respectability symbols to no greater degree than do the non-community-oriented. The one crucial difference in status criteria is that the community-oriented look for respectability symbols in those *below* them in the class hierarchy, whereas the non-community-oriented ordinarily are not concerned with such symbols in anyone but members of their own class.

Middle-Class Status Symbols

Members of the middle class who are seeking high social honor share, in general, the status criteria of the community-oriented upper class. Education, church and public service, legal marriage, female chastity, a Protestant work ethic, and, in some contexts, money are all symbols of high status in the middle class. These positive symbols are seconded by a series of negative proscriptions. A man who wishes to maintain high status in the middle class should not be seen working with his hands, drinking in saloons, or attending a marimba dance. He must never be seen without shoes, long pants, and a shirt. The style of his house has less importance as a status symbol and sanitation none at all. These symbols and their function will be discussed in more detail in Chapter VII.

Lower-Class Status Symbols

Status symbols in the lower class have a less clear-cut frame of reference than they do in upper and middle classes. Although the people in the lower class agree on the status symbols to be applied to the classes above them, there is more latitude in status criteria for members of their own class. Virginity for girls for a few years after puberty, shoes, good clothes, an interest in church and school affairs, some ability to read and write, sometimes a concern with "proper" speech, and skills such as carpentering—all these are important to community-oriented members of the lower class who aspire to middle-class membership, who emulate the community-oriented middle class. A few lower-class aspirants to the middle class emulate the non-community-oriented upper- and lower-class highlanders by occasional conspicuous spending on drink and on personal possessions such as fancy clothes. Such behavior is rare and short-lived in the lower class because of the lack of adequate economic resources.

Those who do not aspire to a higher socioeconomic position gain prestige for timely reciprocity as much as anything else. For example, a man who repays a debt when his creditor is in need is held in more esteem than one who repays his debts without regard for the needs of his creditor. Sexual prowess, the ability to dance well and to invent poetic verses, and skill in subsistence tasks all bring some prestige within the lower class. One can also gain high social honor, in the eyes of the middle and upper classes as well as the lower, by assuming extra responsibility, for example by acting as jefe de la minga.

Crime is negatively valued only when the results affect others in the milieu, e.g. when one steals something from a shop and then flees leaving one's relatives to make reparations. A man may actually gain in status for a misdemeanor that affects no one in the lower class. For instance, someone who is arrested for stealing or some other minor offense is jailed for a few days in the middle of town and becomes the center of attention. There are no facilities for feeding prisoners, so his wife, family, and friends bring food to the jail and talk and joke with the prisoner. For a short time, he is the center of his social network. While in jail he can, to some extent, insult policemen without fear of reprisal, and this, too, may slightly enhance his status. Should a man kill someone or in some other manner disrupt social relations in his milieu, however, he may be branded "montuvio" and lose considerable prestige.

In the lower class, considerations such as dress, speech, housing, and material possessions are not important status criteria except as they indicate an aspirant to the middle class. Only community-oriented members of the middle and upper classes apply such status criteria to members of the lower class.

Status Crystallization: Honorary Padrinazgo

Honorary godparents (*padrinos honorarios, madrinas honorarias*) are chosen for any important social event in San Lorenzo. Such an event might be the opening of a new saloon or large cantina, a May Day celebration, the founding of a new barrio, a fund-raising dance for the school, the visit of the Catholic bishop (annual since 1962), or the visit of a naval officer, which is usually accompanied by a fiesta at the naval base. At least once a month there is a celebration that calls for honorary godparents. Honorary godparents have no responsibility for an event; they are not obliged to attend, although they often do, and one may make a speech. Lower- and middle-class honorary godparents attend most events more frequently than do those from the upper class.

The honorary godparent is sent a letter by messenger (a lower-class boy between eight and 15 years old) and is supposed to respond with a monetary gift, the sum reflecting his economic standing in the community. The most anyone might give is 50 sucres, and only the head engineer, the head of the timber company, and the anthropologist were of sufficient economic means to be expected to give as much as this in 1963. The letter to an honorary godparent is always addressed to Don ———, which symbolizes the ultimate in respect.

For an ordinary event, two to four men from each class, and perhaps one or two women from both the lower and middle classes serve as honorary godparents. Non-community-oriented members of the upper class are just as likely to serve as honorary godparents as community-oriented members are. However, they attend the event much less frequently. In the middle class the community-oriented predominate although non-community-oriented persons with very obvious economic or political power are also sought. In the lower class only those Negroes manifesting aspirant respectability symbols in dress and manner are chosen as honorary godparents.

Honorary godparents function as community symbols of success in the social order; they thus crystallize crucial status criteria. Evidence from honorary padrinazgo strengthens and consolidates generalizations from data presented in the past three chapters. If a man can achieve success in the economic order, he need not manifest other symbols of social honor to stand high in status. However, if he cannot demonstrate obvious economic advantage (few men can, and of those who can, few choose to do so), then the status symbols of community orientation and respectability can bring him high prestige.

Social Status in the Class Framework

San Lorenzo illustrates Weber's point that the system of social honor interferes with the strict functioning of the economic order. Achievement in the competition for status may bring San Lorenzeños an extra advantage in economic competition. The reason for this is the favoritism shown by community-oriented upper-class Serranos to those members of the middle and lower classes who manifest community orientation and respectability symbols. They are the first to be recommended for jobs with the Junta Autónoma, and the first to be hired to perform household services; their shops are patronized and their products purchased.

The compadrazgo system provides the only formal bonds between members of the upper class and the middle and lower classes, and these bonds connect an inter-class network of what we have called the community-oriented. In the relations between middle- and lower-class Costeños, status divisions are subordinate to other factors, notably the kinship system discussed in the next two chapters.

In summary, the following points have been made regarding social status and class in San Lorenzo:

(1) Social honor derives to a considerable extent from the economic stituation of members of the upper class.

(2) The community-oriented members of the upper class are cross-ethnic in their social participation, the non-community-oriented much less so.

(3) This bifurcation of values ramifies from the top of the class hierarchy to the bottom.

(4) In the middle class, successful competition in either the economic or the social order can bring high community status, but only those who manifest community orientation and respectability symbols can solidify their socioeconomic bonds with members of the upper class through compadrazgo relationships.

(5) In the middle class, community-oriented values transcend ethnic divisions and bind people of like orientation, but the non-community-oriented are divided by ethnic lines.

(6) Among the community-oriented members of the middle class, respectability symbols are important indices of status.

(7) Some members of the lower class emulate the community-oriented upper and middle classes through conscious adherence to explicit status symbols. The rest of the lower class has its own symbols of social honor, which are based in part on interpersonal relations in day-to-day life.

Family, Household, and Kinship

The family and household organization of highland Ecuadorian mestizos and people who have come to San Lorenzo from outside Ecuador generally resembles that of the United States, except that women are more restricted in their activities. My concern here is not with these families (except as they are involved in the coastal system), but with the family and kinship patterns characteristic of Negroes and light-Costeños from San Lorenzo and the hinterland.

Kinship Terminology

Table IV lists consanguineal terms of address from the reference point of a male or female Ego. Referential terms are the same except that the possessive prefix "mi" is added (e.g., mi papá). Table V lists affinal terms of address and reference from the reference point of a male or female Ego. Unless otherwise indicated, terms of reference are the same as terms of address except for the addition of the prefix "mi."

Cousin terminology is of Murdock's "Eskimo type" (1949: 223–24), with undifferentiated cross and parallel cousin terminology. A lineal emphasis (Murdock 1949: 142) focuses attention on the bilateral or cognatic nature of the kinship terms and suggests that descent is cognatic (Murdock 1960). Apart from lineal relatives, kinsmen are named for the lineal relatives whose role they seem to fit. Hence, a person considered a second cousin in the United States may be called cousin or uncle, depending on the age relationship between him and Ego. If he does not live near Ego or in some way function in Ego's life, he may not be considered a relative at all.

TABLE IV

Consanguineal Terminology

Term	Biological Relationship
Ego's generation:	
Hermano, -a; hermanito, -a; ñaño, -a; ñañito, -a	Br, Si
Primo, -a; primo, -a hermano, -a	FaBrSn, FaSiSn, MoBrSn, MoSiSn, FaBrDa, FaSiDa, MoBrDa, MoSiDa
First ascending generation:	
Papá; papacita; papí; papita; padre[a]; señor[b]	Fa
Mamá; mamacita; mamí; mamita; madre[a]; señora[b]	Mo
Tío, -a; tiíto, -a	FaBr, MoBr, FaSi, MoSi
Tío, -a; or primo, -a[c]	Grandparents' siblings' children[d]
Second ascending generation:	
Abuelo; abuelito; papá grande[a]	FaFa, MoFa
Abuela; abuelita; mamá grande[a]	FaMo, MoMo
Tío, -a; tiíto, -a; tío, -a grande[a]	FaFaBr, FaMoBr, MoFaBr, MoMoBr, FaFaSi, FaMoSi, MoFaSi, MoMoSi
First descending generation:	
Mi hijo, -a; Mi hijito, -a	Sn, Da
Sobrino, -a	BrSn, SiSn, BrDa, SiDa
Sobrino, -a; or primo, -a[c]	FaBrChCh, FaSiChCh, MoBrChCh, MoSiChCh
Second descending generation:	
Nieto, -a	SnSn, DaSn, SnDa, DaDa[e]

[a] Reference only.
[b] Used only as term of address by child who is being punished.
[c] Depending on age in relation to Ego.
[d] If the person lives with or very near Ego.
[e] Sometimes siblings' ChCh if they are very close to Ego, e.g., raised by Ego.

Non-kinsmen who reside in a household become fictive kin and are addressed and referred to as kin. Distant kinsmen acquire closer kinship terms when they live with or near their relatives or have strong emotional ties to them.

Children are named in accordance with the Spanish system: a child is given a first name, which is followed by his father's second or family name (FaFa) and then his mother's family name (MoFa).

TABLE V

Affinal Terminology

Term	Affinal Relationship
Ego's generation:	
Mi hija[a]; mi hembra[b]; mi mujer[b]; mi esposa[c]	Spouse (male Ego)
Hombre; mi marido[c]; mi esposo[c]; mi hijo[d]	Spouse (female Ego)
Cuñado, -a	WiBr, HuBr, WiSi, HuSi
Concuñado, -a	WiSiHu, HuSiHu, WiBrWi, HuBrWi
Hermano, -a paterno, -a; or hermano, -a[e]	Children of step-Mo of Ego by Fa of Ego
Hermano, -a materno, -a; or hermano, -a[e]	Children of Mo of Ego by step-Fa of Ego
First ascending generation:	
Suegro, -a	Ego's spouse's parents
Padrasto	Step-Fa of Ego
Madrasta	Step-Mo of Ego
Tío, -a; tiíto, -a	Parents' siblings' spouses
First descending generation:	
Hijo, -a[f]	DaHu, SnWi
Sobrino, -a	WiBrSn, WiSiSn, HuBrSn, HuSiSn, WiBrDa, WiSiDa, HuBrDa, HuSiDa

[a] Address only.

[b] Reference only.

[c] Reference when legally married or when consensual union has lasted many years; very rare for men to use the term.

[d] Reportedly used in address, but I have never heard it, and doubt that it is ever actually used.

[e] Depending on age, residence, and degree of friendship, other children of one of Ego's step-parents may be called hermano, hermano paterno, hermano materno, primo, primo hermano, tío, or sobrino (or any of the feminine equivalents).

[f] Sometimes "Hijo de" plus name of Sn or Da.

If the father is unknown, a child bears only his mother's family name. If the mother's father was unknown, the child uses his mother's mother's name.

Inheritance and Property Ownership

There are no formal rules of inheritance in the northern sector of Esmeraldas province. Squatter's rights prevail on land; houses and other major possessions, e.g., canoes, are passed on to those making use of them when the builder moves away or dies. Recently, however, in San Lorenzo and to a lesser extent Limones, attempts have been made to establish property boundaries.

According to Ecuadorian law, land is owned without formal written title only if a person can produce three witnesses affirming that he has resided there for at least 30 years. San Lorenzeños consider 10 years' residence sufficient to establish legal ownership, and refer to their "ancient rights" to property if they have lived there for 10 years.

In 1961 there were few if any disputes over property; the land a man worked was considered his. In 1963 several fences were erected in the Old Section No. 1, in the barrio Mayasquer, and in the new barrio Las Tres Marías. This change may have been due in part to conflicts over property ownership between the Junta Autónoma and the people of San Lorenzo. The Junta Autónoma sold land to highlanders without regard for the people living there. When the squatters refused to move, the Junta Autónoma had to adjust property sales. Today local Junta Autónoma officials and townspeople agree that the Junta Autónoma actually owns the Ciudadela, airstrip, railroad tracks, and the New Town; San Lorenzeños avidly deny any Junta Autónoma claim to ownership beyond this.

Only one family in San Lorenzo has a written title to its land—an old family whose head purchased the land from the German company about fifty years ago. On paper it owns the entire point of land that juts out next to the Ciudadela. The family once raised plantains on this section, but now there are more than twenty large houses here. The "owners" said that they now own only their house, the principal Casa de la Marimba (see Map 3, No. 10). They had neither sold nor lent the rest of the land—others simply moved in when they stopped planting it. Except for the couple's children, no one now living on the land knew that it had once been purchased and owned by the couple. The man and woman do not consider themselves the legal owners of more land than they are actively using, and neither does anyone else in San Lorenzo or the hinterland.

Courtship

Courtship is a relatively simple matter. A boy flirts with a girl and perhaps has sexual intercourse with her at the river during the day.

They do not meet at night for fear of the ghosts of their ancestors who may return with evil intent. Girls evidence more fear of ancestral ghosts than boys do. Eventually the boy asks the girl's father, or mother if there is no resident father, if he may take the girl to a saloon or to a movie; this may be either before or after they have had sexual relations. If the courtship is carried to fulfillment, the couple moves into the home of either the boy or the girl.

Sometimes the girl's mother forces early cohabitation by saying that the boy has had intercourse with her daughter and must therefore support her. Ordinarily she first asks a midwife to examine the girl and inform the neighborhood whether or not she is a virgin. If the midwife says she is not a virgin, the mother will try to coerce the boy into cohabiting with the girl. If he refuses, the mother takes the girl to the doctor, who writes a letter to the effect that the girl is no longer a virgin. The letter can then be taken to the comisario, who, on payment of a bribe, will order the boy to support the girl. Young men who come from outside the community are particularly good prey for such tactics. However, the doctor's letter has weight only if the mother has previously had the doctor certify that the girl is a virgin. When a girl begins to show an interest in a certain boy, the mother will frequently have the doctor make out a formal virginity certificate and the comisario put an official seal on it, for a fee. The drawback of this procedure is that the boy may be frightened away if he learns what the mother is doing.

This practice is sung about in the marimba:

Esta marimba que suena	This noisy marimba
Tiene una tabla quebrada.	Has a broken keyboard.
El mozito que la toca	The youth that plays her
Tiene a su mujer preñada.	Has a pregnant wife.

Here the marimba represents a young girl, and the keyboard her virginity. Hence it can be translated, "This young girl is no longer a virgin." If the girl's mother (or some other female relative of the girl) succeeds in trapping the man who had intercourse with her, then "The youth that plays her has a pregnant wife."

When men or women already have children to care for, courtship is very brief—often only one night at a saloon or fiesta. At the end of the evening the man says, "Vamos matando el gallo" (Let's go kill the cock); and the couple retires for the night with the idea of continuing to live together.

Marriage and Residence

The ordinary marriage arrangement is a consensual union; that is, the couple lives together and shares economic responsibilities by mutual consent. Civil marriages, which are not common, usually take place only after consensual unions have shown remarkable stability, or, interestingly enough, after a man has had a fight with his partner in a stable consensual union and wishes to assert his independence. In this case he makes another woman his legal wife before eventually returning to his more permanent consensual spouse. The number of civil marriages performed in San Lorenzo from 1952 to 1962, for people from the hinterland as well as San Lorenzeños, are as follows:

1952	1	1958	19
1953	7	1959	13
1954	13	1960	17
1955	9	1961	14
1956	11	1962	26
1957	13		

Since many certificates are not recorded, these figures are probably low.

Of the 207 couples in San Lorenzo who have been living together for five years or more, 82 reported having been married in a civil ceremony and 125 reported strictly consensual unions. Of those claiming civil marriage, I was able to establish that at least 15 were incorrectly referring to their stable consensual union as a civil marriage. A few other young people simply lied because they thought that the anthropologist would look upon them more favorably (as Protestant and Catholic missionaries do) if he thought they were legally married.

A third type of marriage, religious marriage, is new to San Lorenzo. There were only three religious marriages in San Lorenzo between 1952 and 1962, but in 1963 there were seven. All seven of these religious marriages were motivated by a desire for vertical or horizontal mobility. For example, one couple was married so that their daughter could receive a Catholic scholarship to a colegio in Quito. Several young couples were married to gain the favor of the priest and other community-oriented highlanders. Though many women speak favorably of church marriage, men are openly opposed to it, for they look with definite disfavor on the permanence it implies.

Taboos, Marital Restrictions, and Preferential Marriage

Sexual intercourse between real, fictive, or ritual mothers and sons is considered unnatural and is said never to take place. Father-daughter sexual relations are not necessarily considered unnatural, but respect prohibitions are said to rule out such acts. The great respect of siblings for one another is said ordinarily to prevent sexual relations between brother and sister. As noted earlier, these respect relations are extended to ritual kin through the compadrazgo system. The common practice of making one's siblings and one's spouse's siblings godparents to children serves to extend the respect taboo across affinal lines, thereby uniting an age group through mutual obligations and, at the same time, reducing potential conflict by restricting sexual intercourse to the biological parents of a child.

Figure 4 illustrates this. Consanguineal ties curtail sexual relations between A and B and between X and Y through respect taboos. A and X marry and have a child (C). A_1 and X_1 are the social equivalents of A and X and hence their potential competitors. Since a man is far more likely to make his brother godfather to a child than a woman is to make her sister godmother, fraternal polyandry is structurally nearly impossible, whereas sororal polygyny is structurally possible. In fact, although a few instances of serial polygyny (discussed below) do take on the form of the sororate, no example of the levirate has been found. When a case of the sororate is pointed out, it is always explained that the partners were not aware that the man had previously been married to his wife's sister.

Both men and women in San Lorenzo and the hinterland express a preference for the marriage of first cousins (*primos hermanos*). When pressed for reasons for this preference, they simply shrugged and stated, "It is the custom." I have evidence of only three such marriages in San Lorenzo, although many people report that their parents were cousins. Everyone questioned in the survey of San Lorenzo households reported that although cousin marriage is pre-

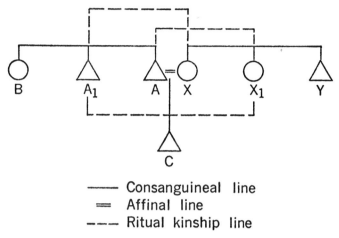

——— Consanguineal line
=== Affinal line
——— Ritual kinship line

Figure 4. Kinship and Compadrazgo Ties

ferred, very few actual cousin marriages now occur. The people themselves offer one of two explanations for this. First, it is against the law for cousins to marry and hence difficult for them to get married in a town where the teniente político is familiar with local genealogy. The last officially recorded cousin marriage in San Lorenzo took place in 1957. This does not, however, explain the absence of consensual unions between cousins. The second reason Negroes give is that there are not enough male cousins permanently residing in San Lorenzo to go around. By this they mean that a woman may not have marriageable cousins whom she expects to remain in town, and on the whole women in San Lorenzo do not wish to move to the hinterland and live a rural life. They are quite explicit about this. Neither of these reasons adequately accounts for the difference between expressed preference and actual practice, but I cannot offer a satisfactory explanation.

Concepts of Family, Household, and Kindred

Abstract discussions of what data to include under the rubric "family" can be interminable. This section is concerned with the same phenomena and problems that M. G. Smith (1962) dealt with in his extensive coverage of Caribbean families. Smith (1962: 10) writes:

The variety of meanings and groups denoted by the word "family" creates special difficulties for the analysis of family relations. Following the distinctions made by . . . the Royal Anthropological Institute, we shall have to deal with (1) *the elementary family,* "a group composed of parents and children"; (2) *the bilateral extended family,* "a roughly defined cognatic group frequently including affines"; (3) *the domestic family,* "a group of relatives and their dependents constituting one household"; and (4) *compound families,* which arise from successive unions or marriages of widows, widowers, divorced, or informally separated parents.

In my discussion of the family, the "elementary," or, as I prefer to call it, "nuclear" family is considered in the section immediately following without reference to the larger kinship structure within which it functions. The domestic family is discussed in the following section, under the heading "household." The section on the "personal kindred" subsumes data on so-called "bilateral extended families," and this term will not be used here. Data on what Smith calls compound families—covering successive unions resulting from separations and death—do not comprise a separate section but are included in various sections of this chapter. By using the terms nuclear family, household, and personal kindred, I hope to avoid the confusion inherent in recognizing four abstractly different family types. Furthermore, this analytic division has the advantage of corresponding to usage in San Lorenzo, where Negroes speak of "mi familia," "mi casa," and "mi parentesco" ("my family," "my household," and "my relatives").

The Nuclear Family

Without recognizing structure as having *phases* (cf. R. T. Smith 1957; Fortes 1958) two types of family might be delineated, the monogamous and the polygynous, and neither type would appear particularly "stable." However, if we regard nuclear families as phases of a single structure, we can identify one family form as "serial polygynous" (Freilich 1961; 960–61). Serial polygyny refers to the expected behavioral pattern of male movement from one spouse to another. In San Lorenzo a man is expected to have a series of wives in his lifetime. Societal norms, expressed in conversation and marimba songs, make the change of mate a male prerogative. Actually, of course, the woman, too, has a series of men. But she is relatively more spatially restricted, and she plays a less active role in any change. Two subtypes representing phases of serial polygyny in northwest Ecuador are discernible: monogamy, in which a man lives with one woman at a time, and polygyny, in which a man lives and shares economic responsibilities with more than one wife at a time.

Serial Polygyny and Monogamy

Norms and values relating to serial polygyny are expressed in conversation and in marimba songs and dances. They are also evident in day-to-day relations between the sexes. Women are expected to trap and hold a man, to make him stay in one place, and, when that is impossible, to travel with him and set up a new home. Men, on the other hand, value the ability to hold a woman's attentions until they tire of her, and the ability to find a replacement for her quickly.

Men value travel for its own sake and say that they are reluctant to take their wives with them on a trip. However, I know of some cases in which a woman refused to go with her husband and the husband later said he had not wanted her to accompany him. A man is supposed to be able to find a spouse wherever he goes so that he need not perform women's tasks—cooking, for example—for himself. When a man changes women, the woman is "left"; she is not expelled from the household but continues in it as before. The father and mother share responsibility for their children, who may either remain with the mother or travel on with the father when the couple breaks up. The choice seems to rest with the father, although no explicit norms govern this. Children may also be raised by other relatives.

These norms and values are asserted even when a marriage has lasted a lifetime. I know of at least twenty nuclear families that have held together for over thirty years; in all cases the woman takes the credit for holding the man and the man expresses regret, together with explicit admiration for his wife's abilities.

Sanctions are severe when a woman attempts to leave her husband or to have an extramarital affair. If the husband learns that his wife has such intentions, he beats her severely and may expel her from the household. He may even kill her, but this is rare and by killing his wife a man exceeds the norms of his milieu. The man to whom the wife is attracted is not blamed, and he makes no effort to protect her. She is free to pursue another man only after her husband has relinquished his role. He need not, however, move out of town or even out of the same neighborhood. The symbolic renunciation of the marriage is a male prerogative that, except in cases of polygyny, women are never allowed to share.

Although men never fight over a woman, women often fight over a man. Few Sundays pass without a fight between women. On Saturday night many men typically go to the saloon without their wives, and there they may initiate a sexual liaison with another woman. When the wife learns of this on Sunday she visits her rival's house, where she calls her a *puta* (whore) and often starts a fight. In one such fight a woman bit off the entire lower lip of her adversary!

Ritual Expressions of Serial Polygyny

Marital norms are given ritual expression in the marimba dance, which is being replaced in San Lorenzo by other emotional outlets (Whitten and Fuentes C., n.d.). Of the principal singers in the marimba, the glosador is always a man and the respondedoras are always two or three women. The glosador always begins the singing with shouts, which are followed by established and improvised verses. The respondedoras harmonize with his long notes and sing set choruses to his verses. As the music crescendoes, the glosador and the respondedoras sing together. While the glosador improvises, yodels, and shouts, the respondedoras frequently sing choruses and verses like these:

Adió', Berejú.	Good-bye, Berejú.
Adió', Berejú.	Good-bye, Berejú.
No quiero, no quiero,	I don't want, I don't want,
No quiero querer.	I don't want to love.
Porque cuando quiera,	Because whenever I love,
Me han de aborrecer.	They will desert [lit. "detest"] me.

Or the respondedoras may sing lines like these (a man is leaving his wife):

Adió' por el hombre.	Good-bye by the man.
Yo ya tengo mi hombre.	I now have my man.
Ay, hombre, espérame, hombre.	Ay, man, wait for me, man.
Sí, hombre, espérame, hombre.	Yes, man, wait for me, man.

While the respondedoras are singing, the glosador sings the following strophes:

Los que están bailando,	Those who are dancing,
Bailen con cuidado.	Let them dance with care.
A debajo 'e casa,	For under the house,
Está el Diablo parado.	The Devil is standing.
No me da la gana	Don't arouse my desire
De bailar contigo.	To dance with you.
Porque cuando bailo,	Because when I dance,
Me duele el ombligo.	My belly button hurts.

These strophes are variations on common themes in the marimba dance. In one very popular combination of these themes, the glosador sings this sequence in the course of about twenty minutes:

Come hear the marimba.
It chases the Devil.
I am the Devil.
I am going on a trip.
Do not dance with me,
Because I might decide
To stay with you.

In response to this, or simultaneously with it, the respondedoras sing these lines:

The Devil is coming.
Good-bye by a man.
I now hold my man.

The respondedoras also insert lines of various strophes between those sung by the glosador. In day-to-day life, neither men nor women are concerned with the Devil, and they are unwilling or unable to discuss the meaning of the references to the Devil in the marimba.

Not only the words of the songs but also the structure of the dance itself suggests the nature of familial relations between men and women. The *bambuco* is now the most popular of the nine marimba dances known in northwest Ecuador (Whitten and Fuentes C., n.d.).[1] In the bambuco a woman (or sometimes two women) takes the initiative in inviting the man to dance. In her right hand she carries a handker-

1. The similarity in name between marimba dances on the coast of Ecuador and national Colombian folk dances in no way implies a similarity between the dances themselves.

chief; the man carries a handkerchief or hat in his right hand. The man and woman move toward one another, and then the man retreats and the woman pursues. She then turns her back and retreats, but as soon as he begins to follow she again turns toward him and he again retreats. This pattern is repeated again and again. The woman steadily advances, pivots, retreats, while the man becomes more and more excited, leaps into the air, stamps his feet in time with the drums, shouts, and waves his handkerchief or hat. He may open his arms as if to capture the woman but, as she turns to him, he retreats.

The marimba dance is known as the *baile de respeto* (dance of respect), but no one could tell me why. Some young people say it is because dancers never touch in the marimba, but this is not so because couples dance in an embrace in the now uncommon *caderona* and *torbellino* dances. More important in interpreting the phrase "baile de respeto," I think, is the way in which the marimba dance re-enacts potential problems between the sexes arising from the practice of serial polygyny. Such problems are re-enacted until dancers and musicians are so exhausted that they are unable to go on. Unlike dancing in a saloon, marimba dancing does not end in a night of new sexual alliances. No new problems arise from a marimba dance: familial components of the social order do not realign afterward. Perhaps this explains the association of "respect" with the marimba dance—respect being equated, in this context, with maintenance of existing marital alliances.

Polygyny

Men in San Lorenzo positively value having more than one wife. Women, on the whole, are not averse to having a man who is both virile and prosperous enough to support two or more women.

In 1963 there were 18 men in San Lorenzo with more than one wife.[2] Of these 18 men, 15 had two wives, two had three wives, and

2. I use the term "wife" when it is difficult to distinguish conceptually between "wife" and "mistress." If I always considered the second wife of a man his mistress, then, in terms of her behavior vis-à-vis that of the man, as compared to other consensual (or even legal) unions, I would have to classify 80 per cent of the young women in San Lorenzo as either mistresses or single women (the latter was done in the national census of 1962), and that is obviously absurd. There are cases in San Lorenzo of a man with both a wife and what may reasonably be called a mistress—a woman with whom he shares sexual relations but little else. For our purposes, a man is considered to have two wives when (1) both women share his life chances

one had four. Living arrangements range from the joint residence in one house by two wives, to wives living in separate households in the same town, to separate households in different towns. Table VI presents the polygynous marriages in terms of four variables: (1) the marriage form (consensual or legal); (2) the wives' residence; (3) the husband's preference (or lack of it) for one wife over another; and (4) the relations between the wives.

Many men and women in San Lorenzo have been part of a polygynous family at one time in their lives. My discussion of polygyny is based not only on observation of the 18 unions shown in Table VI, but also on information about now-broken polygynous unions from informants who either have been members of such families or have had relatives and friends in such families.

There seems to be no hostility between wives so long as they are not competing with each other. When the wives are considered equal, they usually live entirely separate lives and assist the husband in different economic activities. For example, one may work on his farm and the other gather conchas. He, in turn, contributes economic assistance and whatever prestige he has equally to the two households.

More often, however, the husband makes it quite explicit which wife he favors and informs the other that she is free to leave at any time. The slighted woman may justify her subordinate status to herself by asserting that it is better to be the less-favored wife of a "strong" man than the only wife of a lesser man. In such cases, both wives have a set position in relation to the husband and the relative status of the wives is known to the community; they are not in competition. Furthermore, both wives have an advantage; one is a favored wife and the other has the uncommon prerogative of initiating a separation, a prerogative delegated to her by virtue of her subordinate status. In the one case in which two wives occupy one household, one wife is dominant and tasks are rigidly divided between the two women.

Many cases of men with wives in other towns or wives living on their farms are not listed in Table VI simply because I have insufficient data on the character of the relationship. When subsistence and

and style of life; (2) both unions have semipermanent status in the eyes of the parties concerned and of the community; and (3) others in the community, as well as the man and his wives, regard both relationships as marriages.

TABLE VI

Polygynous Marriages in San Lorenzo, 1963

Marriage and Duration[a]	Wives' Residence	Husband's Preference	Relations Between Wives
M-20, C-8	Same house	M favored	Friends, strict separation of tasks
M-28, C-27, C-10	Two in adjacent houses, third in separate part of town	About equal	Two neighbors have violent arguments, no overt conflict with third
C-10, M-4	Separate parts of town	M favored	No overt hostility
M-22, C-3	Separate parts of town	M favored	No overt hostility
M-22, C-8, C-4	Separate parts of town	M favored, C-4 second, C-8 third	No overt hostility
C-2, C-1	Separate parts of town	Equal	Possibly unaware of one another
M-15, C-4	Separate parts of town	M strongly favored	Not friends, but no overt conflict
C-2, C-1	Separate parts of town	C-2 favored	Unaware of one another
C-10, C-1	Separate parts of town	C-10 favored	Overt hostility, physical violence
M-19, C-3	Separate parts of town	M favored	Good friends
C-5, C-2	Separate parts of town	C-2 favored	Friends
M-15, C-10	Separate parts of town	M favored	No overt hostility
M-13, C-5	Separate parts of town	Equal	No overt hostility
C-5, C-3	Separate parts of town	C-5 slightly favored	Enemies, but no overt hostility
M-18, C-4	Separate parts of town	M slightly favored	No overt hostility
C-6, C-4	Separate parts of town	Equal	No overt hostility
C-10, C-3, C-2, C-1	Two in separate parts of town, two out of town in different areas	C-10 favored, others equal	Various degrees of cordiality
C-8, C-6	Separate towns	Equal	No overt hostility

[a] "M" indicates a civil marriage, "C" a consensual union. The figure indicates the number of years the spouses have considered themselves married; in the case of consensual unions, the "marriage" postdates the beginning of sexual relations. "M-20, C-8," then, means that male Ego has been legally married to one woman for 20 years and has had a consensual union with another woman for eight years.

cash economies conjoin, polygyny is often economically advantageous. A man with a farm, a shop, and a cantina can keep all three
operations running profitably if he has one wife living on the farm
and another working in the cantina, while he himself runs the shop.
Polygynous marriages that combine economic diversification and an
explicit preference for one wife over another are as stable as monogamous marriages in San Lorenzo; but whatever marital form is manifest at a given time, the norms of serial polygyny govern it.

Household

Daily life, basic economic reciprocity, and familial relationships take
place in the context of the household, and to some extent between
households. There are two intrinsic concepts in northwest Ecuador,
each crucial to the understanding of household dynamics: the concept of household itself, and the concept of head of household. When
a Costeño speaks of his *casa,* he does not mean simply his physical
house, but the domestic group sharing a house, or part of a house,
which recognizes itself as a distinct unit, usually with only one responsible head.

The concept of household head (*jefe de la casa*) refers to responsibility, not authority, and must be distinguished from the emerging
concept of family head (*jefe de la familia*), which refers to nominal
authority. The newer notion is found among young men in a few
households who have had extensive contact with highland mestizos
and to whom the general concept of headship is important. A few
other men, notably the teniente político and the head of the boys'
school, acquired the new concept while helping with the national census of 1962. But when pressed to place different persons in the community kinship network, they resorted to the concept of jefe de la
casa.

The jefe de la casa is responsible for the actions of the women
and children of the household, and for the animals owned by all
members of the household. When a man is present in the role of husband-father, he is *de jure* head of the house, and he may occupy this
position when he does not regularly eat and sleep in the house—for
example, when he has more than one wife. Nevertheless, as we shall
see later in this chapter, matrifocal households are common. Jefe de
la casa is a prestige position in the community.

Genealogies derived through work with informants provided general information on household composition and important facts about specific households. This information was checked in a house-to-house survey of all 337 Costeño residences. Data for each household were checked with at least two members of the household and with other members of the community familiar with the household. My questionnaire included questions on occupation, household composition (age and sex), genealogy, previous sexual liaisons, the present whereabouts of earlier partners, and the offspring of such unions.

Households in San Lorenzo range from small, matrifocal, patrifocal, and nuclear households to large, bilaterally expanded households containing more than one reproductive or potentially reproductive unit. In general, household composition corresponds to Negro household types reported in studies of the Caribbean (R. T. Smith 1956: 51–150; 1957: 67–75; Clarke 1957; Freilich 1961; Mintz 1961; M. G. Smith 1962). The most efficient and productive way to present the detailed information derived from my survey is to present an inductively derived typology of household structure in San Lorenzo, supplemented by quantitative data and illustrations.

Type I Household

Type I households are made up of a large, bilaterally expanded kinship unit, with one jefe de la casa. They include at least one other active, dormant, or broken reproductive unit besides the family of the household head. Figure 5, showing two examples of Type I households, makes it clear that although a given man (X) may have two families of procreation, he is not necessarily head of two households. Sometimes he heads both households, sometimes he heads only one, and sometimes he heads neither.

There are 69 Type I households in San Lorenzo, 35 of which are headed by a man with a spouse in the wife-mother role; only one man headed such a household without a spouse. Thirty-three of the households were headed by a woman without a man in the husband-father role. In one household there was a dispute between a man and a woman over who was head. This rare case arose when the woman brought home a husband-father after more than ten years without a man in this role, and refused to concede that the responsibility for the household was no longer hers. The other mem-

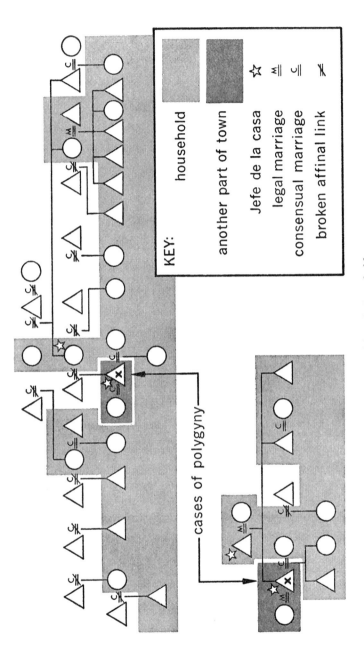

KEY:

household

another part of town

☆ Jefe de la casa

⚌ legal marriage

⚍ consensual marriage

⚡ broken affinal link

— cases of polygyny

Figure 5. Type I Household

bers of the household were not upset by this state of affairs; they felt
that although the woman had a strong claim, the man should be considered jefe. To summarize the data on Type I households (N = 69):

Male Head:		Female Head:	
With spouse	35 (51 per cent)	With spouse	1 (disputed)
Without spouse	1	Without spouse	33 (48 per cent).

The statistics bear out the norm of male headship. Although this
is not reflected in the statistics, the wife of the head ordinarily assumes the man's responsibilities when he leaves or dies. Headship
is not usually passed on to his son, brother, or other male member
of the household.

There are two subtypes of Type I, which we designate as A and B.
Subtype A subsumes the 12 households in San Lorenzo that are
structurally the same as those delineated above, except that fission
in headship has taken place and there are now two heads in the same
household. All these households were headed by men with a spouse

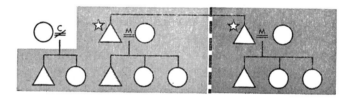

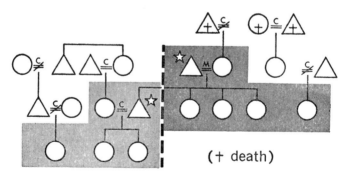

(+ death)

Figure 6. Type I Household, Subtype A

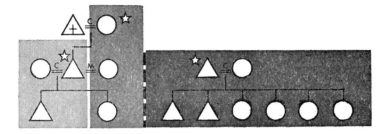

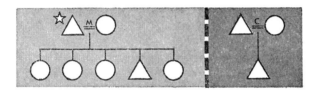

Figure 7. Type I Household, Subtype B (White line between blocks indicates separate part of town.)

in the wife-mother role. It could be said that there are two normative households, although spatially, economically, and socially there is still only the one house. Figure 6 presents two examples to illustrate the dynamics of fission into Subtype A.

Subtype B (Figure 7) also resembles the dominant type, except that it is the product of the fusion of two unrelated families. Of the 29 households in San Lorenzo in Subtype B, 25 were headed by a man with a spouse, three by men without a spouse, and one by a woman without a spouse. In all cases compadrazgo ties made the household structurally similar to Type I.

Type II Household

The second major household type consists of a nuclear family, a broken nuclear family, or one of these two plus other consanguines. In other words, a Type II household contains no more than one reproductive or potentially reproductive unit. Nearly 68 per cent, or 226, of the households in San Lorenzo fall into this category. Some of these appeared at first to be Type I, Subtype B, households, but if they were completely separated from one another by a partition dividing the house, and if they functioned as separate economic

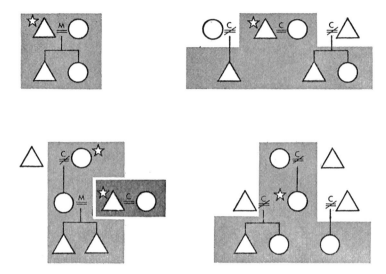

Figure 8. Type II Household

and social units, I considered them Type II households. Figure 8 shows four examples of Type II households. The 226 Type II households can be classified as follows:

Male head:

   With spouse   160 (71 per cent)

   Without spouse 17 (7 per cent)

Female head:

   With spouse   0

   Without spouse 49 (22 per cent).

Type II is obviously the result of fission from a larger structure. Fission may take place after a household unit has consolidated— when, for example, Type I develops into Subtype A (a second head-ship develops) and then fissions into Type II. Or Type II may result from fission in two independent households—when, for example, a young couple sets up a new household. This neolocality is relatively rare in San Lorenzo; ambilocality, in which a couple undergo a sort of trial marriage in the household of the parents of one of them, is more usual.

From the data summarized in Table VII, and from the evidence presented on household typology, the following generalizations can be derived. Men with spouses and women without spouses tend to

TABLE VII
Typology of Household Heads

Household Type	Number	Per Cent of Type	Civil Marriages	Per Cent of Civil Marriages
Type I (N = 69)				
Male head with spouse . . .	35	51	15	43
Male head, no spouse . . .	1	1	—	—
Female head, no spouse[a] . .	33	48	—	—
Subtype A (N = 12)				
Male head with spouse . . .	12	100	4	33
Subtype B (N = 29)				
Male head with spouse . . .	25	86	7	28
Male head, no spouse . . .	3	10	—	—
Female head, no spouse[a] . .	1	3	—	—
Type II (N = 226)				
Male head with spouse . . .	160	71	63	39
Male head, no spouse . . .	17	7	—	—
Female head, no spouse[a] . .	49	22	—	—

[a] No clear-cut instance of "female head with spouse."

head households; men without spouses assume this role less frequently. Except for the one disputed case, women are not responsible for a household if a man is present in the husband-father role. It might be further noted that in all cases of female headship, at least some members of the household were children of the head. This is not true in the case of male heads: men may head households in the procreation of which they have had no part. It can be said that there is a "matrifocal" tendency in San Lorenzo household composition. Since in Type II the family is the household, matrifocal families can also be said to exist.[3]

Household Fission and Fusion

It is important to link the components of the typology and to achieve some notion of the dynamics of fission and fusion in the web of intra- and inter-household relationships, before discussing the personal kindred. Fortes (1958: 4) writes: "Marriage leads to an

3. For a discussion of the possible causation of matrifocal families, see R. T. Smith (1956, 1960) and Kunstadter (1963).

actual or incipient split in one or both of the spouses' natal families and domestic groups, and fission in the domestic group is always translated into spatial representation in the residence arrangements." Obviously, when a boy moves into a girl's home, the move represents fission from his residential group and fusion with the girl's. When the girl has children, her household expands whether or not the man remains with her. If the couple eventually establishes a separate residence, fission has then occurred in both parental households. Type I households are a result of fusion and expansion from Type II households; they may result from normal expansion or from the fusion of two nuclear Type II households. In the latter case, Type II becomes Type IB, and if consolidation occurs—through marriage, the extension of compadrazgo ties, or fictive kinship—Type IB becomes Type IA. When the entire household recognizes one head, the full transition from Type II to Type I has taken place.

The expansion of a household as members acquire spouses and children eventually results in either complete fission into Type II or incomplete fission into Type IA. Since households are constantly undergoing fission, expansion, and fusion, the typology presented here is intended to clarify the principles of household dynamics, and not to classify households as permanent representatives of a particular type.

The normal processes of composition change in San Lorenzo households are complicated by the norms and practice of serial polygyny. Households expand and contract not only as children grow up, marry, and have children of their own, but also as older members bring home new spouses or leave to reside with a new spouse. Figure 9 shows how a household may fission when the spouses separate. Note, however, that the two houses in Figure 9 are actually connected, so that fission has not been completely translated into the spatial representation of living arrangements.

About twenty-five years ago the head of Household B took a second wife and built another house—Household A—onto the one he had shared with his first wife. His daughter moved in with him. His daughter had three childern by three different men, all of whom eventually took other wives and moved on. The daughter's mother cared for the first two children in Household B while the third child remained in Household A. At the time of the interview

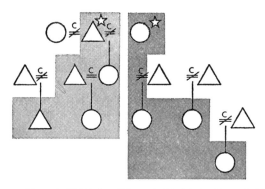

Figure 9. Household Fission (Household A left, Household B right).

(1963), the daughter was living with another man, and a child by him, in her father's household. In the meantime, one of the daughter's daughters had had a child by a man who lived with her only briefly, and that child remained in Household B, with its mother.

This case should illustrate the point that household data alone are not adequate for a full understanding of kinship structure and function. Though it is true that all the members of a household eat and sleep there, and that the household is the basic unit of economic reciprocity, economic reciprocity extends beyond the household. To understand the wider economic and social patterns, and to discuss child-rearing and crisis rites, we must consider the broader context of supra-household kinship organization.

The Personal Kindred

The Concept of Kindred

The basis of supra-household kinship organization is the "personal kindred," a term that I have adopted from Leach (1950: 62) and Davenport (1959) and that I would define as Murdock (1960: 4) defines kindred:

The kindred should . . . be recognized as a bilateral kin group. It is always Ego-oriented, i.e., composed of persons related to a particular individual (or group of siblings) bilaterally (literally "on both sides"). The members of a kindred, other than the core individual and his siblings, need not be, and frequently are not, related to one another. In any society, kindreds necessarily overlap one another. They are not discrete units; a society can never be divided into separate kindreds as it can be segmented into discrete families, lineages, clans, or communities. From the point of view of the core individual or siblingship, the membership of the kindred can be defined in terms of serial links of filiation produced by the ramifying intersection of families of procreation and orientation. The membership cannot be defined, however, in lineal terms by descent from a common ancestor. A kindred therefore is not and cannot be a descent group.

Recent anthropological literature emphasizes the importance not only of distinguishing between linear and nonlinear (cognatic) systems, but also of distinguishing within cognatic systems between groups organized on the basis of personal kindreds (Leach 1950: 61–62; Davenport 1959: 563), and those organized on the basis of "nonunilinear descent" (Davenport 1959).[4]

The distinction between personal kindreds and descent groups seems clear enough if one recalls their differences in point of reference (an individual or siblingship as contrasted with an ancestor or ancestors), clarity of group boundaries (overlapping and diffuse as contrasted with distinct and discrete), and the presence of some variable degree of collateral limitation in the former and no collateral limitation in the latter. (Davenport 1959: 564.)

In view of the current importance properly attached to distinguishing principles of kinship-based group formation within cognatic descent systems, in the remainder of this chapter I will set forth the nature of San Lorenzo personal kindreds so as to demonstrate that a kindred and not a nonunilinear system is involved. It will be demonstrated that the basic social units in San Lorenzo satisfy all Davenport's criteria for personal kindreds as opposed to nonunilinear descent groups.

My reason for using the term "personal kindred" instead of simply "kindred" is that I wish to consider two types of kindred: the personal and the stem kindred. In spite of Murdock's (1960: 4) statement that "because of its lack of discreteness, a kindred cannot be a corporate group," he nevertheless partially concedes, "the so-

4. Davenport (1959) adequately reviews selected ethnographic evidence for the conceptual differentiation, and Mitchell (1963) further describes the problems of using the concept of kindred. These two articles, together with Murdock's analysis (1960) and his criticism of Mitchell's article (1964), cover the literature adequately, and there is no need for a re-review here.

called 'stem kindred' described by Davenport . . . may possibly con-
stitute an exception" (Murdock 1960: 157).[5] As we will see in Chapter VII, under certain conditions—notably mobility into the middle
class—kindreds do take on a corporate character. In the following
chapter I will demonstrate that the "stem kindred"—a corporately
functioning, self-perpetuating kindred, united by consolidated socioeconomic interests and obligations—comes into being in the process
of socioeconomic mobility. In Chapter VIII the functions of the stem
kindred in the political order will be considered.

The Structure and Function of the Personal Kindred

Personal kindreds in northwest Ecuador are, obviously, Ego-oriented, and they include affinal and fictive kin. They are the maximal
kinship units. Although marriage combines the personal kindreds of
the spouses (from the reference point of either spouse), separation
of the spouses does not necessarily lead to fission along lines of the
broken affinal link. That is, a person's in-laws, or selected in-laws,
may continue to be considered part of his personal kindred even
though they are no longer connected through his spouse. Ordinarily,
the personal kindred is strengthened by ritual kinship, i.e. compadrazgo. Members of a personal kindred are distinguishable by local-
ity, prestige, and a system of reciprocal obligations grounded in economic activities.

Personal kindreds are partially localized within a household,
neighborhood, and town, and partially dispersed between towns and
between a given town and the rural hinterland. One often finds a
cluster of Type II households that, when plotted on a kinship dia-
gram, are identical with a single, large Type I household. In fact,
when household membership is plotted through time, the structure
of a defined cluster of households remains about the same, although
there is a great deal of movement within and between the households. The same is true of a series of dispersed households when
their members share overlapping personal kindreds.

A crucial feature of northwest Ecuadorian kindred structure is
that men with status or economic advantage, or both, are more often
included in the kindred a person recognizes than men without par-

5. More recently (1964), Murdock has again acknowledged the corporate or potentially corporate character that kindreds may assume.

ticular status or economic standing. As a result personal kindreds are easier to recognize from the reference point of an important Ego than from that of an unimportant one.

Since the structure of a personal kindred, by its very Ego-oriented character, is idiosyncratic, generalizations based upon precise abstractions are impossible. But the functions of the personal kindreds can be readily discussed, and in a discussion of these functions, the structure should emerge.

Personal kindreds are only apparent when functioning. They function significantly in child rearing, in economic activities, and in life crisis rituals. The personal kindred can and does function in political life, but the quest for personal honor is an individual pursuit.

Child Rearing

Children are raised within the personal kindred of the father or mother or within the personal kindreds of both parents. Ordinarily a child is raised by lineal kinsmen as close as his grandparents or the brother or sister of one of his parents, but in some cases collateral kinsmen (usually first cousins) accept responsibility for a child. Although one of the parents is more likely than a kinsman to raise the child, everyone in the personal kindred is expected to accept the responsibility if called upon. A child may change families and households while he is growing up, but he will always remain within the personal kindred of his mother or father. If a man separates from a woman, he may leave his child in her care, keep the child with him, or ask his mother, grandmother, or sister to care for it. The "abandoned" mother may keep the child, or she may ask her mother, grandmother, sister, brother's wife, or even mother-in-law to care for the child. If she keeps the child or asks some lineal relative to care for it, the man is expected to continue to support it, but if the husband's mother (or other paternal relative) takes the child, the father is no longer expected to provide for it. Inspection of some thirty cases from San Lorenzo indicates that the child is more likely to be raised within his father's personal kindred than his mother's, if for some reason his mother does not choose to raise him. Ordinarily, unless the father and child move away, the mother continues economic aid and maintains emotional bonds with the child, even if he lives with the father or paternal kinsman and regardless of formal separation and allocation of responsibility.

Children are breast-fed on demand for about the first year. Nursing women tease a baby with their breast; they withdraw the breast, tickle the baby on the face with it, cover and uncover it. They do this until tension builds up, and then return the breast to the feeding child. If the nursing woman becomes pregnant, the child is weaned abruptly. Otherwise weaning is gradual, occurring between six months and one and a half years, although ordinarily one year marks the end of breast-feeding. Once he reaches six months, the child is fed a paste made from banana flour and water until he begins to eat adult food.

Little girls ordinarily wear underpants and sometimes a dress from six months of age, but little boys wear only a shirt until they are able to speak well, which is usually sometime after their third year. Toilet training is ignored until about the end of the second year, when children are beaten for eliminating in the house or, in the case of girls, soiling their clothes. Boys are toilet-trained by the time they are given pants. Boys are likely to play and work in public without clothing until they reach puberty, but girls prefer to wear at least pants or a skirt.

When a child misbehaves, he is immediately and harshly punished. The relative who notices the transgression whacks the child with his hand or a stick until he escapes, screaming to everyone in sight. Frequently a punished child marches through the middle of his neighborhood yelling at the top of his lungs and weeping profusely. He will cry and scream much longer and louder before an audience. A punished child may, even at the age of two or three, strike back at his punisher and so incur even more beating. Once the beating and the crying and screaming are over, the matter is forgotten.

Pubescent girls may be beaten if they are suspected of having had sexual intercourse. In fact, women in the mother's personal kindred may ask the midwives or the doctor to examine the girl. If they find that she is not a virgin she may be beaten, but pregnancy, when it occurs, is considered a normal development, and the girl is not punished or made the subject of sanctioning rumors or gossip.

Girls are expected to help with household tasks and economic activities as soon as they are able, but young men are expected to behave irresponsibly, to lie, waste money, and get drunk. Even being arrested for stealing or rape is no disgrace. Only after young men have placed themselves in obligatory situations with other members of their kindred are they held morally responsible for their actions. Young men are nurtured within their kindred without actually reciprocating for a long time, often to age twenty or more, when able-bodied men usually begin taking an active part in mingas. Young men are not given any spending money; they must earn it. Ordinarily boys and young men seek work that will bring them cash, and they avoid subsistence activities. They are not turned out of the house or punished for failing to work, nor are they expected to contribute their cash to the household. In the hinterland, however, boys accompany their fathers or older brothers to fish and to work in the forest at a much younger age than in San Lorenzo.

Economic Activities

Since the function of the personal kindred in socioeconomic mobility is the subject of the next chapter, I shall discuss only ordinary lower-class activities here. The dispersed personal kindred makes possible spatial mobility, which is essential for a subsistence economy with shifting cultivation. When he travels, a Negro ordinarily chooses a route that takes him from relative to relative. He will be housed and fed for as long as he wishes to stay. He reciprocates directly by contributing to the household, and indirectly by obligating himself to extend similar courtesies to his hosts and to persons to whom his hosts are obligated. He must reciprocate when called upon, either personally or through friends and relatives who owe him something.

The absence of inheritance rules, the expanding population, and the necessity to move often in search of a job or new land to work lead to a pattern in which most Negroes expect to move several times during their young adult life. Because of this pattern, a given household may fluctuate in membership between one nuclear family or less at one time and two or more reproductive units at another. Furthermore, the membership of the household may change entirely in five or ten years. Such household change usually represents a spatial reorganization of a personal kindred or of overlapping personal kindreds.

Reciprocal obligations can be broken on good faith only by cash payment for labor. Negroes do not expect cash payment among recognized members of a personal kindred. Hence, a man in need of aid will first approach a member of his personal kindred. Series of reciprocal economic obligations bind the localized segment of the personal kindred together, just as series of reciprocal obligations incurred through spatial mobility bind the dispersed segments. It is by economic reciprocity and the serial nature of such reciprocity that the kindred is most readily definable at any given time. A Negro would feel that he "had to" house members of the personal kindred if he were asked to, and he would "want to" help them if help were needed.

Rituals of Life Crises

A personal kindred ordinarily comes together in one place only at the death of an adult. At the death of a child, the members of the parents' personal kindred who reside in the same community attend the wake and burial. At the death of an adult, the localized and dispersed segments of the kindred gather to pay final homage. The death rituals make it clear that the group I have been calling a personal kindred is not a nonunilinear descent group.

When a child dies, a wake is held the night before its burial. The wake is called an *arrullo* in and around San Lorenzo.[6] Some residents of San Lorenzo tell me that it is properly termed *chigualo*, and that an arrullo is only one type of chigualo song. The dictionary definition of arrullo is "lullaby," but it does not mean lullaby to the Negroes. "Hymn" is probably the closest approximation of their meaning. In the arrullo the dead child, called *angelito*, is dressed in white, laid on a table covered with a white cloth, and surrounded by candles, which are kept burning throughout the night. On his chest are laid flowers, variegated leaves, and white crepe-paper wreaths. The arrullo takes place in the child's parents' home or in the home of a member of the local segment of the kindred. I know of two cases in which the parents wanted no arrullo, but a member of their personal kindred (in both cases a godparent of the child) held one in his home and made all the arrangements.

The mother and close female members of her personal kindred

6. In some parts of Colombia it is reportedly called an *arrollo* (Velásquez 1961a: 49–76; Merizalde del Carmen 1921: 154–55). Arrullos are also sung on special fiestas and saints' days to Jesus, the Virgin Mary, San Antonio, and the Virgin of Carmen.

stand near the child. Other women and men sit on the floor or on benches, talk, and visit. A fairly rapid rhythm is beaten throughout the night on the bombo and two cununos. The bombero may be the father or another member of the parents' close personal kindred, and the cununeros are also members of the kindred. The drummers rotate during the night, and as many as ten men may play in the course of twelve hours. The drummers sit near the child's feet, facing the child. The bombo keeps the body-snatching spirit, Tunda, at bay. Tunda waits near the home for the child's body, but when it hears the bombo it becomes frightened.

Well-known cantadoras, who are not necessarily of the parents' personal kindred, sit or stand to the left of the drummers, while female members of the personal kindred who so desire form a second singing group, to the right of the drummers. Singing alternates between the cantadoras and the large group of female relatives, and is accompanied by the drums.

Anyone in the community is welcome to attend the wake. The ambience is cordial, and not particularly solemn. Children, usually accompanied by their parents, may poke at the deceased and talk as they wish. Women in the parents' personal kindred serve the guests as much aguardiente as they can afford. Usually only close members of the personal kindred, the singers and drummers, and special members of the community (the priest, teniente político, or anthropologist) will be served more than once or twice.

The next day the child is borne to the church for a short Catholic service, and then taken to the cemetery, where he is buried without further ceremony. It is believed that the child goes straight to heaven. Although the arrullo is declining in popularity in San Lorenzo because of the opposition of the priests, it continues throughout the hinterland. When no arrullo is held the relatives still gather, invite cantadoras, sing, and serve aguardiente. The death of a child serves as a catalyst for the intensification of ties among the local members of the parents' personal kindred.

When an adult dies the wake and burial are more solemn affairs, attended by his entire personal kindred. Only local members of his kindred ordinarily attend the first wake, called *alavado* or *alava'o*. The body is laid out in the same way as the body of a dead child. Cantadoras sing essentially the same songs as they sing in the arrullo, but much more slowly, with a different rhythm, and with different inflections.[7] The whole ambience is one of mourning. Today the body is ordinarily placed in the church the night the death occurs, and burial takes place the next morning after a brief service. Sometimes the alavado is held in the church, with the priest's permission. There is little ceremony at the graveyard, and only the very closest female relatives openly weep for the dead.

After nine days the dispersed members of the dead man's personal kindred join the local members at the home of one of them to hold the most important rite, called *novenario*, or more rarely alavado. In this wake the ghost of the deceased is bid a final good-bye and, everyone hopes, it departs from this world for heaven (*Gloria*). Although people "know" that a child goes directly to heaven, they are not sure where adults first go after death, or whether many ever do reach Gloria. For nine days preceding the final alavado, windows and doors are left open so that the ghost of the dead may return. Members of the personal kindred drink to the ghost and socialize. This nine-day period may also be referred to as the novenario.[8]

The ninth-day alavado is more than anything else a dismissal of the dead. The more important the deceased person, the longer, more drawn out, and more intense is the singing. Like the arrullo, the alavado is led by cantadoras living in the community who are not necessarily members of the kindred. Ordinarily, at the ninth-day alavado only one professional cantadora, called the *solista*, leads the singing. Her first shout is always the same:

> "Adioooooooooo, primo hermano, Adiooooooooooo."
> "Good-bye, first cousin, good-bye."

On the second *Adió* everyone joins in and harmonizes. Several more introductory "good-byes" follow before a few of the women slowly sing the first verse:

Vo' vas y me dejas	You go and leave me
Solito con Dios.	Alone with God.

7. In some areas of the Pacific lowlands of Colombia and Ecuador the songs for arrullos and alavados are quite distinct.

8. The second rite, which comes nine days after death (or in some places one week from the day of death), is found among Negroes throughout the entire Pacific lowlands culture area. Usually the nine-day period is referred to as the novenario, and the last rite as *último alavado, última novena, último rosario, última noche,* or, less frequently, novenario.

Then all sing the chorus:

| Hermanito', hermano', | Brothers, dear brothers, |
| Me acompañaran. | They accompany me. |

The singing continues until it is believed that the ties between the members of the personal kindred and the deceased have been severed. Once this separation has been made, people are not supposed to think, talk, or reminisce about the dead person. Such second wakes last from six hours to two days.

Negroes occasionally make special trips to visit the graves of brothers and sisters, and, more rarely, of a parent, if the parent was a particularly important person. These visits are supposed to take place on the anniversary of the sibling's or parent's death, but in practice they may take place almost any time. It is the ties to siblings and filiation to parents that are reasserted, not ties to an ancestor.

Much of the Negroes' folklore centers about unwanted visitations from dead relatives. Both children and adults who have been told of an ancestor fear his return. No one sleeps in a hammock at night because the dead are believed to return there. Women are afraid to have sexual intercourse in the bush at night because their dead relatives may see them there. People who are ill or injured will not go to the cemetery for fear of dying as their relative did. Children flagellate themselves after visiting the graveyard to rid themselves of the *mal aire*.

During the house-to-house survey in San Lorenzo, I found it extremely difficult to check data involving a person who had died. Questions such as "Where did he live?" or "Who lived with him when he was alive?" or "Was he the head of the household?" elicited one response: "He died." Only the informants I worked with daily would give responsive answers to such questions, and even they would never go further back than their grandparents' generation. My references to deceased parents of a dead person in trying to establish kinship relationships carried no meaning whatsoever. The first-generation dead are very seldom referred to in establishing kinship ties, even when they would appear to be essential for establishing a relationship.

The above data clearly establish that the point of reference in northwest Ecuadorian kindred structure is an individual or siblingship, that group boundaries are overlapping and diffuse, and that collateral limitation usually ends with second cousins, since people refuse to trace their collateral relationship through more than one generation of deceased. (Third cousins are made fictive first or second cousins if they are recognized as kinsmen.)

The ceremonies of death dismiss the ancestor from the world and from any significant role in the kinship system. Homage is paid to the dead on the basis of siblingship and filiation to the dead parent, without reference to descent line—real, ritual, or fictive. Hence the nonunilinear descent system suggested by Solien (1959) as probably characterizing the Black Carib of Central America and Jamaican and Haitian Negroes does not exist in northwest Ecuador, even though other aspects of the system are at least superficially similar. I mention this because the corporate, self-perpetuating character of the stem kindred, discussed in the next chapter, may raise the question of whether or not an incipient descent group is developing—that is, whether or not descent from an ancestor more than two generations removed is possibly replacing filiation and the siblingship as the significant reference point in kinship grouping. I wish to avoid such discussion in Chapter VII and so have tried to demonstrate, in advance, the absence of any but a bilateral principle behind the formation of social kin-based groups.

To summarize the data presented in this chapter, it has been demonstrated that the three concepts of mi familia, mi casa, and mi parentesco, held by the Negroes themselves, correspond to the anthropological concepts of nuclear family, household, and personal kindred. Little can be learned from an examination of family structure. Somewhat more can be gained from an examination of household. The maximal and most significant unit is the personal kindred, for it is within the personal kindred that child rearing, economic reciprocity, and rituals of life crises are carried out.

VII

Kinship and Socioeconomic Mobility

In northwest Ecuador, the dynamics of social structure and change emerge most clearly from a study of socioeconomic mobility. In this chapter, therefore, I will first describe three cases of mobility and then construct a model covering not only these cases, but the system of socioeconomic mobility throughout the northern sector of Esmeraldas. A more detailed examination of the middle class in San Lorenzo will then pinpoint the effects of the highland impress on mobility.

The Arisalas of San Lorenzo

Around 1920 Nelson Arisala, his consensual spouse Daisy, and their three small children settled in San Lorenzo. Nelson and Daisy had lived on two rivers in the area and in another small town on the coast. Traveling was never difficult for them because throughout the territory they had relatives who welcomed them into their households. The couple had always shared a house with at least two other families before settling in San Lorenzo. In San Lorenzo, where the family had no relatives, Nelson undertook for the first time the responsibility of being jefe de la casa.

The Arisalas settled down on a small farm on the edge of town, and supplemented their subsistence life by collecting tagua and selling it to buyers who occasionally came to San Lorenzo by boat. They never had any money since Nelson was always either paying a debt or making a loan. They did not want for relatives; a number of other families on the move lived with them for a while and then either settled in their own home in San Lorenzo or moved on. In San Lorenzo the Arisala household always contained more than one family, and at times it included as many as four reproductive units, each of which contributed to the maintenance of the household.

The Arisalas had many children. A few girls found mates and left home, and continued to wrest a lower-class life from the town, forest, river, and sea. Two boys also left home. None of the children who left would lack a place to live or relatives to care for their children; in turn, they would always be ready to bring up children of their relatives, and to shelter a visiting "primo hermano," however long he stayed. One daughter stayed in San Lorenzo and eventually settled down with a newcomer, without any resident kinsmen, who was engaged in commerce. Nelson later took another wife, and went to live with her parents in Colombia. Daisy lived in San Lorenzo with four sons, a daughter, and a second spouse until her death, when Nelson and most of her relatives returned to San Lorenzo to attend the novenario. The life of Nelson and Daisy was typical of coastal-riverine life in Esmeraldas province, and indeed it still is.

Three of the four sons of Nelson and Daisy who remained in San Lorenzo took two or three consensual wives each. The wives lived on their husbands' farms and tended them, while the men, with the help of other wives, opened three shops in town and pursued a variety of economic activities within a day's canoe trip from San Lorenzo. Two wives each maintained a small shop for their husbands, who were in small, nearby settlements. One of the brothers, for example, had three consensual spouses: one lived on a pineapple farm and worked it with her children; another lived in a nearby town, where she and her family of orientation ran a shop; and the third lived with the man in his center of operations, where she helped run his shop while he engaged in the buying and selling of mangrove bark, dried fish, shell-fish, and timber. The Arisala brothers and the husband of the daughter who remained at home—their brother-in-law—also purchased mangrove bark, skins, fish, and other goods from Negroes who did not want to wait for the appearance of a boat to realize a profit. Acting as economic middlemen, the Arisalas then sold their products at a small profit when a boat put in at San Lorenzo. Work was hard and steady; only the promise of future wealth kept the men working. The demand for forest products during World War II brought the

Arisalas a small measure of success, as did the postwar banana boom, during which Negroes aspiring to mobility not only grew and marketed their own bananas, but also marketed bananas they purchased from hinterland Negroes.

When the Arisalas had prospered to the extent that they could be of obvious aid to their kinsmen, they had to make a choice. Either the brothers could assist all their kinsmen and remain in the lower class despite their hard work or they could sever their kindred ties, reciprocate only within their small circle of four men and about ten wives, and rise into the middle class. At this stage in their economic mobility reciprocal contracts with poorer kinsmen could be of no value. They chose to sever their ties with relatives in rural areas and with all those who could not reciprocate on an equal basis. To sever relations was a simple matter. They hoarded surplus cash for the education of their children, or spent it on clothing for their wives and children —the men spent nothing extra on themselves. When they were asked for help, the Arisalas either stated that they could not help, and gave their new expenses as proof, or asked for a delay. By refusing requests for aid, they lost the opportunity to travel and explore new areas, and they committed themselves to one territory, San Lorenzo, within which to pursue their quest for upward socioeconomic mobility.

In the third generation, reckoning from Nelson and Daisy, the Arisala kindred (the reference point now being the siblings who began socioeconomic mobility) was characterized by selected expansion, a tendency to settle in one part of town, and a change in style of life. The Arisalas emphasized education for children, premarital chastity for women, and better housing, with tin roofs, better doors and windows, and more space for fewer people. Although the men continued to practice polygyny, most of them married one of their wives as their children reached adulthood.

The emphasis on mobility and the difficulty of reciprocating on an equal basis forced many members of the third generation to leave town. The men who remained, including affines, took up various political and economic duties. Their income and connections helped their parents build larger shops, expand their farms, and accumulate respectability symbols at a faster rate. Women went to colegios, and, if they returned to town, either did not work at all or became teachers in the local school. These women strongly favored marriage to a light-skinned man, and they looked to the highlanders who were beginning to arrive in San Lorenzo as possible spouses. They were also expected to marry a man without responsibilities to a large personal kindred. The Arisala kindred absorbed affines, but not the relatives of affines, unless it was advantageous to do so.

Some members of the third-generation Arisala kindred moved to Esmeraldas and Ibarra and to Tumaco, Colombia. They continued to reciprocate with the San Lorenzo Arisalas, housing and feeding the children who came to the large towns to attend colegios and look for an appropriate spouse. In return for this they were aided in setting up small businesses.

As the third generation of Arisalas expanded into all economic and political spheres, the position of the kindred was further consolidated by asymmetrical dyadic contracts with key figures in the lower and upper classes. Some of the Arisala men began extending favors to the Rivera brothers. The Riveras, though they had no aspirations to upward mobility, preferred sporadic work in the forest to work in town or on a farm. They frequently organized minga labor groups to bring logs to sawmills in Limones and La Tola, and were recognized as jefes de la minga. By extending favors to the Riveras, the Arisalas gained the power to determine when many mingas would occur. The jefe de la minga would organize mingas on their request, in exchange for a favor such as extended credit in an Arisala shop. But why did the Arisalas want such power? And why did they extend favors to the Rivera brothers in the first place?

At that time San Lorenzo had reached its period of most rapid growth, and wood was at a premium. The Junta Autónoma had established a small sawmill in the center of town and needed timber. Newly arrived upper-class highlanders soon found that mention of the need for timber in one of the Arisala stores often led to rapid delivery of timber to the sawmill. The Arisalas came to be middlemen in mestizo-Negro social relations, as well as economic middlemen. This situation produced an in-migration of young, lower-class Negroes of the favored personal kindred of the Rivera brothers; they became part of a labor force indirectly controlled by the Arisalas through a series of dyadic contracts. Eventually some of these lower-class Negroes severed their kinship ties and began to rise economically and socially.

In return for indirectly arranging for many mingas, the Arisalas

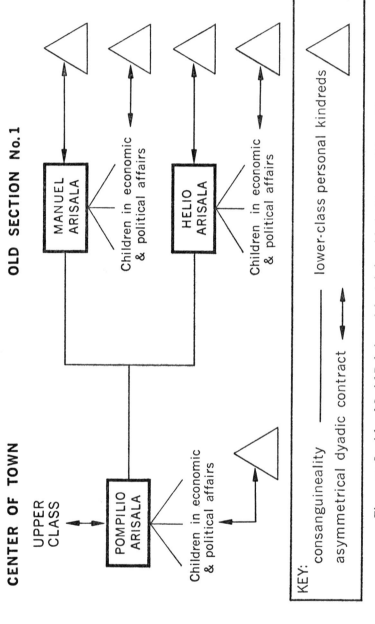

Figure 10. Spatial and Social Relations of the Arisalas with the Upper and Lower Classes

received such favors as the only license in San Lorenzo to sell aguardiente, which was at that time distilled and distributed by a government monopoly. Members of the kindred were placed in political positions in which graft further enhanced their already favorable economic position. The Arisalas' position on the receiving end of asymmetrical dyadic contracts with upper-class newcomers allowed them to re-extend their dyadic contracts with other Negroes, asymmetrically now, for they had become middle-class.

The structure of the neighborhood (Old Section No. 1) in which most of the Arisalas live resembles that of a large, bilaterally expanded household or a series of dispersed smaller households. Pompilio Arisala is especially responsible for relations with the upper class, while socioeconomic relations with the lower class are the responsibility of the two other Arisala brothers. Pompilio, the central figure, manifests all the prestige symbols mentioned earlier. He even tries to speak what he considers "better" Spanish. For example, he realizes that Costeños drop their *d*'s between the vowels *a* and *o*, as in *alava'o*, and has carried his knowledge to the extreme of insisting that the correct pronunciation for cacao is *cacado*. He dresses like an upper lower-class American, as does his wife, his daughters, and to a lesser extent his sons. His two daughters who have reached marriageable age are legally married to highland mestizos. Pompilio's very large shop, the largest in town, is the one closest to the center of town, and is in the best spot to attract the highlander's business (see Map 3, p. 210).

Pompilio, his two brothers, and his brother-in-law, together with all their children, make up a functionally corporate, though bilateral, kindred from the reference point of the above siblingship. Unending dyadic contracts bind the kindred together, and tie it to important members of the upper class and to large lower-class kindreds. These serial connections are further reinforced by compadrazgo relationships. The Arisalas are godparents to their sibling's children and children's children, and to the children of lower-class Negroes with whom they have established strong dyadic contracts. Members of the upper class are godparents of Arisala children, but no Arisala is a godparent to an upper-class child. Figure 10 illustrates these social and spatial relationships.

The Arisala case has been described in some detail because it exemplifies the height of kindred rise in a propitious economic framework. So far as I have been able to determine, every town of 500 people or more in northwest Ecuador has a kindred that has risen in the same way as the Arisalas of San Lorenzo. The only rural middle-class kindred I know of, which is localized on the Santiago River, operates in the same manner as middle-class kindreds in towns. Like the town kindreds, it, too, is in the third generation.

The Downfall of the Rodríguez Kindred

Two other kindred situations in San Lorenzo must be mentioned before a model of kinship and socioeconomic mobility can be presented. The first involves a kindred that forty years ago (about the time the Arisalas began their rise) occupied the same position in San Lorenzo the Arisalas do today.

In the late 1880's, long before Nelson and Daisy Arisala came to San Lorenzo, Donald Rodríguez moved from Iscuandé, Colombia, and settled in Mataje, on the Colombian border. Donald's sons went to Borbón and Concepción as agents of either the German or the English company (reports vary), and eventually settled in San Lorenzo with their adult children to establish far-flung commercial relations. From the early 1920's to 1940 they dominated San Lorenzo's economic and political life. Light Costeños who resided in the center of town, they were probably the "white" family referred to by Ferdon (1950: 18). The next generation of the Rodríguez kindred, the fourth, were adult residents of San Lorenzo at the time I made my study of the town. Their fathers, too, were still living in San Lorenzo in 1963. In the fourth generation the kindred was unwieldy, the need for aid outweighed the resources of the town, and dyadic contracts even within the kindred often could not be fulfilled. Members of this kindred had established too many asymmetrical serial dyadic contracts with the lower class. Most members of the lower class felt that at least one member of the Rodríguez kindred owed them something. The overall effect was the economic leveling of the members of the kindred. The downfall of this fourth-generation mobile kin group (reckoning from Donald, who settled in Mataje) exactly coincides with the rise of the third-generation Arisalas.

Many of the young members of the Rodríguez kindred who remain in San Lorenzo have turned to Communism, in hopes of regaining their lost position in the community and the region. They also actively, even frantically, join in formal group activities and frequently try to organize new formal associations. It is the fourth generation that is most desperately seeking economic and social re-establishment. In other areas of Esmeraldas province, too, Communism has a great appeal for now poor, but previously important, young men belonging to large, consolidated kindreds that have lost the economic viability they once had.

The Rise of the Mina Kindred

Several families now living in San Lorenzo have severed their ties with members of their dispersed personal kindred, and reciprocate only within a small, local, active group. They are most often the children of stationary parents, and have begun to rise by opening saloons, cantinas, and shops that are often operated by a wife while the men engage in day-to-day labor. In a few of these families the parents have given their sons economic freedom and have encouraged them to enter local politics, to try by less radical means than Communism to win some concession from the now-dominant Arisalas.

The Mina half-brothers, each with one consensual and one legal spouse, have already accrued enough economic and political capital to be considered middle-class. They are preparing their sons for higher education and subsequent business and political careers in San Lorenzo. Because the Mina brothers are very light mulattoes, they have the social advantage of being favored to some extent by many highlanders.

As the Arisala kindred continues to expand, some people in the upper and lower classes, especially newcomers, are beginning to turn to the members of the smaller Mina kindred as political and economic middlemen. Asymmetrical serial contracts are being established from the top of the class pyramid to the bottom, without Arisala control. It is possible that the Arisala kindred may relinquish more contracts to the rising Mina kindred or another rising kindred in the future.

Kinship and Mobility: A Model

By abstracting data drawn from these and other cases, a model can be developed that should make clear the salient features of the usual manner of socioeconomic mobility from the lower to middle class, and the effects of the changing socioeconomic scene upon it. In this model I begin by considering a segment of a lower-class personal kindred that has become localized, and I refer to this situation as the first generation of socioeconomic mobility since the process begins with localization.

First Generation

A family or a group of relatives establishes itself in a town and begins commercial relations and small-scale cash farming. These enterprises keep the participants settled in one place, while serial dyadic contracts continue with a dispersed personal kindred or overlapping personal kindreds. Although the settled group may make more money than other members of the kindred, the leveling effect of symmetrical dyadic contracts with a number of kinsmen keeps the members of the first generation from advancing economically. Also, because their work ties them to one place their own spatial mobility is restricted, although they continue to contribute to the spatial mobility of others.

Second Generation

In this generation, ties to the large dispersed personal kindred are severed, and reciprocal contracts within a small, localized kindred become intensive. All able-bodied members of the local kindred, including affines, contribute to one another's economic advance. Some capital is expended on the children's education and dress. Political activities become increasingly important to the furtherance of economic interests. In the town the kindred is definitely established as upward-mobile, and members enter the middle class as they continue shopkeeping and expand commercial interests. They are especially active in buying forest and sea products from lower-class Negroes and marketing them later at a profit. They become middlemen in the economic order. Polygyny, which reaches its height in this generation, makes possible considerable diversification of economic activities.

Third Generation

It is with the third generation that the stem kindred (Davenport 1959: 565; called "nodal kindred" by Goodenough 1962: 10–11) clearly emerges as the operative kinship group. Davenport illustrates the use of the term as follows:

Among the small farmers of County Clare in Ireland (Arensberg and Kimball 1940: 61–157), for example, an agnatic line of titleholders constitutes the genealogical line of landholders toward whom a small personal kindred have definite obligations. . . . As a consequence of the permanence of the farmstead and the continuity provided by the line of successive titleholders, *the kin unit itself has a kind of perpetuity.* The term suggested for this kind of organization is "stem kindred." [Emphasis mine.]

Perpetuity of the kin unit in northwest Ecuador is dependent not on a farmstead but on consolidation of socioeconomic interests. In the third generation the kindred expands, draws together in one section of town, and if successful, consolidates its economic position through social and political connections. The Ecuadorian situation seems to me structurally similar to the Irish one; the consolidation of socio-economic interests, like the succession of titleholders, endows the kin unit itself with a kind of perpetuity.

The difficulty of reciprocating within the kindred on a symmetrical basis forces some members of the third generation to sever relations and leave town. Those who remain pursue all sorts of economic activities. Many, but not all, of them cultivate "respectability symbols." They stop dancing the marimba and stop public drinking in saloons, and they may show at least nominal interest in the activities of the Catholic Church, though only the women actually attend church. The emphasis on respectability crystallizes in the attitudes and actions toward women. They are educated in colegios, expected to remain chaste before marriage, and encouraged to marry a middle-class man, preferably a light-skinned highlander. The only profession allowed them is teaching.

In the delineation of the kindred the agnatic line becomes ascendant, but there is still no concept of relationship through a common ancestor. Men pursue polygynous affairs, but usually marry one of their wives as their children reach adulthood. Some members move to nearby cities, where they aid their kinsmen by housing, feeding, and clothing their children who have come to attend a colegio or to find an appropriate spouse. When a girl marries she either integrates her spouse (but not his kinsmen) into her stem kindred, moves to another town and continues to aid her kindred through her in-laws, or severs relations with her stem kindred.

In this generation of socioeconomic rise, the successful stem kindred comes to dominate, albeit indirectly, a large portion of community politics and economics. From the reference point of second-generation men, propitious relations with key figures in all three classes lead to an unending series of contracts that function in various spheres of community activity. The stem kindred functions corporately, but without coercion or authority.

The dominant stem kindred in any community becomes very valuable to members of the upper class who wish to accomplish some task with the use of lower-class labor. A case in point is the Arisalas' intervention to supply the newly arrived highlanders with the lumber they needed. By helping the upper class, the responsible heads of the Arisala stem kindred placed themselves in the favored, lower half of asymmetrical dyadic contracts. Because of this they were able to extend favors downward to lower-class Negroes without trapping themselves in a disadvantageous position. In this case, the upper class received lumber, the lower class a guaranteed market for the fruits of their minga operations, and the dominant middle-class stem kindred favors that were necessary for continued mobility; all those involved benefited. This is only one example of a standard way to accomplish a task in San Lorenzo, although each group in each class does not always receive such obvious benefits.

To recapitulate, asymmetrical serial dyadic contracts originate in the middle-class stem kindred and extend from there into the upper and lower classes. This is true in northwest Ecuador whether or not the town has a resident upper class, as San Lorenzo does. In return for favors extended to members of lower-class kindreds, a dominant middle-class stem kindred controls a striking proportion of the labor force and, when called upon, can mobilize a good part of the Negro lower class for political or economic action. In return for the occasional exercise of this power, the middle-class stem kindred receives the favors it needs to maintain its widespread commercial interests.

Asymmetrical contracts extending up and down in the class hierarchy link the dominant middle-class kindred to other reciprocating groups on the bottom and to important economic and political groups on the top. The network of relationships radiating from the stem kindred defines it as the necessary mediating agency for a community's socioeconomic activities. It is the third-generation middle-class stem kindred that facilitates the conjoining of cash and subsistence economies in northwest Ecuadorian communities.

Although an investigator would find a dominant middle-class stem kindred in any sizable town in northwest Ecuador, the dominance of any particular middle-class stem kindred is short-lived. Natural increase, together with the prosperity that keeps members of the third generation from moving on, makes the upward-mobile kindred unwieldy in the fourth generation.

Fourth Generation

Members of the kindred remain in the middle class and retain their respectability symbols and some upper-class contacts, but their control of economic and political affairs weakens to the point where they cease to be useful to the upper and lower classes. They still have prestige, but their power is gone. Because the kindred expands faster than the economy, serial dyadic contracts within the stem kindred become impossible to fulfill. Small, rising, third-generation kindreds compete with them successfully. Factions develop that eventually create fission within the unit. The eventual dispersion of the kindred allows remaining members to hold on to whatever socioeconomic position they still have for some time, but they are unable to perpetuate their middle-class standing, as a unit, to the next generation.

The ambitious young men of the fourth generation, who do not receive the rewards they expected, are likely to marry into a rising kindred or to turn to Communism to regain their lost standing. Women in this stem kindred strive to marry out of the community and look for a man in a rising kindred, preferably a light-skinned Costeño or a highlander.

Implications of the Model

The model of kinship and mobility presented here demonstrates that Negroes and light Costeños in the lower and middle classes interact within the same kinship structure. The model, represented in Figure 11, points out the difference in function of the kinship structure in the two classes. Lower-class kindreds (personal kindreds) aid members in spatial mobility and subsistence economics. Middle-class kindreds (personal and stem kindreds) aid members in socioeconomic mobility. Mobile kindreds vary with respect to

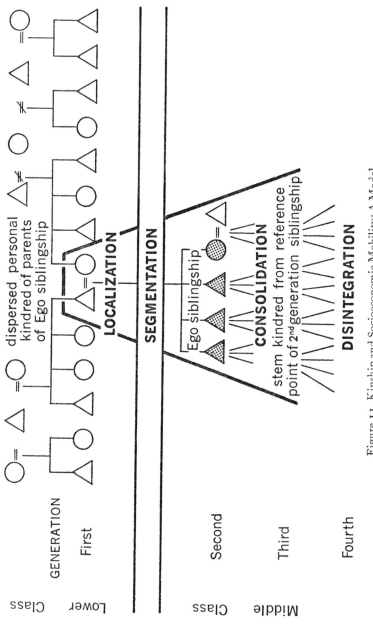

Figure 11. Kinship and Socioeconomic Mobility: A Model

generation: the small rising kindred is evident in the second generation of socioeconomic mobility; the corporate, established kindred
represents the third generation; and the large, disintegrating kindred characterizes the fourth generation. The term "stem kindred"
subsumes the dynamics of perpetuity and continuity through the
agnatic line that are apparent in the second, third, and fourth generations of socioeconomic mobility.

Within the kindred, members fare as follows. Members of the
second generation move up and consolidate their economic and political position as their sons and daughters reach adulthood. These
sons and daughters, the members of the third generation, help their
parents consolidate their economic and political position, but as their
own children reach adulthood they become involved in the process
of disintegration. Members of the fourth generation enjoy economic
advantages as children, only to lose them as adults.

Kindreds are adaptable to the economic situation of northwest
Ecuador. No Costeño need lack for shelter or food at a subsistence
level, nor find travel a problem, so long as he reciprocates. Socioeconomic mobility is possible provided that segmentation from the
large kinship network is initially effected by a mobile kin unit. An
upward-mobile group of reciprocating kinsmen is well adapted to a
static economy; if successful, it becomes the locus of community
action during the third generation and maintains its middle position
in relation to others. During boom periods a dominant middle-class
third-generation kindred expands its activities and uses its advantageous position to indirectly control the labor needed by the upper
class. Such boom periods are also advantageous to second-generation
mobile kindreds. Given slow, steady economic growth, second- and
third-generation mobile kindreds should be equally adaptable; they
are always producing more members, who, with the support of the
established members of the kindred, may enter expanding economic
pursuits.

Figure 12 sets forth the class structure of San Lorenzo, the major
ethnic divisions, and the basic bifurcation in values, and illustrates
the position of the dominant stem kindred in the structure. It is immediately evident that the people in the middle class fall into more
analytic categories than people in either of the other two classes.
This is due not to the imagination of the anthropologist, but to the

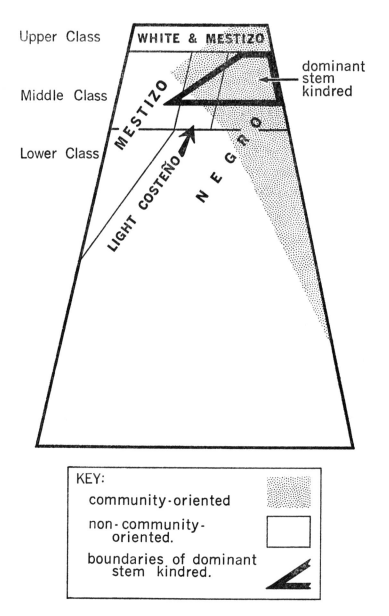

Figure 12. The Dominant Stem Kindred in San Lorenzo's Social Structure

fact that the dynamics of change are most apparent in the middle class. Social categories such as those presented in Figure 12 should represent potential variables in the dynamics of a system. They may aid or hinder mobility; they may seem either to offer opportunities for advancement or simply to justify a person's present position. The following discussion seeks to place the middle-class social categories in the broader system.

The Negro Segment of the Middle Class

The dominant stem kindred encompasses about half the people in the Negro segment and extends, by marriage, into the light Costeño and mestizo segments of the middle class. The other middle-class Negroes are almost all members of either fourth-generation, disintegrating kindreds or second-generation, rising kindreds. The very few middle-class Negroes with no real kinship affiliation have come to San Lorenzo from larger towns, either to seek work or to fill a post to which they have been appointed, e.g., as schoolteacher, lumber appraiser, or SCISP worker. In 1963 there were only two completely unattached men, the lumber appraiser and a new schoolteacher; two new women schoolteachers were equally unattached. Such "loners" ordinarily attach themselves to a stem kindred and function as kinsmen. Often, in fact, a third-generation stem kindred favors an unattached person for political offices. I have never known a Negro man to successfully launch a serious economic or political undertaking without the backing of a major stem kindred. Furthermore, when single newcomers do become established, their brothers often join them, and they begin a rise similar to that described for the Arisalas.

A young Negro woman who is appointed to a teaching post in a San Lorenzo school may become the mistress of a member of the dominant stem kindred or, alternatively, the mistress of a middle- or upper-class mestizo. Usually this kind of sexual liaison leads to a real tie between her kindred in another town and the man who keeps her in San Lorenzo. Unless marriage takes place, however, the tie is an unstable one.

Community orientation and the display of respectability symbols are very important to middle-class Negroes. Certain men and women must manifest such symbols and orientation vis-à-vis the community-oriented segment of the upper class in order to win all the favors they need to maintain themselves in the middle class. Everyone in the kindred, however, need not manifest such symbols. Ordinarily the men responsible for dealing with the upper class manifest such symbols, but many other members of the kindred do not.

Displaying the proper respectability symbols and a community orientation can and does win members (even of poor, lower-class kindreds) favors from the upper class, favors such as employment as cook or laundrywoman. Community orientation and the manipulation of respectability symbols also enable some members of the lower class to bypass the middle-class stem kindred and establish asymmetrical contracts directly with members of the upper class through compadrazgo relationships. The doctor, for example, now has nine ajihados and must treat them without pay. By themselves, however, such favors, though promoting horizontal mobility, do not establish a sufficient base for mobility from the lower class to the middle class.

If we consider the social structure of San Lorenzo in static terms, the situation may appear quite confused. But if we think in terms of social dynamics, the picture is quite clear: kinship affiliation and reciprocity within the kin unit define the position of any one person in relation to others. The quest for status manifested in respectability symbols and community-oriented behavior unites the mobile kindreds, through community-oriented men and women, to community-oriented members of the upper class.

The way in which the priest was supplied with the lumber he needed to build a school and a dormitory before teaching and medical nuns arrived in 1963 is a striking example of how this unity makes community action possible. None of the sawmills could supply the amount of lumber needed for the amount of money the priest allotted. The sawmill managers agreed, however, to cut logs for a small fee if the priest could supply the logs.

The priest announced his need for logs at a women's meeting of Acción Católica. The next day fifty able-bodied men went to the forest to cut logs for the priest. The Rivera brothers and a man named Caicedo (an important lower-class jefe de la minga favored by the Minas) served as minga heads, even though none of them liked the priest. In five days the necessary logs were delivered to the three sawmills; the minga heads delivered them to the amazed sawmill owners with the simple explanation that they were "for the priest." Later Luis Mina and two Arisalas told the priest that the people of the town wanted him to have the logs. This action is inexplicable until we perceive the relations between the community-oriented upper class, the dominant and aspirant middle-class stem kindreds, and the lower-class personal kindreds, and reciprocal work relations. The priest is convinced to this day that God had an active hand in the minga.

The Light-Costeño Segment of the Middle Class

The light-Costeño ethnic group is in a slightly different position. Except for the policemen, who are rotated, all the light Costeños are affiliated with either the principal fourth-generation kindred or one of two second-generation rising kindreds. But they are favored by both community-oriented and non-community-oriented members of the upper class. Some light Costeños are also linked to the dominant Negro stem kindred. All in all, the light-skinned Costeños of San Lorenzo are in an advantageous position. It is possible for them to marry into a highlander family and even to move into the upper-class coastal system.

It was through a young woman of the fourth-generation Rodríguez kindred that the timber company moved so easily into San Lorenzo's socioeconomic system. She had been living with a man who worked for the company (as accountant and paymaster) in Tumaco, Colombia, and suggested San Lorenzo as a base for operations when Colombian labor laws and unionization began encroaching on profits. When the company did come to San Lorenzo her father and uncles asked minga heads to work for the Cuban head of the company. This they did, and two systems combined to the benefit of all. A segment of the fourth-generation kindred, centered around the young woman, severed relations with the rest of the kindred and began a new socioeconomic rise in the community.

Highland Middle-Class Mestizos

Middle-class mestizos who marry into a Negro or light-Costeño kindred do so without having to fight an anti-Negro ethos. In fact, they are respected for their choice by the majority of highlanders. In Ecuador the ethos of free racial mixture is a strong one; despite the harmful actions and the derogatory terminology the highlanders may use in their dealings with Negroes, they value the principle of accepting them as potential marriage partners.

Mestizo men who marry a Costeña enter a new system. The Costeños feel that simply by marrying a well-brought-up middle-class girl, her husband acquires obligations to the entire kindred, from the reference point of her brothers and parents. The mestizos in San Lorenzo who have married into the coastal system have, in fact, adopted the system, and it has been to their advantage to do so. One Junta Autónoma employee of the non-community-oriented upper class married a light Costeña of the fourth-generation Rodríguez kindred. His wife is the daughter of a woman who owns the Hotel Pailón. She herself runs the Salón Ibarra, while two of her half-brothers are boat pilots for the Junta Autónoma and operate a ferry service between Limones and San Lorenzo.

One middle-class mestizo married a girl from the Arisala kindred, a daughter of Pompilio. He eventually quit the Junta Autónoma to devote full time to his business activities, which include a share in the monopoly on the San Lorenzo–Limones ferry service operated by the men mentioned in the preceding paragraph.

The man who married into the Rodríguez kindred has accepted compadrazgo relations only with members of the upper class. Nothing can be gained in his case by extending ritual kinship beyond the already too large stem kindred of his wife. His wife, too, has refused to aid her kinsmen, thereby restricting the circle within which she will reciprocate. The middle-class mestizo and his Negro wife, Pompilio Arisala's daughter, have effectively extended compadrazgo ties upward into the upper class and laterally within their own stem kindred.

Other mestizos fare almost as well socially, but not economically, by becoming community-oriented, establishing relations with prominent Negroes and light Costeños, and winning the approval of the community-oriented upper class. These mestizos are active in formal groups, and they may have compadrazgo ties to Negroes and light Costeños.

Most mestizos, however, are non-community-oriented and have no kinship ties to the Costeño community. They do not form a group in the sense of having structured interaction among themselves.

Negro house on the Cayapas River

The center of town

Old Section No. 1

"Street" dividing the barrio Cuba from the Zona Centrales

The New Town

The port

The railroad

The airstrip

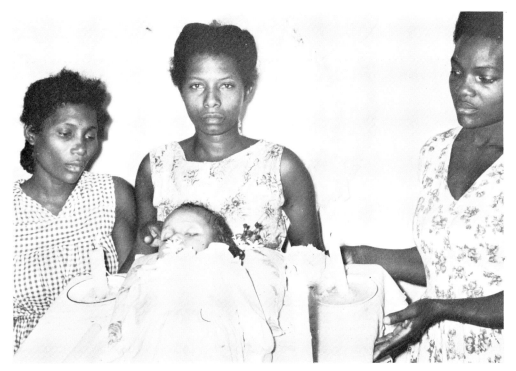

The end of an arrullo

Funeral procession for an adult

Marimba orchestra

¡ Baile marimba !

Loading coconuts at the new pier

Washing clothes in the Río Nadadero Chico

Drying fish at La Tolita de Pailón

They derive their identity as a social category only as the rest of the community perceives them—and they are generally perceived with disfavor. Members of the upper class feel it below them to associate on an equal basis with these mestizos, and the Costeños have no reason to do so.

These mestizos are the members of the community who are most intensely interested in national politics and in the development of a labor union. They feel the world is unjust. They are quickest to resort to physical violence in any small crisis, and to react emotionally to any provocation. They appear to satisfy Banfield's (1958: 9–10) criteria for social atomism expressed in the ethic "Maximize the material, short-run advantage of the nuclear family; assume that all others will do likewise." (Banfield 1958: 85). They alone react to economic success with conspicuous consumption. They neither share nor give, and are reluctant to borrow for fear that no one will trust them if it is known they are in debt. They never attempt to extend obligations beyond the nuclear family. They are subservient in their relations with those economically above them, and consider the people even slightly below them their decided inferiors. They compete with their equals. In all their interpersonal relations, they operate according to the naked market principle. They do not seek status, they do not participate in horizontal mobility, and they do not enter the coastal kinship system in any way.

The Junta Autónoma strike was the first real group action of highland mestizos. Since the strike, many attempts have been made to enlarge the small union of Junta Autónoma workers by incorporating it in a regional or national movement. Thus far factionalism and the indirect control of members of the upper class have kept such efforts from succeeding.

A Broad Base for Social Cooperation

With the exception of the atomistic mestizo element and most of the upper class, nearly everyone in San Lorenzo has some affinal or consanguineal tie, if not both, to everyone else, though the affinal link may no longer be active—for example, when the parents of a child have separated. The Arisala and Rodríguez kindreds unite at many points through children with one parent from each kindred (though in all cases the parents are now separated). Nevertheless, the

Arisalas think of themselves as a group distinct from the Rodríguez for all ordinary purposes. This extensive kinship network, kept potentially viable through constant references in daily gossip, does not function in normal activities. It is in times of crisis that appeals to common kinship are made. In a crisis a person can easily justify loyalty to someone by bilaterally reckoning some consanguineal and affinal series of links to him. Generally speaking, however, the only functional relationships are those with the personal kindred or stem kindred.

As a person gains in class standing or social honor, kinship ties with him become more and more desirable, and gossip, particularly among the less well-to-do, is often directed toward establishing links with him. The members of the lower class who like minga labor, for example, reckon their relations from the jefe de la minga because he is crucial to them. Those who have other aspirations organize their functional personal kindreds differently.

Because of the entangling lattice of real kinship ties in San Lorenzo, conflict between kindreds vying for prestige and economic advancement does not occur. When conflict does occur between individual men or women—and such conflicts are always erupting—people do not form opposing groups behind the antagonists, but rather develop many buffer groups between them. Although conflict between individuals is common, conflict between kindreds, classes, and status or ethnic groups is nonexistent. As we saw in Chapter II, conflict between ethnic groups did occur in San Lorenzo during the period of railroad construction, but with the extension of affinal bonds between some of the mestizos, the Negroes, and the light Costeños, the system is now too complex for ethnic conflict per se. Compadrazgo relationships complement the kinship network by reuniting collateral relatives and extending binding ritual kinship to non-relatives.

Ethnic, status, and class groupings in San Lorenzo are at once divided and united by kinship relationships. Kinship ties and relationships between kindreds range from the top of the class hierarchy to the bottom. Though the life chances of Negroes and light Costeños are dependent on their network of kinsmen, the network of kinsmen is dynamic and sensitive to changes in economic conditions and the system of social honor. Highland mestizos are both being integrated into the coastal system and serving as agents of structural change.

Changes in social structure are brought about by the operation of power. The next chapter, on the political order, is concerned with formal and informal power in San Lorenzo and hence with the capacity and potential of the social structure to change.

VIII

The Political Order

Weber's (1958: 194) conceptual framework for the analysis of community in a societal context has ordered the presentation of data in the study. My purpose in this chapter is not to analyze political structure per se, but to relate politics to the data already presented on class, status, and kinship in order to see San Lorenzo in a larger context.

Whereas the genuine place of "classes" is within the economic order, the place of "status groups" is within the social order, that is, within the sphere of the distribution of "honor." From within these spheres, classes and status groups influence one another and they influence the legal order and are in turn influenced by it. But "parties" live in a house of "power."

Their action is oriented toward the acquisition of social "power," that is to say, toward influencing a communal action no matter what its content may be. In principle, parties may exist in a social "club" as well as in a "state." As over against the actions of classes and status groups, for which this is not necessarily the case, the communal actions of "parties" always mean a societalization. For party actions are always directed toward a goal which is striven for in planned manner. This goal may be a "cause" (the party may aim at realizing a program for ideal or material purposes), or the goal may be "personal" (sinecures, power, and from these, honor for the leader and the followers of the party). Usually the party action aims at all these simultaneously. Parties are, therefore, only possible within communities that are societalized, that is, which have some rational order and a staff of persons available who are ready to enforce it.

Politics can be defined as the sphere of human activity in which power is manifestly paramount. Power is the ability to influence activities (Weber 1958: 184; see also Russell 1962; Lasswell and

Kaplan 1950: 74–102). The term "rationalization" will be used instead of Weber's "societalization" to refer to the systematic, centralized arrangement, secularization, and impersonalization of power (Weber 1958: 51, 239; Schermerhorn 1961: 7). The formal political order at the provincial level can be discussed in terms of the executive, legislative, and judicial offices and the electoral tribunal.

Executive Branch

The Governor of the province is the head of the provincial executive structure and resides in the capital city, in this case Esmeraldas. The Governor is appointed by the President of the Republic through the Ministry of Government, one of the eight ministries appointed by the President. At the canton level a jefe político is designated either by the Governor of the province or by the Ministry of Government. The Ministry of Government has the first right to designate the jefe político; if it does not choose to exercise this right, the choice is delegated to the Governor. The Governor in turn may delegate the choice to the leaders of the party in the canton.

The jefe político has *de jure* control of the military personnel stationed in the canton, and with the comisario is responsible for internal security and for commercial relations within the canton, with other cantons, and with other countries. Because of the increase in foreign interests, this is quite an important responsibility in such rich forest cantons as Eloy Alfaro, the canton in which San Lorenzo is located.

The executive representative of the parish is the teniente político, and his office the tenencia política. The teniente político is chosen either by the Ministry of Government or by the Governor of the province. Officially, he is not chosen by the jefe político, though members of the party in power or other friends of the jefe político may be instrumental in gaining an appointment for him. The teniente político deals with all civil and minor criminal cases in the absence of a comisario nacional de policía.

San Lorenzo is the seat of the parish of San Lorenzo, which extends north from Najurungo on the railroad tracks to Molina, encompassing the island of Tatabrero in the Canal de Bolívar, and east from La Tolita de Pailón in the Bahía de Pailón to San Antonio (see Map 2, p. 14).

Executive officers at each level of government are responsible for the efficient running of parish, canton, and province, and are first to be blamed when dissatisfaction arises. Their offices are foci for political conflict.

The Governor of the province and the lesser executive representatives in the cantons and parishes have, to help or hinder them, an elected council, which deals with four aspects of social administration: education, public health, public works, and sanitation. At the provincial level this is called the *consejo provincial*, which is headed by the elected mayor of the capital city. Half the members of the provincial council are elected every two years. In the cantons the analogous body is the municipal council. In Ecuador the boundaries of the municipios and cantons are coterminous, but the municipio functions in the social, not the political, sphere. Members of the municipal council are elected every two years; the body itself elects a president and vice-president.

In theory, a Junta Parroquial is a party organization set up for political purposes (Blanksten 1951: 63). In the Sierra it is usually sponsored by the Conservative party. The Junta Parroquial of San Lorenzo is a bipartisan parish council that makes recommendations to the municipal council and badgers it to follow them. It contains five men, supposedly appointed by the president of the municipal council. In the eyes of the municipal council, the Junta Parroquial is responsible for public works in San Lorenzo. In practice, however, the Junta Parroquial is made up of prominent members of the two major coastal parties (Socialists and Liberals) who do no more than make recommendations to the municipal council.

If members of the Junta Parroquial or other San Lorenzeños object to the workings of the municipal council, they may appeal to the provincial council. Usually such an appeal is honored only if it involves party conflict.

Legislative Representation

Esmeraldas province sends two senators to the national Senate and three or four deputies to the Chamber of Deputies. The senators are elected every four years, at the same time as the President, and the deputies are elected every two years. The number of senators is fixed; the number of deputies depends on population. The functional channels of communication from senators or deputies to canton and parish open and close according to personal favor and graft. Such favors and graft in turn depend upon political party affiliation.

Judicial Structure

In the provincial capital of Esmeraldas five or six provincial judges, appointed to four-year terms by appropriate superior courts, make up the court of justice. The superior court judges are in turn appointed to four-year terms by the supreme court. The supreme court is made up of 15 judges, elected for a six-year term by the Congress meeting in joint session. The provincial court of justice functions as a labor tribunal as well, and is the final court of appeal at the provincial level for any labor dispute.

The court of justice appoints a judge called the Comisario Nacional de Policía for each canton. This judge presides over cases involving misdemeanors, referring criminal cases to the provincial courts and theoretically civil cases to the teniente político. In rare cases of urbanized parishes, a comisario is assigned to a parish. Because of the national concern over San Lorenzo and the town's theoretical political importance, a comisario was assigned to it in December 1961, even though, as we have seen, San Lorenzo and the surrounding parish could in no way be considered urban.

The comisario is also official arbitrator in labor disputes, interprets laws pertaining to labor, management, and unions, and is responsible for the internal security of the canton (or parish). The chief of police is officially under the comisario and works closely with him. A central office of rural police assigns policemen throughout the coastal region. Customs inspectors are not under the comisario but under home offices in Quito and Guayaquil.

Electoral Tribunal

Like all Ecuadorian provinces, Esmeraldas has an electoral tribunal charged with the duty of organizing and controlling all elections. Every legal political party in each province sends three names to the tribunal as candidates. The tribunal then selects one principal and one substitute for each province for each party. The provincial tribunal is made up of five members designated by the supreme electoral tribunal. The supreme electoral tribunal is composed of seven men, three appointed by Congress, two by the President, and two by the supreme court. They have a four-year term and cannot resign without the consent of the appointing organ.

The provincial tribunal is supposed to appoint sub-officials to set polling places, called *mesas* (tables) throughout the province. These officials are responsible for the legal conduct of an election, and for counting and recording votes. The electoral tribunal and its representatives are supposedly the officials closest to the actual electorate —that is, the tribunal is ideally of and for the people. Under popular pressure, or in time of crisis, mesas may be established for an election without executive or legislative approval. It is not uncommon for the military to intervene in the name of the *electoral* when it appears that the executive, legislative, or even judicial branches are not fulfilling their function.

Political Action and the Formal Structure

The Governor of the province changes as the President of the Republic changes, or as the President or Ministry of Government see fit to replace him. The Governor must hew to the national party line. When the Governor of the province is replaced, and he frequently is, the entire provincial political structure is replaced. For example, José Velasco Ibarra once chose seven different Ministries of Government in 21 months; with each federal change, the political personnel of each province, canton, and parroquia also change. His successor by military coup, Julio Carlos Arosemena, made two such changes in 1962. Even when the Governor does not change, changes can be made at canton and parish level through appeals to the Governor, Ministry of Government, or the President. When changes take place, supporters of the party in opposition make major decisions on new candidates for office.

The municipal personnel normally change every two years, but they may change more frequently in response to electoral demand. Such demand usually arises in any political crisis, and it may in times of political stability. It is through political parties that members of the municipal councils are appointed, though the members' political orientations do not always coincide with those of the party in power at any given time.

In practice then, political and municipal personnel change frequently, and parties are at the base of the process deciding which man should occupy what position. Ordinarily, the process is as follows. The President or Ministry of Government names the Governor, who supposedly concurs completely with the President's policies. The Governor then requests a list of possible new jefes políticos, tenientes políticos, and even comisarios from whatever party he favors. The party leaders send in their lists, usually indicating a favored man for each position. Although even judges may be appointed in this way, political party leaders within a given province may not choose their own judges. The comisario for San Lorenzo, for example, was chosen by political heads of Guayas province.

When a political party has a man in an authoritative position, active party members receive social and economic favors. For example, taxes are levied more heavily on members of opposition parties. Lucrative commissions such as a monopoly on alcohol distribution are granted active party members, and they are not charged for legal transactions. Also, the teniente político or comisario can declare meetings or other political parties subversive and have the police break them up. Lower-class members of successful parties find more jobs and have less difficulty holding their jobs.

Ecuadorian national politics are unstable, and the personnel at the national level can change at any time. Hence parties at the local level must stand in constant readiness to exploit situations stemming from national political flux. Economic success is so dependent upon political favoritism within the victorious party and discrimination against an opposition party that parties must keep active at all times. Within any community or canton aspiring businessmen find it necessary to take an active part in party politics, or at least to keep in the favor of more than one party. Furthermore, members of the lower class must be able to change party affiliation whenever they think it expedient. Because of its role in economic competition, the party system in San Lorenzo must be understood if we are to have a clear picture of the dynamics of power within the social structure.

Parties in San Lorenzo

The party system is more complicated in San Lorenzo than is common on the coast or elsewhere in Ecuador. In addition to the Liberal party, which is the traditional coastal party, and the Conservative party, the traditional Sierra party, San Lorenzo has Socialist, Communist, and Independent parties. Perhaps the last is not a political party strictly speaking but its position will be made clear presently. I will first discuss the ideology and then the membership of these parties.

The Conservative party is a traditional highland party, which advocates the union of Church and State in political life. It is anti-Communist and anti-Socialist, and can be considered rightist. Conservatives often look to the Catholic Church for direction. The Independents, too, are a traditional highland party. They form a party only in the sense that they tend to act in a political bloc. They are forever seeking the ideal party and may often be found in new parties named after a caudillo (cf. Blanksten 1951), who usually emerges in an unstable situation and gathers a party around him.

The Liberal party is the traditional coastal party. It is avowedly anti-clerical and anti-Communist. It favors the status quo, and can be considered middle-of-the-road. At times there are rival Liberal parties in San Lorenzo and other northwest coastal towns. The Socialist party can best be characterized as the Liberal party's chief competition on the coast. In many communities it functions as the opposition that reaps the benefits when the Liberals are in national disfavor. There may be more than one Socialist party in San Lorenzo at a given time. The Socialists are slightly to the left of the Liberals. Like Communist parties everywhere the Communist party in San Lorenzo is not seeking favors within the system so much as it is seeking to overthrow the system—i.e., Church, State, and private enterprise—itself. Unlike the other local parties, it looks outside the country for guidance and help, notably to Russia and Cuba, and receives literature on political and labor organizations from these countries.

As nearly as I can reconstruct the situation, political favors were formerly divided between the Liberal and Socialist parties or between rival Liberal parties. In recent years, the alternation has been between Conservatives and Liberals. By 1963, however, the Conservative and Liberal parties had united to the apparent exclusion of the other three parties. To explain how such a union between a highland pro-clerical party and a coastal anti-clerical party came about requires an analysis of party membership and its relationship to the socioeconomic structure set forth in the preceding chapters.

Parties and Membership

In the house-to-house survey of San Lorenzo I did not ask a specific question on party affiliation, but probed the responsible adults in each household about the parties they favored, the parties they thought represented their interests, and the parties to which they owed at least nominal allegiance. The answers to these questions, plus observation of actual behavior and intensive interviews with party leaders and people active in politics, enabled me to arrive at the membership of each party. It must be remembered that there are no written membership lists, and that since parties visibly function only in political crises, individual affiliation may vary with the political situation, in accordance with factors to be described below.

The two highland parties in San Lorenzo, the Conservatives and the Independents, reflect both class and status divisions. The Conservative party includes most of the community-oriented members of the upper class and a handful of men (three or four) from the community-oriented middle class. All the non-community-oriented members of the upper class, the middle-class mestizos (except for the three or four Conservatives), and all the lower-class mestizos are Independents. However, most upper-class men who call themselves Independents side with the Conservatives except when they perceive an advantage in temporary affiliation with another Sierra party.

The Independents have no leader and no meeting place. They do not discuss politics or act as a political group outside obvious political contexts, and then they exert power by backing whatever leader seems able to procure some obvious and immediate benefit. Such behavior is known as *caudillismo*, and is characteristic of the political behavior of the country as a whole, though less so of the northern sector of Esmeraldas.

The Conservatives ordinarily congregate in the church for announced political meetings, but they also discuss politics at the gatherings of the many voluntary associations in which, as we have seen, the community-oriented middle-class plays a major part. Conservatives may back a caudillo, but only if he manifests respectability symbols and community orientation and does not seem anti-clerical. The Junta Patriótica was conceived and organized by members of the

Conservative party and has had considerable political impact, though it claims to be a nonpolitical organization.

The most important party on the northern Esmeraldas coast is, and reportedly has been at least since the turn of the century, the Liberal party. Natives of the northern coast ordinarily announce themselves either for the Liberals or against them, and in the latter case it is the fact of opposition to the Liberals, rather than commitment to another party, that is important. In fact, one will often find a faction of the Liberal party making up the political opposition in a town. It was supposedly the Liberal party that initiated many of Ecuador's land and labor reforms, though such reforms had no particular bearing on northern Esmeraldas. The Liberal party is the only party to be mentioned in songs sung at wakes for both adults and children. For example, in a common arrullo song, cantadoras sing a verse instructing the dead child to walk along the clean road to heaven while between each line a chorus of female relatives sings, "For me, I like the Liberals."

At present, the dominant stem kindred in San Lorenzo, headed by the Arisala siblingship with the support of the personal kindreds of prominent lower-class Negroes, is the basis of Liberal party strength. The party meets in the home of Pompilio Arisala, the man whose shop is the center of relationships between highland mestizos and middle-class Negroes. The Arisalas, in cooperation with others, revived the Junta Parroquial at the same time that the upper class founded the Junta Patriótica. In 1963 the vice-president of the municipal council was Pompilio Arisala, and the teniente político was the brother-in-law of Pompilio's brother.

Splinter groups of Liberals often set themselves against the dominant kindred. Such splinter groups may be created by dissatified younger members of the kindred with few, or declining, opportunities, or by members of other rising second-generation kindreds.

In San Lorenzo highlanders tend to regard all Liberals as members of a unified party. This may have led Liberal splinter groups there to call themselves Socialists rather than simply Opposition Liberals. The local Socialist party currently revolves around the small, strong, rising second-generation stem kindred referred to in Chapter VII as the Mina kindred. This kindred has also attracted followers from among the less radical members of the large fourth-generation Rodríguez kindred and from another previously important but now disintegrating kindred. Some of the younger Arisalas are also allied to the Socialist party in San Lorenzo.

The Communist party is making inroads both on the coast and in the highlands. Since direction for party action comes from outside the country, it is not really of the same order as the parties discussed above. In San Lorenzo as in other northwest Ecuadorian communities, active Communists are often young male members of fourth-generation disintegrating stem kindreds. Also, a very few upward-mobile men of the Negro lower class who have no affiliation with a middle-class kindred have found the idea of overthrowing the existing social, economic, and political orders appealing. Three lower-class highland mestizos have also become very active in the local Communist party.

In 1963 Communists established the Club Deportivo to attract more of the lower class to their following. A social club, it features a small orchestra, composed of a few avowed Communists and members of second-generation mobile kindreds ordinarily allied with the Socialists. The club immediately became the center of economically lucrative social interaction, for it offered music, beer, and aguardiente not only on Saturday night but also on Sunday afternoon, when cargo boats put in and the town receives most of its consumer goods. The clubhouse also serves as the Communists' meeting place.

Although the Club Deportivo won the Communist party greater popularity and perhaps a measure of respect, the party won no new members. More than any other political party in San Lorenzo, the Communist party is plagued by internal friction. The Communists put immediate political objectives before all else, and to these ends always sought to bring crises to a head. In doing so, however, they always lost political ground, for reasons that will shortly be made clear.

Inter-Party Cooperation and Competition

The number of ideologically conflicting parties in San Lorenzo might appear to suggest entrenched political conflict, reflecting important social cleavages. This is not the case. At the time the railroad was completed, there were reportedly three political groupings in San Lorenzo: the highland Independents, the coastal Liberals, and Op-

position Liberals or Socialists (reports vary on the name of the opposition to the Liberals). The Liberals dominated the political scene
and for a while the Independents dominated economic activities.
This was a time of open conflict between parties. The growth of the
Conservative party began with the development of the community-
oriented highlanders' interest in the town, which occurred some time
after the Junta Autónoma branch office in Ibarra was moved to San
Lorenzo.

The community-oriented highlanders expressed an interest in "re-
spectable" Negroes and light Costeños. As we have seen, most of
the native townspeople manifesting respectability symbols and community orientation were either from the third-generation dominant
stem kindred or from mobile second-generation kindreds. An informal alliance developed between the heads of the third-generation Arisala stem kindred and the community-oriented upper class.
Through kinship ties and serial dyadic contracts linking middle- and
lower-class Negroes, the situation developed to the point at which,
in 1963, the upper-class community-oriented Conservatives and the
middle- and lower-class Liberals worked as political allies. Also,
through affinal links, some middle-class Independents were incorporated into the dominant stem kindred. The political alliance between Liberals and Conservatives was strengthened by the participation in Acción Católica and church activities of women from the dominant kindred, and by nominal support of other members of the
Arisala kindred.

The most prominent rising second-generation kindred, the one
reckoned from the Mina siblingship, became the core of the Socialist
party. The Catholic clergy in San Lorenzo felt the leftist orientation
of the Socialists to be a distinct threat, and were quick to call prominent Socialists "Communists." Because of the Church's influence, the
party affiliation of the Minas makes it difficult for them to cement
sociopolitical relationships with members of the Conservative party.
Some Independents were drawn to the rising Socialist party, chiefly
because the Minas are ethnically light Costeño, but also because the
Socialists were willing to rally to a caudillo whenever such a move
seemed likely to strengthen the party.

Because they associate the Liberals in San Lorenzo with strong
Negro ethnic identification, Independents may embrace any party

except the Liberal party for immediate political action. Rather than back a given party, however, they generally look to a strong man, and because of this, any member of the upper class who wishes to do political battle for any reason can usually count on the Independents' support. Ethnic identity between the upper class and highland middle class assures the Independents an important place in the political life of San Lorenzo, even though in other ways they are not truly incorporated into the community network of social relationships.

The Communists' relationships have not yet been so firmly established that their allies and competitors, real and potential, can be clearly discerned. In 1963 they were rejected by the Liberals because they represented a threat to the political status quo, and rejected by the Conservatives because they were openly anti-Catholic (not just anti-clerical). I have known Socialists and some Independents to swing their support to the Communist party for certain purposes. Other Independents, though, supported the Conservatives in these instances. More than action initiated by other parties, perhaps, Communist action crystallizes political, social, and economic conflicts, and forces San Lorenzeños to take sides. In 1961 there was no Communist party in San Lorenzo; in 1963 it was still small, but it was growing in influence and membership.

The military coup of August 1963 forced the Communist party leaders to leave town. Those who did not escape were arrested, but they were allowed to return to San Lorenzo a few days later. The Communist party is said to still exist in San Lorenzo, but the presence of formal military rule has forced it to go underground.

Figure 13 illustrates the relationships between political parties in San Lorenzo in 1963. The two large rectangles (A and B) represent the basic political division between the Liberal-Conservative bloc and the others. The smaller rectangles represent relative size of party membership. The large rectangles are not completely closed, for although the Conservatives are allied with the Liberals, they also occasionally ally with the Independents and the Socialists, either to oppose the Communists or to find support when the Liberal party seems unable to function.

An example of an exceptional break in the Conservative-Liberal alliance occurred in the spring of 1963, when Esmeraldas province went on strike against the rest of the nation. The strike was initiated

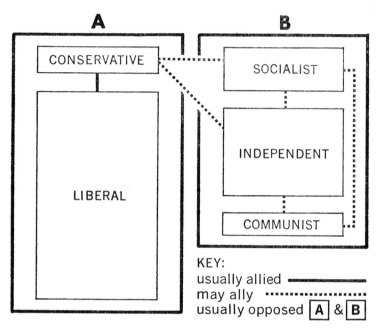

Figure 13. Party Opposition and Alliance

by the Liberals in the capital city of Esmeraldas, and carried on by the Liberals in Limones and other important towns. The strike was called to protest a segment of the boundary between Esmeraldas and Pichincha. Esmeraldas claimed the right to tax an increasingly important town on the Quito–Esmeraldas highway near Santo Domingo. Essentially, the strike consisted of closing all public offices, closing the Esmeraldas airstrip, and forbidding ships to enter or leave harbors. The railroad was blocked at La Boca, and the road to Esmeraldas barricaded. All shopowners were urged to close their shops, and officials encouraged to resign. Mail and other public services were discontinued. The Communists in San Lorenzo, Limones, and Esmeraldas were the first to propose violence to break the strike. Rioting in Esmeraldas resulted in the death of several persons. In San Lorenzo violence was threatened if townsmen participated in the strike. It appeared that the Independents and Socialists would ally with the Communists in opposition to the strike, and the Conservatives, too, looked upon the idea of Liberal participation with great disfavor. In the face of this opposition the Liberals simply ignored orders to go on strike, and, as it turned out, San Lorenzo was the only town in the entire province with a population of 500 or over that did not join the strike. By giving way to the pressure from the other political parties, the Liberals of San Lorenzo actually gained in prestige; by immediately advocating violence, the Communists lost prestige, even though superficially it might appear that everyone had allied with the Communists against the Liberals.

Thus far no political party in San Lorenzo has been able to gain the clear support of the Junta Autónoma's head engineer, nor has any party in San Lorenzo been able to claim the comisario as a member. A party member in either of these positions would greatly aid the party in competition with the others. To date, the head engineer has concerned himself only with highland politics and the comisario with "el mame."

A Broader Basis for Political Action

Affinal links between members of personal and stem kindreds of important people may provide avenues of political reconciliation between parties, at least for a brief span of time. These avenues of political conciliation are not ordinarily emphasized, but they may be if political conflict seems likely to damage the established social, economic, or political position of prominent individuals. Figure 14 illustrates how some prominent members of different parties are related to one another through series of affinal links. Each of the kindred segments depicted in Figure 14 has structured socioeconomic relationships, established through serial dyadic contracts, with lower-class Negroes. Since the personal kindreds of these lower-class Negroes overlap, the party allegiance of a given group of Negroes is often not clear, whereas allegiance to one or another of the stem kindreds is quite clear.

As the fourth-generation stem kindreds segment and disintegrate, lower-class Negroes tend to emphasize their ties to the dominant middle-class stem kindred and therefore to the Liberal party. However, the overlapping of allegiances makes political action by one party in opposition to another very difficult to sustain for long. Also, the overwhelming allegiance to the dominant stem kindreds places great responsibility on the core siblingship to do something for all supporters, which makes action somewhat more slow and ponderous

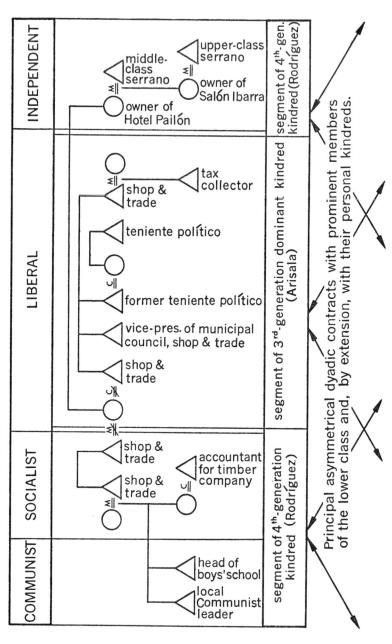

Figure 14. Party Affiliation and Kindred Structure

for the stem kindred than it is for second-generation aspirant kindreds with their small sphere of influence in (and hence responsibility to) the lower class. The connections within the middle class resulting from kinship ties, as well as the factors listed above, keep the community from dividing on political lines alone. The following case shows how clear-cut bipartisan action can be undertaken in San Lorenzo.

In April 1963 the Junta Autónoma made an arrangement with the leaders of the municipal council (who were residents of Limones, not San Lorenzo), whereby the Junta Autónoma would donate the part of the town designated on Map 3 (p. 210) as "Parque 24 de Mayo," plus the adjoining areas, if the council would undertake to tear down what is now the eastern center of town when San Lorenzo opened as a free port. The Junta Autónoma had set aside this area for customs warehouses, but feared retaliation by townsmen if it took responsibility for the demolition. The Junta Autónoma further agreed to help rebuild shops and municipal offices on the site of the New Town. An agreement to this effect was reached in the middle of May, and members of the Liberal, Communist, and Socialist parties heard about it soon afterward.

Early on the morning of May 24, lower-class Negroes tore down the Junta Autónoma and hotel fences in the center of town, cut the grass, weeds, and bushes with machetes, and erected signs saying "Parque 24 de Mayo" in the area so designated on Map 3. May 24 was chosen for its symbolic significance; this was supposedly the date that the people of San Lorenzo revolted against the English around the turn of the century. While the Negroes worked, the heads of the Communist, Socialist, and Liberal parties shouted encouragement. Everyone called everyone else "primo hermano." The Salón Acapulco opened, music was played, and middle-class Negroes and light Costeños of all political parties bought drinks for the workers. All the participants were related to one another in some way or another. Furthermore, no upper- or middle-class highlander, except those married to Costeños, had any inkling of the movement to establish the park before work actually started.

By August 1963, the park was a source of pride for all San Lorenzeños, although for most highlanders (including the community-oriented), who had not been involved, it was a subject for jest. The

Junta Parroquial had been quick to point out to the municipal council that it could not give a park to the Junta Autónoma because San Lorenzo already had a park, and the Junta Autónoma made no more attempts to raze the center of town.

Clearly, the bases for political parties are divers in San Lorenzo. The Socialist and Liberal parties are primarily kinship-based, though membership depends on the mobility level (second, third, or fourth generation) of the kinship unit. The Conservatives are a class and status grouping, composed of community-oriented upper-class highlanders and a few middle-class community-oriented highlanders. The Independents are for the most part middle- and upper-class Ecuadorian highlanders and foreigners. The Communists seem to represent the more dissatisfied elements of the middle and lower classes from both the coast and the Sierra. Cooperation and competition between these groups is partly buffered by shifting kinship emphases.

Before proceeding to an analysis of power relations in San Lorenzo, it is important to note the increasing number and importance of formal associations. Organizations such as Acción Católica, the Junta Patriótica, the Junta Parroquial, and the Club Deportivo, to mention only those with tangible political influence in 1963, were potential bridges of class, status, and kinship boundaries. We are now in a position to answer the key question about the operation of political power: How is something accomplished in San Lorenzo? I will begin by presenting four cases of collective action, both successes and failures, for the achievement of a political goal. It is hoped that these cases will establish a basis for a summary of power relations and social dynamics in San Lorenzo that will have application to social systems in general.

Tenure in Office

Though any teniente político's stay in office is precarious, some incumbents manage to secure a relatively more stable position in the administrative structure than others. The first two cases illustrate two attempts by tenientes políticos to remain in office, one a failure and the other a success.

Case I: A Teniente Político Is Ousted

From 1959 to June 1962 the Liberals, with the approval of interested members of the upper class (Independents and Conserva-

tives) named every teniente político of San Lorenzo. Though opposing factions always managed to have the teniente político removed
from office eventually, the Liberals always named his successor. In
June 1962 the leaders of the Socialist party, in agreement with Conservative members of the upper class, named the teniente político,
using the Junta Patriótica as a unifying organization. Their candi-
date, Juan Valdés, was a middle-class light Costeño who had recently come to San Lorenzo from Borbón, where his father ran the
largest shop in town. He had no job and expressed a strong interest
in politics. He did not commit himself to any one party, but participated actively in all formal organizations, became a secretary of the
Junta Patriótica, and was very active in Acción Católica.

    Though Juan Valdés retained the support of the Conservatives,
he lost the support of the Socialists very rapidly, principally because
the Socialists were badgered continually by other San Lorenzeños
for having no control over him. The badgering revolved around the
fact that Valdés had neither kinship nor compadrazgo ties with any
of the Socialists. The Socialists lost prestige every time Valdés acted,
for it was never clear whether he acted as a party man or out of self-
interest. The Socialists finally brought matters to a head by embark-
ing on a deliberate program of lawbreaking. Members of the upper
class urged Valdés to act, and he finally had some Socialists arrested
and ordered them to pay nominal fines. The Socialists gathered in
his office, and loudly told Valdés that he could not jail members of
his own party, and that he was acting solely out of self-interest. The
comisario remained aloof, claiming the dispute was a civil matter.

    The argument attracted a crowd, and, when it grew sufficiently
large, leaders of the Socialist party demanded that Valdés resign.
He refused, and called the Socialists "Communists." The crowd
became abusive, whereupon Valdés called in the lieutenant of the
naval base (who was also standing in the street) to put down the "insurrection." The lieutenant ordered the people in the crowd to dis-
perse, and, when they persisted, went to the naval base and returned
with the captain and sailors, who placed the town under martial rule.

    A few days later the sailors arrested leaders of the Socialist party,
together with some known Communists, and sent them to Quito as
political prisoners. The town reacted quickly, under the leadership of
the Liberals, protesting that the military was violating the wishes of
the electorate. The prisoners were returned to San Lorenzo after a

day and a half in Quito, and were given a hero's welcome on their return. Valdés moved to the naval base. A few leading Socialists and Liberals petitioned the Governor of the province (a Liberal) to remove Valdés, claiming that he was acting against the best interests of the community and that the navy was meddling in domestic politics. The Governor summarily dismissed Valdés. The captain of the naval base was eventually transferred to the only post in Ecuador less desirable than San Lorenzo—the Napo River.

The salient features of this case study can be summarized as follows. (1) Valdés had known political aspirations. (2) He was a joiner, an active participant in all formal organizations. (3) The Socialists who had backed Valdés renounced him quickly because they had no personal control over him, or so it appeared to others in the community. (4) The leading opposition party took no action against Valdés except in concert with the Socialists. (5) The conflict was complicated and prolonged, but not resolved, by the intervention of the military acting in the guise of suppressing an insurrection. (6) The Socialist party gained in group prestige as Valdés, who was the central figure in the conflict, lost in personal prestige. (7) The military itself lost prestige by intervening in opposition to the wishes of the community.

Case II: A Teniente Político Remains in Office

After the dismissal of Valdés, the Liberals were asked to pick a teniente político. Without consulting members of the upper class, they chose a Negro, Gonzalo Calzada, who had come to San Lorenzo with his sister in 1949. His sister married an Arisala, a man who was to hold the post of teniente político off and on for eight years. Gonzalo Calzada was a member of the Junta Patriótica, the Junta Parroquial, and Acción Católica, though he never took part in these groups' activities. A community-oriented member of the middle class, he manifested all the important respectability symbols and was well-regarded, though not well-known, among upper-class members of both the Independent and the Conservative parties. At the time of his appointment, he was foreman at one of the sawmills. He had never openly participated in political activities, but he was nevertheless known to be a strong Liberal.

Several times in 1963 the Socialists and Communists, and on one occasion some Independents, attacked Calzada and petitioned to have him removed from office. The Liberals made no public comment, nor did Calzada. The Liberal party, not Calzada, seemed to absorb both criticism and praise, so that the man himself never became a political issue. The upper class found that they could easily accomplish their ends with Calzada in office, and resisted moves to force his resignation. Members of the community who tried to force Calzada out of office ran into resistance from the upper class and the dominant stem kindred. Further, it was known that the naval officers would regard any attempt to expel Calzada as an insurrection.

After the strike of 1963, when the Socialists replaced the Liberals in the provincial government of Esmeraldas, the Socialists were ordered to pick a new teniente político and a new comisario. The Socialists were again thwarted by military intervention to "stabilize" the situation—but this time with the approval of the town. The interference of the military was part of a national movement to rid the country of Communism, a movement which led to the exile of the President of the Republic and his replacement by a military junta.

Rather than taking over the community, as the ruling military junta directed, the naval lieutenant, acting as commandant, arrested a few Communists and sent them to Quito, and then let Gonzalo Calzada remain in office, to the satisfaction of the upper, middle, and lower classes alike. The blow to the Socialists was mitigated to some extent when Calzada intervened in their behalf by asserting that they were not Communists.

The differences in the fates of Juan Valdés and Gonzalo Calzada can be summarized as follows. (1) Gonzalo Calzada had no known political aspirations. (2) He did not join in the activities of the formal groups to which he belonged. (3) He was attacked by the opposition party, not his own. (4) He was considered to be personally committed to his party through kinship alliance with the dominant stem kindred, which indeed always supported him. (5) He was supported in a crisis by the military, who were acting in accord with the wishes of most of the community. (6) He himself never became the center of controversy.

Enforcement of a Community Ordinance

A town ordinance in San Lorenzo requires that cows be tethered and pigs be penned. The ordinance was never put into effect until June 1963, when there were thirty cows in the town of San Lorenzo and many more pigs. The need to clear the streets of cattle and pigs had been pressing since at least 1955, when a series of attempts began to tether or pasture the cows and pen the pigs. All these attempts originated with a political party: either by the party that had just come to power through the appointment of a teniente político, or by the party in opposition. In all cases the teniente político was the center of political conflict.

Lower- and middle-class members of all parties owned cows and pigs. Tethered cows and penned pigs must be fed, and feeding is an expense. If cows are pastured instead of tethered, someone must watch the pasture, a chore made particularly unpleasant by ticks and vampire bats. The obvious choice is to let the cows and pigs forage at will in town. Whenever a party initiated action to get the cows and pigs off the streets (an undertaking that always originated at the request and often the insistence of members of the upper class), it was immediately thwarted by combined opposition from other parties. The resulting impasse frequently ended with the changing of tenientes políticos.

Case III: The Ordinance Is Ineffective

In 1961 a zealous new teniente político, appointed through the influence of community-oriented members of the upper class, ordered the police to shoot all pigs appearing on the main street. Ten pigs were shot—and the teniente político left office the next day. In 1962 the priest hit two cows with a machete when they entered the churchyard and church, and one of the cows died. Again the teniente político became the center of political controversy: he was blamed by one side for not having enforced the ordinance against cows earlier, and by the other side for not arresting the priest. He, too, left office. In short, the problem of cows and pigs on the streets of San Lorenzo always seemed to precipitate a political crisis that was resolved to the detriment of the teniente político and his party. But in June 1963, without undue difficulty, the cows were pastured and the pigs penned—an event as striking as the priest's minga.

Case IV: The Ordinance Is Enforced

In 1963 everyone seemed to feel that the freedom of the cows and pigs should be restricted, but an attempt by anyone to initiate the action necessary to achieve this was such a good opportunity to challenge political authority, and thus create a situation of possible political change, that nothing could be accomplished.

In June 1963 Luis Mina, the leader of the Socialist party, decided to impress the municipal council by presenting a letter formally requiring a number of civic improvements, such as better electricity, more schoolteachers, and better sanitation, but its real purpose was to show the council that the head of the Socialist party was indeed literate and conversant with legal formalities. Mina asked a newly acquired compadre, the local physician, an upper-class community-oriented highlander, to write a correct and eloquent formal letter for him to sign. The doctor agreed, but on the condition that he also include a strong plea for enforcement of the pig and cow ordinance. Mina reluctantly agreed. The doctor then asked the teniente político (Gonzalo Calzada) and other members of the Liberal party if they would again try, through the municipal council, which was then in their control, to rid the town of cows and pigs if he got the Socialists to initiate the action. The Liberals said they would. The doctor also contacted the priest, who spoke in favor of the action at a women's Acción Católica meeting.

Instead of taking direct action on receipt of the letter, the municipal council petitioned the Governor, a Socialist, to direct the comisario to enforce the ordinance in San Lorenzo; this the Governor did. When the comisario began to carry out his order, the Socialists, the Liberals, and the Conservatives all felt they had won a victory, and prepared to fight the opposition. The Independents owned no cows or pigs, and so did not oppose the comisario's move. The Communists, however, immediately threatened the teniente político and the comisario, expecting to be supported in their threats by the Socialists. They did not realize that the Socialists believed themselves fully responsible for the comisario's action. Finding only a small group of Communists in opposition, the comisario declared their opposition criminal, and levied fines against them, from which he realized a good profit that no one begrudged him. Within a week there was not a cow or pig on the streets of San Lorenzo, and everyone but the Communists felt he had benefited by this change in some way.

These four cases show that in San Lorenzo, one self-interested person or political party could not successfully undertake direct political action without becoming a focus of political crisis. Since crises ordinarily terminate with a change in the teniente político, action by one side presents an ideal opportunity to the opposition. Because of the presence of a literate upper class, formal community-oriented organizations, and a comisario appointed from outside the town, successful political action could be initiated from a variety of sources. In successful political programs, opposition could not focus on an individual man or party as a point of conflict until the action had already been partially carried out.

Power in San Lorenzo

Successful competition in politics is a necessary condition of socioeconomic mobility of second-generation kindreds, and of socioeconomic domination by a third-generation stem kindred. Members of fourth-generation disintegrating kindreds seek to reclaim their economic and social position through political action. If it were not for the complicating factor of the entry of highlanders into this coastal community, which has given it an upper class and an ethnically divided middle class, it could reasonably be established that the middle-class stem kindred is the locus of community power, and that its power is always threatened by rising stem kindreds and influential members of disintegrating kindreds. In the changing structure, the stem kindreds seem to function as "veto groups" (Riesman 1955: 246–51) in relation to one another.

Kinship dynamics establish important loci of power in the sense that no open political action can be undertaken without the alignment of kinship units for and against it. At the same time, class and status interests may support or compete with cooperating and competing kinship units.

Power, the ability to accomplish something, depends on manipulating a situation in such a manner that rival factions do not conflict as they pursue their separate interests. Successful political activity in San Lorenzo occurs only when the "veto group" phenomenon can be circumvented. To circumvent it, members of the upper class initiate action through formal organizations, using the manifest motive of community welfare. Because the formal organizations adopt this ethic and work toward the same goals, the personal and party sources of political activity remain diffuse. Continuance of activity in the pursuit of these welfare goals reinforces the community orientation and establishes a tangible raison d'être for the formal organization.

Persons wishing to attain a given political end pave the way by acting simultaneously through a coastal non-radical party (in San Lorenzo the Socialist party) and through the party with a man in office (usually the Liberal party in San Lorenzo). If the goal is to be attained, members of both the party in office and at least one of the stronger opposition parties must see more personal or party advantage in working for the goal than against it. It must initially be unclear if the party in office or the opposition party is working for the goal. Of course it must be clear that the upper class (or some members of it) would like to see the goal achieved, but potential opponents must not be able to pinpoint just who is behind the political action. Usually, only when the person or party initiating the action is known can people in San Lorenzo recognize the motives behind it and the possible outcome.

Ordinarily the attainment of a political goal will increase the political strength of the opposition party, and may even lead to its installation in office for a time. Rotation in office does not disturb interested members of the upper class, for they work both with the party in power and with the non-radical opposition. The ties binding interested members of the upper class and political aspirants are ordinarily formalized in compadrazgo relationships, which outlast the aspirant's time in office.

The process is apparently even more effective if, once action has begun, resistance arises from sources inadequate to stop it. In the face of such resistance, groups working toward a goal reinforce the cooperative aspects of their organization, thereby thwarting potential internal cleavage. In San Lorenzo the Independents and the Communists offer such resistance. Neither group has sufficient kinship ties or dyadic contracts with other members of the community to counteract the power of the community-oriented upper class, the dominant middle-class third-generation stem kindred, and the principal second-generation stem kindreds when they are acting in concert.

Given this system, in which the locus of power remains obscure, Independents, Communists, or others outside the system can still initiate successful action for their own benefit by influencing a member of the upper class or a Socialist or Liberal aspirant to office. The strike of the Junta Autónoma workers, most of whom were Independents, was successful because local officials refused to back the head of the Junta Autónoma and jail the leading strikers. The ground had already been laid for the strike with both Liberal and Socialist party leaders, and through them with all active party members.

Things are accomplished in San Lorenzo when the Liberal and Socialist parties act in concert. This harmony is reached when members of the upper class initiate action indirectly, through formal organizations, supported by ritual kinship ties with organization members. The formal organizations, then, seem to diffuse power among the classes and status groupings, just as the bipartisan kinship and ritual kinship structures diffuse power among the parties. The structure of power, though obscure, is discernible. Activities bringing parties into sharp conflict emphasize the potential of each party and clearly define the lines of socioeconomic cleavage, but they do not terminate in successful goal-oriented action.

When political action fails in San Lorenzo, the social structure emerges in strongest relief; when political action succeeds, the social structure is most obscure. Thus we might say that power decreases as structure becomes defined, and hence power operates most effectively when the social context is most amorphous. By this I simply mean that when power is successfully wielded in the community, the various kinship, status, and class lines are least apparent, and when the manipulation of power fails these lines become clearer as people seek to assign blame and struggle to find personal or group satisfaction.

In San Lorenzo even organizations designed to wield power, such as the navy, cannot accomplish their goals unless the prerequisites set forth above for the exercise of power have already been satisfied. Such open power organizations may then complete a goal-oriented action in harmony with previously established tendencies, but they will only delay termination of an action when they move against the force of community power.

Conclusion

In a little more than twenty years, San Lorenzo has developed from a relatively isolated, predominantly Negro village with a population of between 500 and 700 into an ethnically and culturally heterogeneous town with a population approaching 3,000. The future of San Lorenzo, once completely dependent on events beyond the control of its inhabitants, is now at least partially in their hands, and responsive to the pressures generated by formal voluntary organizations as well as to developments in the larger society.

The social changes that have occurred in San Lorenzo, and by implication throughout the northern sector of Esmeraldas province, were stimulated by the construction and completion of the Quito–San Lorenzo railroad, which for the first time placed San Lorenzeños in sustained contact with people from the Sierra. During the construction and completion of the railroad and the development of the town and port, highlanders settled in the town and the surrounding area and established themselves in new social positions. Changes in social structure in the contact situation may be summarized in the following five points.

(1) Highland Ecuadorians (mestizos and whites) and some Europeans entered the social structure as a new upper-class elite; highland mestizos entered the social structure as a new segment of the middle and lower classes. The period immediately following their entry was characterized by ethnic-based conflict.

(2) During the completion of the railroad, a bifurcation in values emerged between those people who were community-oriented and those who were non-community-oriented. This bifurcation ramified from the top to the bottom of the class hierarchy, cutting across ethnic lines.

(3) Dyadic contracts, compadrazgo relationships, and affinal links solidified the relationships between the community-oriented high-landers and some of the community's Costeños, especially those hav-ing economic advantage, high social honor, and political importance. These middle-class Costeños were members of the third-generation dominant kindred, a second-generation aspirant kindred, or a fourth-generation disintegrating kindred.

(4) The ingress of the Serranos complicated but did not signifi-cantly change the nature of the traditional social structure, which is based upon the rise and fall of kindreds from generation to genera-tion. It was through the kindred structure that cash and subsistence economies were effectively linked.

(5) Membership in political parties underscored class, ethnic, and status cleavages. These divisions are most evident when political goal-oriented behavior fails, and most obscure when political goal-oriented behavior succeeds. Community power, i.e. the ability to ac-complish something by community action, seems to operate most successfully in those contexts in which the lines defining segments of the social structure are most obscure.

The ramification of kinship into new contexts has important im-plications for social dynamics. Unlike the unilineal and bilineal kin-ship systems that tend to break down in societies undergoing inter-cultural contact and economic rationalization (cf. Mair 1963: 82–84), the cognatic descent system, based on personal and stem kin-dreds, seems highly adaptable to expanding and changing functions. It operates successfully in both lower- and middle-class life, and also in mobility from the lower to the middle class. The flexibility inher-ent in kindred-based group organization seems to promote interper-sonal realignments between and within kindreds. The potential for these realignments inherent in the kinship system allows members of kindreds to meet new situations arising from an expansion of scale without abandonment of the traditional kinship system, on which economic, social, and political activities are based.

Another interesting aspect of social dynamics is the extension of a traditional labor form to the new context of cash labor. A variant of traditional labor reciprocity allowed a new timber export company to quickly rationalize lumber operations to the mutual benefit of both workers and management. The coordination of minga and cash labor was facilitated by the correspondence of traditional time concepts with the needs of the timber business, and by kinship bonds that supplemented other reciprocal obligations between the middle and lower classes and between the company and the middle class. In this connection, it should also be noted that the one sawmill owner who insists on using only the minga system is rapidly losing his former competitive advantage to the other owners, who are introducing rational organization into the old system. The Negroes are indeed adapting their traditional labor organization system to new contexts, and not attempting to retain a system in the face of expanding opportunities.

New to San Lorenzo's social structure is the growth of formal associations oriented toward the economic, social, and political orders: e.g., a labor union, Acción Católica, and the Junta Parroquial. Formal organizations absorb the criticism that might otherwise thwart the actions of a person or a known interest group. Acting through the new formal associations keeps originating forces diffuse, making it difficult for opposition to organize and preventing individual initiators from becoming the centers of social and political conflict.

These formal organizations, then, increase the ability of San Lorenzeños to accomplish something in the community. They seem to operate most effectively when the initiator of a given action is not an outspoken leader in any of the organizations. By introducing an action through one or more formal organizations, and simultaneously paving the way with friends representing different factions in the community, an innovator can circumvent the danger of conflict over the question, "Who is getting what from this?" which almost invariably arrests a given action. I suggest that this reasoning represents that of the prominent Negroes who join all formal associations (that is, lend their name to the associations), but refuse to become publicly involved in their activities. It allows those interested in accomplishment to remain behind the scenes in the new world of formal power and to operate effectively, without evoking suspicion, in the traditional world of social manipulation.

Furthermore, since the new formal associations have effectively demonstrated that they indeed can influence national decisions for the good of San Lorenzo, Negroes joining the associations but not participating gain prestige from the associations' accomplishments, even though they have had no hand in them. Their prestige as men who can accomplish things increases among other Negroes, and the manner in which things are in fact accomplished becomes even more obscure.

Although I have not directed my attention to the Negro entrepreneurs in the changing system, it is worth noting here that Geertz's conclusions on the entrepreneurs in pre-take-off Indonesian society (Geertz 1963: 151–52) apply equally to their Ecuadorian counterparts: "The major innovations and innovational problems the entrepreneurs face are organizational rather than technical. . . . The function of the entrepreneur in such transitional but pre-take-off societies is mainly to adopt customarily established means to novel ends."

Another important change in San Lorenzo's social structure is the increase in the number of officials responsible to different government organizations, e.g. customs officials, the comisario, the representative of the Ministry of Development, as well as the naval officers. The effect of this increase is not yet clear, but the officials may serve as checks on one another and thereby discourage usurpation of authority. It has been pointed out that the military and the comisario can only act effectively when their actions are equivalent to, or at least do not conflict with, established, community-based, goal-oriented behavior. The increased number of officials may increase the local entrepreneurs' freedom of action, by allowing them to act in a traditional way on the local level without fear of direct, unrestricted interference from a national official.

Finally, although there are increasing economic opportunities for everyone in San Lorenzo, the opportunities do not always, from the standpoint of the lower class, appear to offer a clear advantage over more traditional ways of earning a livelihood. When new opportunities coincide with the traditional work pattern and offer a greater than usual economic gain, remarkable successes, of which the new timber export company is one example, can occur.

Generalizing about change in San Lorenzo, we can say that the social structure has moved toward increased rationalization while at the same time expanding traditional ways of getting things done. How is this possible? I submit that the rationalization of the social structure functions to effectively link the northern Esmeraldas community with the greater Ecuadorian society, while the structure's traditional aspects serve to accomplish things within the community. Rationalization is a community-nation link; traditionalism is an intracommunity means of achieving noncoercive social control and social manipulation.

Witness again, for example, the fact that those Costeños who are able to accomplish the most while causing the least social conflict in San Lorenzo are members of large traditional kinship groups and at the same time lend their names, but not their energies, to formal organizations. Costeños who actively participate in these organizations but do not have significant kinship relationships with prominent San Lorenzeños cannot achieve their political goals. The highlanders who are involved in national bureaucracies and active in the formal organizations can achieve their political goals *provided* they work through successful Costeños. The formal organizations provide a viable link between the national agencies responsible for development and the traditional sources of community power, the stem kindreds.

Newly arrived officials often voice considerable frustration over their inability to "do" anything in San Lorenzo—their usual response is to decide that the town has not yet developed sufficiently to warrant their presence. They are especially disappointed that the New Town is unpopulated, that there are no warehouses, and that the potential of the forest remains essentially untapped. But perhaps most frustrating of all to the more important newcomers from the Sierra is their inability to achieve things within the local social system. Phenomena such as the priest's minga, the removal of cattle from the streets, and Gonzalo Calzada's tenacity in office are utterly mysterious to them. These new officials have thus far remained cut off from the life of the town, banding together in one another's company and consoling one another with talk of how things are accomplished in other parts of the country.

Communism, too, has been unable to gain a foothold in San Lorenzo. Perhaps the Communists have been so notably unsuccessful because they attack both the traditional and the new, rational way of doing things. They simply offer no reasonable substitute for the system as it now operates.

In the coastal towns in which Communism has had greater success, e.g. Limones and Esmeraldas, there appear to be no viable links between the upper and lower classes. The growth of the middle class in both Esmeraldas and Limones has been based on extensive commercial relations with the outside world. Members of the middle class in these towns are economically more successful than their San Lorenzo counterparts, but at the same time they are more frustrated in attempts to climb further in the class hierarchy. In San Lorenzo the middle class does not seem to have reached the limits of its advance, and hope for greater success and the belief that such success is possible are manifest. Labor unions in the lumber business, too, have been more successful in Limones and Esmeraldas than in San Lorenzo. Like Communism, the labor union provides a new way of accomplishing something for those who are dissatisfied with the usual social channels. To date, the majority of people in San Lorenzo have been able to act to their satisfaction within the system, and perhaps for this reason Communism and labor unions have had very little success there in recruiting members and in carrying out any action.

San Lorenzeños, then, do not seem particularly prone to accept new ways of accomplishing things at the community level. They are willing to incorporate newcomers and to expand their traditional methods, but they are not willing to give up proven methods of accomplishing things. At the same time, they welcome the development of new organizations, or new ways of doing things, which offer a concrete impact in the larger society. Their major criticism of new officials, Communists, and labor union leaders is that they show too much concern with how things are done in San Lorenzo, and too little concern with how to get things for San Lorenzo from the greater society. San Lorenzeños have thus adjusted to change both by adapting their social system to new contexts and by keeping out or absorbing potentially disruptive forces.

The prominence of traditional lifeways in San Lorenzo should not be interpreted as evidence of culture lag. As Godfrey and Monica Wilson (1945: 111) put it: "In the historical moment autonomy in the narrower relations, subordination in the wider, is structural *flexibility* combined with *traditionism*. Flexibility is the autonomy of a group from the past; traditionism is its subordination to the past."

San Lorenzeños have achieved a degree of flexibility built on, but

not completely subordinated to, traditional methods of coping with
emergent problems. The Wilsons (1945: 112) have discussed the
significance of flexibility and traditionalism in social structure as they
apply to social change:

The combination of flexibility with traditionism is a necessary condition of
differentiation in the historical moment. If there be no flexibility—that is,
no autonomy in the narrower historical relations—there can be no change,
and therefore no differentiation between generations. If there be no subordination to the past, succeeding generations cannot benefit from the activities of those preceding them—the cultural heritage is lost. Flexibility
and traditionism, allowing of development, are therefore a necessary condition of civilization.

Change has not been a disrupting element in the social structure of
San Lorenzo. By extending traditional lifeways into new contexts,
the Negroes and their lighter relatives have retained their own
power structure, centered on kindred interaction. Furthermore, they
have begun to control aspects of the new economic opportunities,
especially in the lumber and shellfish industries. The native townsmen are themselves agents of change so long as they control a large
share of power, of the ability to get things done.

In the historical moment of this study the Negroes are adapting.
The adaptability and flexibility of a system can be observed either in
the micro-setting, as they have been in this book, or in the macro-
setting, i.e. in the stages of growth of a society. For Ecuador the
crucial stages lie ahead. San Lorenzo has become a dynamic part of
a developing nation, an active element in the growth of a plural society. Whether San Lorenzo will eventually be torn by racial and
socioeconomic strife, merge gradually and effectively into an economically expanding plural society, or develop along other lines that
cannot be foreseen now depends on the development of the greater
society—and on the ability of San Lorenzeños to maintain some
adaptive power in a changing society in a changing world.

Postscript: San Lorenzo in 1965

In May 1965 I paid a brief visit to San Lorenzo, during which I was able to observe the major changes that have occurred over the past two years.

The tenuous rule of the military junta now in power in Ecuador has brought no real change to San Lorenzo's power structure. The teniente político has left town, having accepted a position as administrator and buyer for the timber company station at Borbón. The captain of the naval base is now the official representative of the executive branch of the government. The same man has continued as comisario, but he is now living in the house of the former teniente político, in the barrio Las Mercedes, where he is far more integrated in community life than he was in 1963.

The Junta Autónoma is struggling to maintain the railroad and to keep it in operation from San Lorenzo to Quito, but it has been nearly overwhelmed by problems arising from insufficient funds and rapid natural deterioration. While the railroad has deteriorated, the port has developed. It is now completely marked by buoys, and the pier is considered finished. The lumber and concha industries have expanded, although almost none of this trade is going to the highlands. Most of the lumber is going directly to the United States, while the conchas (and other forest and sea products) are sent by boat to Esmeraldas and Guayaquil.

The most striking change in San Lorenzo is the growth of the New Town. This growth represents a triumph not of the Junta Autónoma, but of the Combonianos. Soon after the military junta took over, the Junta Autónoma was petitioned by Acción Católica to al-

low the people of San Lorenzo to use the unexploited facilities of
the New Town. The captain of the naval base concurred, and the
Junta Autónoma turned development of the New Town over to the
priest and his various development committees. From their own
funds, the Combonianos built a new hospital. Ground was broken
on August 10, 1964, on the site once set aside for the Protestant
Evangelical hospital, and the hospital was expected to open in December 1965. The Combonianos also opened the New Town's school,
which they run as a trade school, with 20 complete sets of wood-
working equipment, including a few electric saws. Children learn
to make such articles as chairs, tables, doors, and shutters, as well as
the wooden handles and bases of tools. Their fathers obtain the raw
lumber, and the children, with the help of the younger of the two
priests, cut it into boards at the Italian sawmill, which they are allowed to use free of charge.

One residential section in the New Town has been completed. It
includes 16 wooden houses with tin roofs, the building of which was
made possible by loans from the Combonianos' banking organization
in San Lorenzo (to which the priests added enough to stimulate bor-
rowing). For the most part, the people building homes in the New
Town are small-scale cash farmers, many of them newly arrived
Costeños whose children have commercial activities in San Lorenzo.
In another section of the New Town, known as barrio Kennedy, 22
cement houses are being constructed by the Combonianos. Their construction was made possible by a loan from the Banco de Vivienda,
a government lending institution established to encourage the development of rural housing. The priests will serve as rental agents
for the houses.

San Lorenzo itself appears the same: there has been almost no
building since December 1963 except in the New Town. The airstrip
is overgrown with bushes that are more than ten feet tall, and two
houses have been built on the strip itself. A new airstrip, to be located
east of the town, is under consideration. The navy has begun con-
structing a bridge to span the swampy inlet between Las Tres Marías
and the naval base. The priests and nuns have stocked their medical
dispensary and are giving sewing classes to adult women. A second
physician is now residing in town, in barrio La Samuela. Although
two members of the Peace Corps lived in San Lorenzo from fall

1963 to spring 1965, they seem to have had absolutely no impact on San Lorenzo or the people.

There is little work with crafts now; very few people have time to make paddles, bateas, baskets, hammocks, or sleeping mats to sell. Almost every able-bodied man in town works in the lumber business for wages, while concha gathering and household tasks occupy the women. Indeed, San Lorenzo has taken on a new cast; on weekdays it is a town of women, children, and old folks. Men return to town only to spend the weekends or to load a ship that is about to leave the port. Ships of 4,000–5,000 tons come to San Lorenzo almost every month now, to pick up the raw timber bound for Mobile, Alabama. Smaller ships carry lumber from the Italian mill to the United States. The development of the timber and lumber trade has been greatly encouraged by the military junta's establishment of stable taxation, and there is much public discussion about a large-scale program of conservation in northern Esmeraldas, hopefully to be supported by funds from the United States Agency for International Development.

Prices have risen in San Lorenzo, especially for food and crafts. Coconuts worth one sucre in 1963 now sell for three, bateas that cost five to eight sucres two years ago sell in town for 15 sucres or more, and most other prices are similarly inflated. Corn, an important staple in the Colombian Pacific lowlands, is now being raised in northern Esmeraldas by the slash-mulch system.

The effect of these changes has not been uniform throughout the class structure. In the upper class, only the owners of the Italian sawmill and the timber exporting company have improved their financial situation since 1963. The German sawmill owner receives some income through marginal business contacts with the timber company, but his overall income is about the same. The Ecuadorian mill suffers losses because of uncertain railroad conditions. The engineers once responsible for the development of the New Town have not received credit for its growth, and have been unable to keep up with the natural deterioration of the railroad and other Junta Autónoma facilities. Their own residences look better than ever, owing to a campaign to beautify the Ciudadela with palm trees, flowers, and a new road, but their morale is low. The Italian sawmill owners, the head of the timber company, and the younger priest are by far the out-

standing figures in the upper class. The first two control a large part of the economy of San Lorenzo, and the last dominates most of the town's viable social groupings. No one person or group (with the probably short-lived exception of the military) is particularly important in political affairs.

The middle-class mestizos, with the exception of those who had married into the Negro group by 1963, are discontented. The personnel who make up this ethnic category have changed almost completely in the past two years. The middle-class Negroes seem, above all else, to be waiting. Major figures of all kindreds are involved in the lumber business in one way or another. Economic positions are being maintained, but until a political crisis arises there is little opportunity for one kindred to restaff the political offices at the expense of another kindred. The middle class is now benefiting economically, and, it seems, waiting politically. Potential favoritism is concentrated in the hands of the naval captain and men in frozen administrative positions. Graft is minimal, and favors must be given with care.

The fluctuating Ecuadorian political situation, which allowed mobile kin units to dominate a community, has been suspended, but the stability imposed by the military junta is probably only temporary. The present situation is not viewed with resentment, or even dislike. Rather, prominent members of kindreds and formal groups seem to be waiting for something to happen, storing their power potential, so to speak, until it can again be used in a dynamic and fluctuating political order. Meanwhile, the younger priest, with the support of the military and the assistance of Acción Católica (whose membership includes all factions of aspirant, dominant, and disintegrating kindreds), is able to bring about improvements in education and medical care.

Among lower-class Negroes, the primary tendency is toward increasing dependence upon the timber business. The wages it pays are high by Ecuadorian standards, and wage labor now offers a clear-cut advantage over subsistence tasks. The cultivation of corn and the decline of crafts are the only changes at the subsistence level. The concha business is apparently still expanding. In the past year two new concha pens, with residences on top, were built in the little bay adjoining the Ciudadela, to make a total of four large pens in that inlet alone. Tens of thousands of conchas are shipped weekly to

Guayaquil and Esmeraldas. Mangrove stripping continues, along with fishing and similar pursuits. Many Negroes are profiting from tourism, by selling clay figurines from various archaeological sites and by offering their services as guides to these sites.

The stigma attached to the marimba dance among people in the middle class and the upward-mobile members of the lower class seems to be declining. Many Negroes express pride in their distinct coastal heritage, and regard their music as a prominent part of this heritage. The young priest, too, supports ethnic identity among the Negroes. In December 1963 he took a San Lorenzo marimba band to Quito, where it won first prize in a folklore festival.

The Negroes of San Lorenzo, then, are tending to take increased advantage of their environment. Expanding economic opportunity has made intensified exploitation of their environment possible. They may also be moving toward increased self-identification as an ethnic group. There is no apparent trend toward increased integration between Serranos and Costeños. Relations in the town might better be characterized as "stabilized pluralism." It may be that a more dynamic politico-economic structure is necessary to bring ethnic groups together in mutual striving toward a more rewarding future. If the apparently imminent fall of the military junta occurs, such a dynamic structure will probably become characteristic of the country once again.

Appendix

Town Ecology

The town ecology of San Lorenzo can be described from two frames of reference, both of which I have used in this study. The first is based on such major landmarks as the Hotel Imperial, the Salón Ibarra, and the railroad station; the second is based on barrios. In San Lorenzo, the "image" (Gulick 1963) that a person may have of his barrio and the barrio system varies with the time he has spent in San Lorenzo and with his place of origin. Highlanders tend to use only the first frame of reference, based on major landmarks, even after many years in town. Lower-class newcomers from the coast generally refer to the barrio system as it applies to their part of town. After several years they usually form a hazy conception of barrios on the other side of town, but they seldom recognize divisions that are not adjoining their own. Middle-class Costeños tend to use both frames of reference, depending on the reference point of the person being addressed.

The major features of San Lorenzo are given on Maps 3 and 4. Map 3 represents the first frame of reference, Map 4 the second. Since the landmarks indicated in Map 3 have been mentioned frequently, I will briefly describe the details of Map 3 before going on to discuss the barrio system, depicted in Map 4.

Map 3

The legend indicates the symbols for the Catholic church, the two schools, the water tanks, and the railroad. Enclosed within dotted lines are the three sawmills (S_1, S_2, and S_3), which are owned, respectively, by an absentee Ecuadorian, a resident German, and three resi-

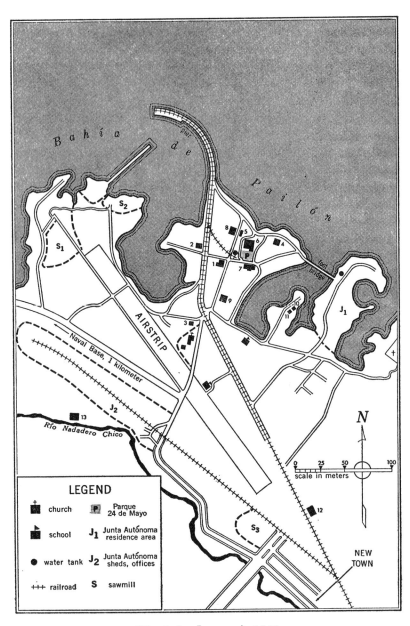

Map 3. San Lorenzo in 1963

dent Italians. The enclosed space next to S_2, with a narrow pier extending toward the central pier, was the site of an American-owned shrimp-processing plant in 1961. The plant was in operation for less than one year, and by 1963 the company had moved to Guayas province (see Chapter III) and the building and pier in San Lorenzo were in decay. Also enclosed in dotted lines are the residential and shed-office areas of the Junta Autónoma (J_1 and J_2, respectively). J_2 includes the offices of the engineers, topographer, and former secretaries, and the medical dispensary, radio shack, mechanics' sheds, and warehouse, as well as a camp for middle-class Junta Autónoma employees. The Parque 24 de Mayo, indicated by a P, is discussed in Chapter VIII. Parallel lines represent the dirt streets and major pathways. Many of these streets and paths were given names in 1957, when the railroad was completed, but few people in town remember the names of more than the main streets, and many people know none of them. The streets with paved sidewalks indicate the beginning of the New Town. Also on the map is part of the cemetery (indicated by a †). It has not been possible to show more than the northwestern corner of the New Town or to include the naval base.

The school next to the airstrip was a girls' school in 1963, and the other one a boys' school. The "new school" lies one kilometer from the southeast edge of the map, on the other side of the New Town. The area indicated as the Catholic church includes, besides the church, a dormitory for the nuns, living quarters for the priests, a medical dispensary, a large theater used for plays and public meetings, and a playground. The small Protestant church (next to the theater) is not shown on the map because it has no social significance and is not a major landmark for anyone in San Lorenzo. (There are only four Protestants in town, and they are all highlanders.)

Other buildings not indicated in the legend have been numbered as follows.

The three shops of the Arisala brothers, whose role in the community is discussed at length in Chapter VII, are numbered 1, 2, and 3. The Hotel Pailón, which was built by a light-Costeño San Lorenzeño during railroad construction (see Chapter II), is represented by 4; the Salón Ibarra, which is owned by the daughter of the woman who owns the Hotel Pailón, by 5; the French-built Hotel Imperial, supposedly on the site of the old English and German

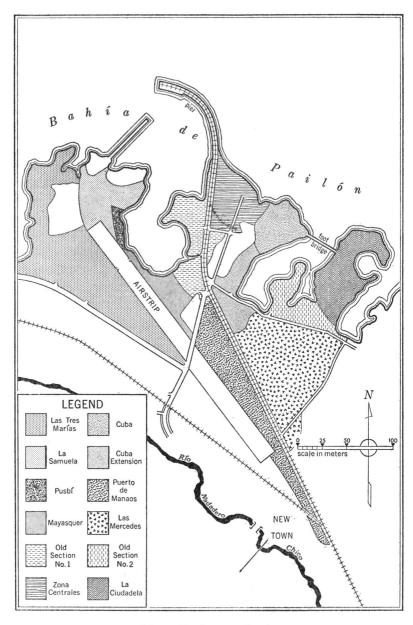

Map 4. San Lorenzo Barrios

central offices, by 6. The Parque 24 de Mayo is directly behind the Hotel Imperial. Number 7 stands for the Salón Acapulco, the only saloon open in San Lorenzo in 1963.

The building that houses the administrative offices of the teniente político, the comisario, the comisario's secretary, and the rural police is represented by 8. The jail, with separate, completely unfurnished rooms for men and women, is in the same building, directly below the offices. The local theater, run by a junta of nine upper- and middle-class Junta Autónoma employees and former employees, plus one light Costeño (the owner of the Salón Ibarra), is indicated by 9; the leading Casa de la Marimba (discussed in Chapters V and VI) by 10; and the Communist-run Club Deportivo by 11. The railroad station and the pumping station are indicated by 12 and 13.

These are the significant landmarks of San Lorenzo, and all of them have been mentioned in the text. Residential patterns are better discussed in relation to the barrio system.

Map 4

The present-day barrio system of San Lorenzo reflects, at least in part, the history of the town's growth. According to elderly informants, the effects of English and German exploitation, with the concomitant development of San Lorenzo as a trading town, forced a wedge, now called the Zona Centrales, between what I have called Old Section No. 1 and Old Section No. 2. The town then expanded from the Old Sections toward what are now the barrios La Samuela, Pusbí, and Mayasquer to the west, and Las Mercedes to the east. Cuba and its extension grew out of the Zona Centrales with the coming of the railroad. Las Tres Marías and Puerto de Manaos, the last barrios formed, developed only after the railroad had been completed. The individual barrios, ranging from west to east, are discussed in detail below.

Las Tres Marías

Las Tres Marías declared itself an official barrio in January 1963. The newest barrio in San Lorenzo, it is also the most vigorous in terms of the inhabitants' identification with the barrio and their interest in improving it. It has a president (whose personal qualities are discussed in Chapter V) and a development and maintenance committee. Las Tres Marías was formerly a part of La Samuela, and is still regarded as part of the older barrio by most of the people who live east of Pusbí. A high percentage of the Negroes living in Las Tres Marías are new immigrants to San Lorenzo, primarily from the rural coastal regions of the department of Nariño in southwest Colombia, and from the islands between San Lorenzo and Colombia. They have a strong sense of barrio identity, and for the most part are little integrated into the life of the rest of the town.

The people of Las Tres Marías located a shell mound on the western edge of their barrio and used these shells to pave the streets, giving the barrio an attractive overall appearance. A road was built from the center of the western edge of the barrio to the road leading to the naval base in June 1963; by August 1963 thirty new houses were under construction. What makes this rapid growth most interesting is that Junta Autónoma officials, charged with the development of the town, refuse to admit the existence of Las Tres Marías. To date there is no electricity in the barrio, and the land is officially the property of absentee highlanders who reside in Quito.

La Samuela

La Samuela now includes only those Negroes living on the bay side of the airstrip. The barrio no longer has a president or a committee, and no cooperative work to clean or develop the barrio has been undertaken for at least four years. Like Las Tres Marías, La Samuela is inhabited only by Negroes, most of whom have emigrated from Colombia or are the children of Colombian emigrants. Many people living in the eastern part of town regard everything west of the Catholic church as part of La Samuela.

Pusbí

Pusbí is named after a small stream in Colombia that runs into the Mira River, a stream that the thirty or forty Negroes living in Pusbí (or their parents) originally came from. All the residents are related to one another in some way; they did not all move to San Lorenzo at the same time, but followed one another. Pusbí is recognized as a barrio only by those who live in it and by Negroes living directly adjacent to it. It has neither president nor committee.

Mayasquer

Mayasquer, inhabited by Negroes, is named after a small river running into the Mira River in Colombia, though no one in the barrio claims to have lived there. According to Merizalde de Carmen (1921: 143) slaves were brought to the Mayasquer River area to mine placer gold. Residents of Mayasquer are unclear about whether or not it is indeed a barrio; the young people say it is, but the older people often disagree and say it is not. Kinship ties, common territory, and reciprocal work obligations that occasionally bring the residents together in general clean-up parties make Mayasquer a loosely defined unit. Everyone living to the east of the Catholic church and many people living to the west of it recognize Mayasquer as a barrio. A water spigot on the dividing line between Mayasquer and Pusbí serves that entire part of town (water is available when the electricity is turned on; see Chapters III and IV).

Old Section No. 1

This section has no name, though some of the younger residents are beginning to refer to it as Imbabura, the name of the road that runs along the railroad track. As described in Chapters VII and VIII, the Arisala stem kindred and allied lower- and middle-class Negroes dominate every aspect of life in Old Section No. 1.

Zona Centrales

The Zona Centrales evidently first became a distinct district of the town during English and German exploitation, and has been the center of town since the period of railroad construction. This is the zone designated for warehouses and customs offices by the Junta Autónoma.

The Zona Centrales contains most of the principal shops in town, the central administrative offices, the jail, and the Salón Ibarra. It is also the area in which members of the disintegrating fourth-generation Rodríguez kindred live; they occupy most of the homes in the Zona Centrales. This kindred entered the middle class during the period of English and German exploitation.

Adjoining the Zona Centrales, indicated by a blank space on Map 4, is the area used by the Junta Autónoma for workers' camps during railroad construction and to a lesser extent afterward. Today these camps house transient railroad workers and a small number of former Junta Autónoma employees. This unnamed section on the border of the Zona Centrales also contains the police living quarters, the Salón Acapulco, a poolroom, the theater, and the Protestant church.

With the exception of residents of Las Tres Marías and Puerto de Manaos, no one in San Lorenzo has difficulty defining the boundaries between the Zona Centrales and the beginnings of the workers' camps and the adjacent barrios.

Cuba and Extension

Cuba, once a part of the Zona Centrales, was officially founded between 1957 and 1958 (reports vary) with a formal ceremony that certain highlanders were invited to attend as honorary padrinos. This marked the first formal attempt to incorporate these highlanders into community affairs, and initial contacts between aspiring Costeños and upper-class newcomers were made at this time. Cuba is the center of activities both for the second-generation Mina kindred and for the Communists. Both Communist highlanders and the Communist members of the fourth-generation Rodríguez kindred live there. Together with the Zona Centrales, Cuba houses most of the ethnic category referred to in this study as light Costeño.

The "extension" of Cuba is a unit that was recognized as part of what is now Cuba by both residents and nonresidents before Cuba was officially proclaimed a barrio. All residents of the extension consider themselves separate from Cuba. Objectively, the inhabitants of Cuba are much lighter, ethnically, and further left in political orientation than the residents of the extension.

Puerto de Manaos

Puerto de Manaos was inaugurated and named when it was officially announced in 1962 that San Lorenzo was a free port for Brazil, an event discussed in Chapter II. This barrio has little to unify it beyond a name and a president. It has never had a minga to clean up the barrio or to build a road or pathway. Many of the residents are unaware that they live in an official community unit. Ethnically and culturally heterogeneous, it contains aspiring Negroes from San

Lorenzo as well as a few highland Negroes and mestizos. Like Las Tres Marías, it is not really integrated into the life of the community, but unlike Las Tres Marías, it lacks a self-identity and ethnic homogeneity. There are many new, small shops here, as well as the small Hotel Carchi. The barrio is expanding west along the railroad and toward the airstrip.

Las Mercedes

Las Mercedes was officially inaugurated in 1959, but it no longer has a president or a committee. An all-Negro residential area, it is characterized by much upward socioeconomic mobility, or potential mobility, from the lower to the middle class. Two saloons, closed in 1963, several carpenter's shops, 10 new cantinas, and many small shops are located in this district. Las Mercedes is recognized as a community unit by all residents and most nonresidents. Its position in the community resembles that of La Samuela before the rapid growth and separation of Las Tres Marías, except that the Negroes living in Las Mercedes are predominantly from Ecuador, not Colombia. The second community water spigot is located on the edge of Las Mercedes, near the railroad.

The barrio has benefited from the attention of the Junta Autónoma, which widened the road and dug drainage ditches along the road in April 1963. The main reason for the Junta Autónoma's interest lay in the chief engineer's desire for a better road on which to drive between his home in the Ciudadela and his office. April was the only month in 1963 when his jeep was running, which is why that month was chosen to improve the road. When the Junta Autónoma started work on the road, a cooperative barrio clean-up movement sprang up that soon spread to other barrios.

Old Section No. 2

This barrio contains the main Casa de la Marimba and the Club Deportivo. Otherwise it is simply a Negro residential area in which some of the town's oldest families reside. Pile houses are now being built over the water since there is no more room on the little peninsula itself. This entire point of land was once farmed by the head of the Casa de la Marimba and his wife (see Chapter VI).

Some residents of other barrios consider this section part of Las Mercedes, and others call it El Punto (The Point). Residents of the barrio see themselves as a unit, defined by location and kinship ties. Kinship ties between residents of this barrio and lower-class residents of Old Section No. 1 and Mayasquer are especially complex.

La Ciudadela

La Ciudadela is not really a barrio in the same sense as the others. Nevertheless, it is a functional social division since about half of the upper class lives there. Residents of the Junta Autónoma buildings have a tennis court and water tank at their disposal. Important tourists often stay at the Ciudadela rather than one of the hotels, for only at the Ciudadela can one find running water most of the day and flush toilets.

Summary

The barrios represent potential cooperative work units, which sporadically form to improve roads and pathways and to clean up around all homes. Such cooperative work ventures are now known as mingas, but they do not follow the pattern of the lumber mingas described in Chapter IV. Usually, cooperative barrio work is stimulated either by an undertaking of the Junta Autónoma (improvement of the road in Las Mercedes, for example), or by the construction of a new road in a new barrio (e.g., construction of the new road in Las Tres Marías). When such a project is begun in one barrio, people in neighboring barrios begin to clean up around their own houses, or to widen a path or road, or even to clear extra ground.

The locus of responsibility for cooperative work varies with the age of the barrio. In the older barrios, cooperative efforts are initiated by important members of the dominant stem kindred or large personal kindreds. Such activities in newer barrios are initiated by formal committees with a selected president. The new barrios are far easier than the older ones for an outsider to recognize, since they have more clear-cut boundaries and formal names.

All the barrios contain shops serving the basic needs of their residents, and all of them have cantinas. Mayasquer, Old Section No. 1, the Zona Centrales, Old Section No. 2, and Las Mercedes all have marimba houses though only the one in Old Section No. 2 is used

for community dances. (The others are used for practice.) In 1961
there were two saloons in Las Mercedes, one in Puerto de Manaos,
and one under construction in Mayasquer, but by 1963 only the saloon in the unnamed section adjoining the Zona Centrales remained
open. In 1963 most political activity was initiated and carried out by
inhabitants of Old Section No. 1, the Zona Centrales, and Cuba, with
the support of members of the upper class residing in La Ciudadela
and, in one case, the Zona Centrales.

No one I know in San Lorenzo is aware of all of the barrio names
or their boundaries. In general, people can clearly identify only the
barrio in which they reside. The only eastern barrio that people from
the west side of town ordinarily speak of is Las Mercedes, while
those in the east speak only of La Samuela in the west. Many of
the residents of Old Section No. 1 and No. 2 make fun of the barrio
system as new, and say that formal town districts are unnecessary.
The Zona Centrales, however, seems to be known to most people in
town, not just as a general business district and the center of town,
but as a bounded barrio.

Glossary

Aguardiente. Cane liquor
Ahijado. Godchild
Ají. Hot pepper (capsicum)
Alavado (alava'o). Wake for an adult; song from the wake
Arrullo (arrollo). Wake for a child; song from the wake; hymn to saint or deity
Barrio. Community district
Batea. Large wooden bowl
Bombero. Man who plays bombo
Bombo. Drum resembling bass drum
Bruja. Witch, mystical being
Brujo. Sorcerer, witchfinder
Cantadora. Singer
Cantina. Small bar
Cantón. Canton; region
Carrilano. Railroad laborer
Casa de la Marimba. Site of marimba dance
Ceviche. Fish or shellfish prepared with ají, lemon, onion, and tomato
Colegio. High school, academy
Comadre. Godmother and mother with respect to each other
Comisario nacional de policía. Local representative of the supreme court of justice
Compadrazgo. Ritual kinship; relationship between parent and god-parent
Compadre. Godfather and father with respect to each other
Concha. Small salt-water mussel
Conchera. Woman who gathers mussels
Costeño. Person from the coast

Cununero. Man who plays cununo
Cununo. Cone-shaped drum resembling conga drum
Espanto. Magical fright; apparition
Ferrocarril. Railroad
Glosador. Lead singer in the marimba band
Grito. Glosador's stylized shout in marimba songs
Guarda espalda. Person who assists and protects a brujo
Jefe de la casa. Head of a household
Jefe de la minga. Head of a minga
Jefe político. Chief executive officer at the canton level
Madrina. Godmother
Mal aire. Dangerous air radiating from the dead
Mal de ojo. Involuntary evil eye
El mame. Graft
Marimba. Folk dance; xylophone
Mestizo. Person of white and Indian descent
Minga. Reciprocal work group
Montuvio. Monolingual Spanish-speaking Indian from the coast; dirty, antisocial person; anyone from Guayas or Manabí provinces
Municipio. Municipality
Novenario. Second wake for an adult
Padrinazgo. Relationship between godparent and godchild
Padrino. Godfather
Papachina. Edible tuber resembling taro
Parentesco. Kindred
Pasmo. Folk illness
Pildé. Vine with hallucinogenic properties
Primo hermano. First cousin
Rascadera. Edible tuber resembling taro
Respondedora. Cantadora in the marimba band
Serrano. Person from the highlands
Solista. Lead respondedora in marimba band or at wake
Susto. Fright, usually magical
Tagua. Palm-nut ivory, used in making dice, jewelry, and toys
Teniente político. Local representative of the executive branch of the government
Yuca. Sweet manioc
Zambo. Person of Negro and Indian descent

References Cited

Acosta-Solis, Misael

    1944   Nuevas contribuciones al conocimiento de la Provincia de Esmeraldas. Vol. I. Quito, Publicaciones Científicas.

    1959a   Las manglares del Ecuador. Quito, Junta Autónoma del Ferrocarril Quito–San Lorenzo.

    1959b   El Noroccidente Ecuatoriano. Quito, Junta Autónoma del Ferrocarril Quito–San Lorenzo.

    1960   Maderas económicas del Ecuador y sus usos. Quito, Casa de la Cultura Ecuatoriana.

American Republics Series

    1960   Ecuador. Washington, D.C., Pan American Union.

Arensberg, Conrad M., and Solon T. Kimball

    1940   Family and community in Ireland. Cambridge, Mass., Harvard University Press.

Banfield, Edward C., with the assistance of L. F. Banfield

    1958   The moral basis of a backward society. Glencoe, Ill., Free Press.

Barrett, S. A.

    1925   The Cayapa Indians of Ecuador. 2 Vols. New York, Heye Foundation.

Bartholomew, J. G.

    1930   A literary and historical atlas of America. Revised by Samuel McKee, Jr. New York, Dutton.

Blanksten, George I.

    1951   Ecuador: constitutions and caudillos. University of California Press, Berkeley and Los Angeles.

Borhegyi, S. F.
    1959   Pre-Columbian cultural connections between Meso-america and Ecuador. Middle American Research Records 2, No. 6. New Orleans, Middle American Research Institute.

Bott, Elizabeth
    1957   Family and social network. London, Tavistock.

Buitrón, Aníbal, and Barbara Salisbury Buitrón
    1947   El campesino de la Provincia de Pichincha. Quito, Caja del Seguro.

César Cubillos, Julio
    1955   Tumaco: notas arqueológicas. Bogotá, Minerva.

Cieza de León, Pedro de
    1932   Parte primera de la crónica del Perú. Madrid, Edición Espasa–Calpe.

Clarke, Edith
    1957   My mother who fathered me. London, Allen and Unwin.

Coe, Michael
    1960   Archeological linkages with North and South America at La Victoria, Guatemala. American Anthropologist 62: 363–93.

Collier, Donald
    1946   The archeology of Ecuador. In Julian H. Steward, ed., Handbook of South American Indians, Vol. II.

Conforti, Emilio A.
    1962   Estudio preliminar para un proyecto de desarrollo regional de la "zona influenciada por la linea ferrea Ibarra–San Lorenzo (Provincias Carchi, Imbabura, Esmeraldas)." Quito, Technical Assistance Board, United Nations. Ms.

Costales Samaniego, Alfredo
    1957   Algunas artefactos prehistóricos de los Esmeraldeños. Llacta Año II, Vol. III. Quito, Instituto Ecuatoriano de Antropología y Geografía.

Davenport, William
    1959   Nonunilinear descent and descent groups. American Anthropologist 61: 557–72.

Dozer, Donald M.
    1962   Latin America: an interpretive history. New York, Mc-
            Graw-Hill.
Eichler, Arturo
    1955   Snow peaks and jungles. New York, Crowell.
Eisenstadt, S. N.
    1954   Reference group behavior and social integration: an
            explorative study. American Sociological Review XIX:
            175–85.
Elías Ortíz, Sergio
    1946   The native tribes and languages of southwestern Co-
            lombia. In Steward, Vol. II.
Elliot, Elisabeth
    1961   The savage my kinsman. New York, Harper.
Erasmus, Charles J.
    1956   Culture structure and process: the occurrence and dis-
            appearance of reciprocal farm labor. Southwestern Jour-
            nal of Anthropology 12: 444–69.
    1961   Man takes control. Minneapolis, Minn., University of
            Minnesota Press.
Estrada, Emilio, and Betty J. Meggers
    1961   A complex of traits of probable transpacific origin on
            the coast of Ecuador. American Anthropologist 63:
            913–39.
Ferdon, Edwin N., Jr.
    1950   Studies in Ecuadorian geography. Monographs of the
            School of American Research 15. Sante Fe, N.M.,
            School of American Research and the University of
            Southern California.
    n.d.   Characteristic figurines from Esmeraldas. Papers of the
            School of American Research. Santa Fe, N.M., School
            of American Research and the University of Southern
            California.
Fortes, Meyer
    1958   Introduction. In Jack Goody, ed., The developmental
            cycle of domestic groups.
Foster, George
    1948   Empire's children: the people of Tzintzuntzan. Insti-

tute of Social Anthropology Publication No. 6. Washington, D.C., Smithsonian Institution.

1961   The dyadic contract: a model for the social structure of a Mexican peasant village. American Anthropologist 63: 1137-92.

1963   The dyadic contract in Tzintzuntzan II: patron-client relationships. American Anthropologist 65: 1280-94.

Franklin, Albert B.

1943   Ecuador: portrait of a people. New York, Doubleday.

Freilich, Morris

1961   Serial polygyny, Negro peasants, and model analysis. American Anthropologist 63: 955-75.

Fuentes Contreras, Aurelio

n.d.   Breve análisis de la patología medicina y problemas sanitarios de San Lorenzo y sus posibles soluciones. Ms.

Garces G., Jorge A.

1942   Plan del Camino de Quito al Río Esmeraldas. Quito, Publicaciones del Archivo Municipal XIX.

Garcilaso de la Vega

1723   El Inca: primera parte de los comentarios reales. 2d ed. Madrid.

Geertz, Clifford

1963   Peddlers and princes: social change and economic modernization in two Indonesian towns. Chicago, University of Chicago Press.

Gillin, John

1949   Mestizo America. In Ralph Linton, ed., Most of the world.

Goodenough, Ward H.

1962   Kindred and hamlet in Lakalai. Ethnology I: 5-12.

Goody, Jack

1958   The developmental cycle in domestic groups. Cambridge Papers in Social Anthropology 1. Cambridge, Eng., Cambridge University Press.

Guevara, Dario

1957   Las mingas en el Ecuador. Quito, Editorial Universitaria.

Gulick, John
   1963   Images of an Arab City. Journal of the American Institute of Planners 29: 179–98.

Harner, Michael J.
   1962   Jívaro souls. American Anthropologist 64: 258–72.

Hauser, Philip M., ed.
   1961   Urbanization in Latin America. New York, Columbia University Press.

Hernández de Alba, Gregorio
   1946   The highland tribes of southern Colombia. In Steward, Vol. II.
   1948a   Sub-Andean tribes of the Cauca Valley. In Steward, Vol. IV.
   1948b   Tribes of the north Colombia lowlands. In Steward, Vol. IV.

Herring, Hubert
   1961   A history of Latin America. 2d ed. New York, Knopf.

Herskovits, Melville J.
   1958   The myth of the Negro past. Boston, Beacon Press.

Horn, Eugene F.
   1947   Forest resources of western Ecuador. Agriculture in the Americas 7: 46–49.

Houssin, Jacques
   1954   Informe sobre las posibilidades de explotación de madera en la zona por la cual atraviesa el ferrocarril a San Lorenzo. Quito, Editorial La Union, reprinted by the Junta Autónoma del Ferrocarril Quito–San Lorenzo.

Jaramillo Alvarado, Pío
   1954   El Indio Ecuatoriano. 4th ed. Quito, Casa de la Cultura Ecuatoriana.

Jayawardena, Chandra
   1963   Conflict and solidarity in a Guianese plantation. London School of Economics Monographs on Social Anthropology 25. Oxford, Humanities Press.

Jijón y Caamaño, Jacinto
   1941   El Ecuador interandino y occidental antes de la conquista Castellana. Vol. I. Quito, Editorial Ecuatoriana.
   1943   ———. Vol. II. Quito, Editorial Ecuatoriana.

Kahl, Joseph A.
    1957   The American class structure. New York, Rinehart.
Karsten, Rafael
    1935   The head-hunters of western Amazonas; the life and
            culture of the Jibaro Indians of eastern Ecuador and
            Peru. Societas Scientarum Fennica, Commentationes
            Humanarum Litterarum (Helsinki), Vol. 7, No. 1.

    1954   Some critical remarks on ethnological field research in
            South America. Societas Scientarum Fennica, Commen-
            tationes Humanarum Litterarum (Helsinki), Vol. 19,
            No. 5.
Kluckhohn, Clyde, *et al.*
    1951   Value and value-orientations in the theory of action. *In*
            Parsons and Shils, eds., Toward a general theory of ac-
            tion. Cambridge, Mass., Harvard University Press.
Kolberg, Joseph
    1897   Nach Ecuador. Strasbourg, Munich, and St. Louis, Mo.
Kubler, George
    1946   The Quechua in the colonial world. *In* Steward, Vol. II.
Kunkel, John M.
    1961   Economic autonomy and social change in Mexican vil-
            lages. Economic Development and Cultural Change 10:
            50–63.
Kunstadter, Peter
    1963   A survey of the consanguine or matrifocal family.
            American Anthropologist 65: 56–66.
Lasswell, Harold D., and Abraham Kaplan
    1950   Power and society. New Haven, Conn., Yale University
            Press.
Leach, Edmund
    1950   Social science research in Sarawak. Colonial Research
            Studies 1. London, Colonial Office.
Linke, Lilo
    1955   From the jungle. Américas, Vol. 7, No. 8.
    1960   Ecuador: country of contrasts. 3d ed. London, Oxford
            University Press.
Linton, Ralph, ed.
    1949   Most of the world: the peoples of Africa, Latin Amer-

ica, and the East. New York, Columbia University Press.

Mair, Lucy
1963   New nations. Chicago, University of Chicago Press.

Mellafe, Rolando
1964   La esclavitud en Hispanoamérica. Buenos Aires, Editorial Universitaria.

Merizalde del Carmen, Padre Bernardo
1921   Estudio de la costa Colombiana del Pacífico. Bogotá.

Mintz, Sidney W.
1961   A final note. Social and Economic Studies 10: 528–35.

Mintz, Sidney W., and Eric R. Wolf
1950   An analysis of ritual co-parenthood (compadrazgo). Southwestern Journal of Anthropology 6: 341–69.

Mitchell, William E.
1963   Theoretical problems in the concept of kindred. American Anthropologist 65: 343–54.

Montagu, Ashley
1960   An introduction to physical anthropology. Springfield, Ill., Thomas.

Murdock, George P.
1949   Social structure. New York, Macmillan.
1960   Cognatic forms of social organization. In Murdock, ed., Social structure in Southeast Asia. Chicago, Quadrangle Books.
1964   The kindred. American Anthropologist 66: 129–32.

Murra, John
1946   The historic tribes of Ecuador. In Steward, Vol. II.
1948   The Cayapa and Colorado. In Steward, Vol. IV.

Niles, Blair
1923   Casual wandering in Ecuador. New York, Century.

Paredes Borja, Virgilio
1963a   Historia de la medicina en el Ecuador. Vol. I. Quito, Casa de la Cultura Ecuatoriana.
1963b   Suma de la historia de los conocimientos médicos en el Ecuador: I (?–1914). Medicina y Ciencias Biológicas (Quito), I: 43–51.

Parsons, Talcott
  1954 An analytic approach to the theory of social stratifica-
       tion. *In* Parsons, Essays in sociological theory. Glencoe,
       Ill., Free Press.
Petersen, William
  1961 Population. New York, Macmillan.
Prescott, William H.
  1874 History of the conquest of Peru. 2 Vols. Philadelphia,
       Lippincott.
Radcliffe-Brown, Alfred R.
  1957 A natural science of society. Glencoe, Ill., Free Press.
Riesman, David, Nathan Glazer, and Reuel Denney
  1955 The lonely crowd. New York, Anchor Books.
Royal Anthropological Institute
  1951 Notes and queries in anthropology. 6th ed., London,
       Routledge.
Rubio Orbe, Gonzalo, Reinaldo Torres Caicedo, and Alfredo Cos-
    tales.
  1961 Problems confronting the city-planner and administra-
       tor in the town of Esmeraldas, Ecuador. *In* Hauser, ed.,
       Urbanization in Latin America.
Rumazo, José
  1948 Documentos para la historia de la audiencia de Quito:
       Pedro Vicente Maldonado. 2 Vols. Madrid, Afrodisio
       Aguado.
Russell, Bertrand
  1962 Power: a new social analysis. London, Allen and
       Unwin.
Sáenz, Moisés
  1933 Sobre el Indio Ecuatoriano y su incorporación al medio
       nacional. Mexico, Secretaría de Educación Pública.
Saunders, J. V. D.
  1961 Man-land relations in Ecuador. Rural Sociology, Vol.
       26, No. 1: 57–69.
Schermerhorn, Richard A.
  1961 Society and power. New York, Random House.
Simpson, Alfred
  1886 Travels in the wilds of Ecuador and the exploration of

the Putumayo River. London, Low, Marston, Searle, and Rivington.

Smith, M. G.
1962   West Indian family structure. Seattle, University of Washington Press.

Smith, Raymond T.
1956   The Negro family in British Guiana: family structure and social status in the villages. London, Routledge.
1957   The family in the Caribbean. *In* Vera Rubin, ed., Caribbean studies: a symposium. Seattle, University of Washington Press.
1960   Community status and family structure in British Guiana. *In* Bell and Vogel, eds., The family. New York, Basic Books.

Solien, Nancie L.
1959   The nonunilineal descent group in the Caribbean and Central America. American Anthropologist 61: 578–83.

Stevenson, W. B.
1826   Relation historique et descriptive d'un séjour de vingt ans dans l'Amérique du sud. 2 vols. Paris.

Steward, Julian H., ed.
1946   Handbook of South American Indians, Vol. II: The Andean civilizations. Bureau of American Ethnology Bulletin 143. Washington, D.C., Smithsonian Institution.
1948   ———. Vol. IV: The Circum-Caribbean tribes. Bureau of American Ethnology Bulletin 143. Washington, D.C., Smithsonian Institution.

Stirling, Matthew W.
1938   Historical and ethnographical material on the Jivaro Indians. Bureau of American Ethnology Bulletin 117. Washington, D.C., Smithsonian Institution.

Suárez Veintimilla, Mariano
1942   El ferrocarril Quito–San Lorenzo. Appendix to Jorge A. Garces G., Plan del Camino de Quito al Río Esmeraldas.

Uhle, Max
1927   Estudios Esmeraldeños. Anales de la Universidad Central (Quito), Vol. XXXIX, No. 262: 219–79.

Velásquez M., Rogerio

1961a   Rítos de la muerte en el alto y bajo Chocó. Revista Co-
         lombiana de Folclor (Bogotá), Vol. II, No. 6: 9–76.

1961b   Instrumentos musicales del alto y bajo Chocó. Revista
         Colombiana de Folclor (Bogotá), Vol. II, No. 6: 77–
         111.

Villavicencio, Manuel

1858   Geografía de la República del Ecuador. New York,
         Craighead.

Von Hagen, Victor W.

1940   Ecuador the unknown. New York, Oxford University
         Press.

1949   Ecuador and the Galápagos Islands. Norman, Okla.,
         The University of Oklahoma Press.

1955   South America called them. 3d ed. New York, Duell,
         Sloan.

Warner, W. Lloyd, Marchia Meeker, and Kenneth Eells

1960   Social class in America. New York, Harper.

Weber, Max

1958   From Max Weber: essays in sociology. Translated and
         edited by H. H. Gerth and C. Wright Mills. New
         York, Oxford University Press. A Galaxy Book.

West, Robert C.

1952   Colonial placer mining in Colombia. Baton Rouge, La.,
         Louisiana State University Press.

1957   The Pacific lowlands of Colombia: a Negroid area of
         the American tropics. Baton Rouge, La., Louisiana State
         University Press.

Whitten, Norman E., Jr., and Aurelio Fuentes C.

n.d.   ¡Baile marimba! Negro folk music in northwest Ecua-
         dor. Journal of the Folklore Institute, in press.

Wilson, Godfrey and Monica

1945   The analysis of social change. Cambridge, England,
         Cambridge University Press.

Wolf, Teodoro

1879   Viajes científicas por la República del Ecuador, No. 3:
         Provincia de Esmeraldas. Guayaquil.

1892   Geografía y geología del Ecuador. Leipzig, Brockhaus.

Index